MAKING POLICY IN THEORY AND PRACTICE

Edited by Hugh Bochel and Sue Duncan

First published in Great Britain in 2007 by

The Policy Press
University of Bristol
Fourth Floor
Beacon House
Queen's Road
Bristol BS8 1QU
UK

Tel +44 (0)117 331 4054
Fax +44 (0)117 331 4093
e-mail tpp-info@bristol.ac.uk
www.policypress.org.uk

British Library Cataloguing in Publication Data
A catalogue record for this book is available from the British Library.

Library of Congress Cataloging-in-Publication Data
A catalog record for this book has been requested.

ISBN 978 1 86134 903 3 paperback
ISBN 978 1 86134 904 0 hardcover

Cover design by Qube Design Associates, Bristol
Front cover: photograph supplied by kind permission of www.alamy.com
Printed and bound in Great Britain by Hobbs the Printers, Southampton

Contents

List of tables and figures

Tables

Figures

List of abbreviations

BSE	bovine spongiform encephalopathy
CCT	compulsory competitive tendering
CNAA	Council for National Academic Awards
DCLG	Department of Communities and Local Government
Defra	Department for Environment, Food and Rural Affairs
DfES	Department for Education and Skills
DWP	Department for Work and Pensions
EIA	environmental impact assessment
EITC	Earned Income Tax Credit
EMA	Education Maintenance Allowance
EPPI-Centre	Evidence for Policy and Practice Information and Coordinating Centre
ESPACE	European Spatial Planning: Adapting to Climate Events
ESRC	Economic and Social Research Council
GOs	Government Offices for the Regions
GSRU	Government Social Research Unit
HIA	health impact assessment
HR	human resources
IPPR	Institute for Public Policy Research
IT	information technology
LAA	Local Area Agreement
NAO	National Audit Office
NHS	National Health Service
NICE	National Institute for Health and Clinical Excellence
OECD	Organisation for Economic Co-operation and Development
OSI	Office of Science and Innovation
PMSU	Prime Minister's Strategy Unit
PSA	Public Service Agreement
QAA	Quality Assurance Agency
RIA	regulatory impact assessment
ROAMEF	Rationale, Objectives, Appraisal, Monitoring, Evaluation and Feedback
SDA	Service Delivery Agreement
SIA	social impact assessment
SSM	Soft Systems Methodology

Notes on contributors

Catherine Bochel is Senior Lecturer in Social Policy at the University of Lincoln.

Hugh Bochel is Professor of Public Policy at the University of Lincoln.

Martin Bulmer is Professor of Sociology at the University of Surrey.

Elizabeth Coates is an ESRC CASE PhD student in the Department of Sociology at the University of Surrey, in collaboration with the Government Social Research Unit, HM Treasury.

Louise Dominian is Regional Lead for Police Reform at the Home Office.

Sue Duncan is the Government Chief Social Researcher and head of the Government Social Research Service, based in HM Treasury.

Angela Evans is the Welsh Assembly Government's Chief Social Researcher.

John Hudson is Lecturer in Social Policy at the University of York.

Marion Kerr is Deputy Director in the Department for Children, Schools and Families.

Jane Mark-Lawson is Senior Associate, Breen and Partners, and formerly a Deputy Director in the Department for Education and Skills.

Andrew Massey is Professor of Politics at the University of Exeter.

Warwick Maynard is a Project Leader in the Home Office's Strategic Policy Team.

Edward C. Page is Sidney and Beatrice Webb Professor of Public Policy at the London School of Economics and Political Science.

Richard Parry is Reader in Social Policy at the University of Edinburgh.

Martin Powell is Professor of Health and Social Policy at the University of Birmingham.

Jamie Rentoul is Head of Strategy at the Healthcare Commission.

Louise Shaxson is an independent consultant working in the area of the evidence base for public sector policy and strategy.

Robert Walker is Professor of Social Policy at the University of Oxford.

The views expressed in this book are the authors' own and do not necessarily reflect those of their employers.

ONE

Introduction

Hugh Bochel and Sue Duncan

This book seeks to review policy making in the public sector. It is different from others in bringing together academic theorising with the 'real-life' experience of those responsible for making policy (or, more properly, for advising elected representatives). It seeks to draw on both academic and practitioner perspectives on policy analysis. To some extent this reflects much of the reality of policy analysis as it operates in the 'real world', drawing on tools and techniques of policy analysis and combining these with knowledge of specific issues, so that those responsible for the formulation, implementation and evaluation of policy can undertake these in an informed manner.

This has been a challenging endeavour; while academics have long played a role in contributing to the development of specific policies, whether commenting or advising, they rarely come face to face with policy makers in discussing the process, rather than the substance, of policy making. The two very different perspectives rarely come together in productive dialogue.

We have taken as our starting point *Professional policy making for the twenty-first century* (Cabinet Office Strategic Policy Making Team, 1999), not because the Labour administration of the time in any sense invented the art of modern policy making – the tradition is a long one – but simply because the document lays out nine competencies that it suggests together comprise the policy-making process. Some are better known than others; for example, 'evidence-based' and 'joined-up' policy making have been the subject of much debate, whereas concepts such as 'inclusive' or 'outward looking' generally have a lower profile. Each chapter in this volume examines one of these nine elements, exploring the academic literature and measuring it against experience, with extensive use of examples. The process described here is not unique to the UK; the art of policy making is being refined on an international scale and some of the approaches described here are mirrored in other countries. This book therefore sets the current state of British policy making in a wider context, both internationally and historically.

Analysing the policy process

As the state grew in size and responsibilities, particularly from the mid-20th century, governments began to gather increasing amounts of information relevant to their areas of activities, from the economy and defence to transport, health, education and urban planning. The postwar period saw an acceptance of a greater role for the state as a 'problem solver' and the use of approaches that sought to examine 'problems' and develop options for reducing or solving them. Although this tradition is much longer, the postwar period was, to some extent, linked to the development of 'social science' that aspired to be like 'real' science, with a view that knowledge of society could inform decisions that would make society better. During the 1960s in particular, these developments came together to produce a form of policy analysis associated with the role of governments as problem solvers. At roughly the same time there was also a growth of academic interest in the analysis of the policy process, and particularly of how issues and problems reached the policy-making agenda and how decisions were made. Consequently greater attention was paid to policy formulation, decision making, the exercise of power by different groups, the role of the media and so on. These developments all contributed to the development of policy analysis.

While the term 'policy' appears relatively simple, in reality it is used in a wide variety of different ways. Hogwood and Gunn (1984) identified 10 different uses of policy:

1. A *label* for a field of activity: this may be applied to broad areas, such as 'environmental policy' or 'social policy', or to more specific areas, such as community care, pensions policy or housing policy.
2. An *expression of general purpose* or desired state of affairs: such as a statement outlining a desire to reduce unemployment or inflation.
3. *Specific proposals:* such as the Labour Party's commitment in their 1997 General Election manifesto to halve child poverty by 2010 and to end it by 2020.
4. *Decisions of government:* for example, in responses to domestic or international challenges, such as avian flu or European Union (EU) enlargement.
5. *Formal authorisation:* such as in the passage of legislation through Parliament.
6. *A programme:* a relatively specific sphere of government activity, such as Sure Start.
7. *Output:* what government delivers, which can clearly be very varied in nature, such as increases and reductions in taxation to renewable energy, or the building of hospitals or schools.
8. *Outcome:* what is achieved; these can be hard to distinguish from outputs, but the study of outcomes should be based on an assessment of whether a policy is achieving its stated aims, as opposed to a focus on what is being delivered.
9. *A theory or model:* policies frequently involve assumptions about cause and effect, including that if governments do one thing, then another will follow.
10. *A process:* the making and implementation of policy is a continual process that cannot easily be analysed through the examination of specific decisions, and the introduction of one policy will itself have implications for other policies.

In the past the policy process was frequently depicted as a number of stages, such as formulation, implementation and evaluation. Today, however, it is more likely to be seen as a continual, iterative process, which is unlikely to be ordered in a sequential fashion, a view that is much more likely to reflect the realities of contemporary society and politics (see, for example, Parsons, 1995; Spicker, 2006). Nevertheless, despite their shortcomings, stagist approaches retain some value, for example in encouraging analysts to consider the order in which things should occur, and in providing some structure for analysis. Such approaches are now widely used to inform policy making, with, for example, HM Treasury's *The green book* (2003) identifying the ROAMEF cycle:

1. A *Rationale* for policy
2. Identification of *Objectives*
3. *Appraisal* of options
4. Implementation and *Monitoring*
5. *Evaluation*
6. *Feedback*.

Such approaches are often associated with 'rational' approaches to policy making, which assume that a given problem will be tackled through a series of cumulative and logical steps in a search for the best response (Simon, 1945/57, 1960). While this approach is helpful, in that it suggests that it is possible to approach policy making in a systematic fashion, it has been widely criticised for failing to reflect the situations that policy makers generally face. In particular, the formulation and development of policy rarely proceeds in such an orderly fashion; policy making is a complex process involving many different actors, and it involves conflict over aims, goals and values. In government, too, it takes place in a political environment and this makes an already complex activity even more complicated; the political process is a constant influence on the process of policy making and it is some of this complexity that this volume aims to unpick. In reality there are many push and pull factors that are constantly working for and against each other. While the rationalistic model of decision making is somewhat utopian, it has nevertheless continued to influence attempts to improve the quality of decision making, arguably including much of the 'modernisation' agenda with which this book is concerned. It is important therefore to be aware of the strengths and weaknesses of these approaches (see also, for example, Parsons, 1995; Bochel and Bochel, 2004).

The most widely known alternative model is 'incrementalism', initially developed in Lindblom's (1959) article 'The science of "muddling through"'. Lindblom argued that pure rational decision making is rarely, if ever, achieved, that policy makers are often more concerned with coping with problems than solving them, that policy makers tend to stick with the known, accepted, familiar and manageable, and that 'muddling through' is an important part of decision making. While this may reflect the reality of policy making in a political environment, it is perhaps not so much a matter of 'muddling through', as juggling the many and diverse influences that impact on the policy process. These include, among other things, political ideology, public opinion, the media, a range of other organised interests and the power of the ballot box. Policy making does not occur in a vacuum; it is subject to all sorts of wider influences. There are also a variety of other views that are critical of both rationalism and incrementalism, such as Dror's (1964) 'optimal model' and Etzioni's (1967) 'mixed-scanning', both of which aim to produce models that are descriptive of the reality of policy making and prescriptive in that they suggest that policy making would be improved through the use of these approaches (Parsons, 1995; Bochel and Bochel, 2004).

Modernising policy making

While it is important to recognise that a government demonstrating a concern with the processes of policy making and implementation is not new, it is probably true to say that the level of attention paid to the policy process under Labour has not previously been equalled in the UK. At the heart of much of the change has been the idea of 'modernisation', which is in itself part of a wider emphasis on modernising public services, including the civil service (Cabinet Office, 1999). There is obviously scope for wide-ranging debate about what 'modernisation' is, but Newman (2001) has provided a thorough exploration and critique of many of the issues around modernisation and governance.

The backdrop for New Labour's attention to the policy process can be seen as dating back at least as far as the 1960s and 1970s. During this period there were a number of developments intended to improved policy making. These included, for example, attempts to develop more rational (Simon, 1945/57, 1960) decision making in relation to public expenditure, through the Public Expenditure Survey Committee (PESC), established in 1961, the Programme Analysis and Review Committee, set up in 1970, and a growth in the use of planning units within government departments, and to improve collaboration between government departments, such as the Joint Approach to Social Policy. In 1968 *The Civil Service, vol 1* (Fulton Committee, 1968) argued that the civil service was largely the product of a 19th-century philosophy, and that this was inadequate to meet the demands of the 20th century. Following the report, over time, a series of reforms were introduced, including the creation of a civil service department, and of the civil service college (now the National School of Government), to provide further training for civil servants. In 1971 the Central Policy Review Staff was established within the Cabinet Office, with the intention that it should define government strategy and provide a framework for the formulation of government policies, and in 1975 a Policy Unit was created to provide advice specifically for the Prime Minister. At this time there was also a renewed interest in the potential contribution of research, including social research, to policy making (for example, Rothschild, 1971).

Under the Conservatives from 1979 to 1997, not only were there major policy shifts, such as an emphasis on policies designed to reduce the role of the state and to give individuals greater power and responsibility over their own lives, and large-scale privatisation, there were also significant changes in the processes of formulation and implementation of policies. One of the most obvious changes was the greater reliance on the private sector and the market, including not only in relation to the former nationalised industries and public utilities, but also through the 'contracting out' of particular operations in central and local government. These in turn required the development of new regulatory mechanisms, such as the Office of Gas and Electricity Markets (OFGEM) and Office of Water Services (OFWAT), to oversee the operation of these new markets. The Conservatives also sought to make greater use of the private and not-for-profit sectors in the delivery of services, including in areas such as community care and social housing.

Another significant change came with the report by Sir Robin Ibbs, *Improving management in government: The next steps*, which argued that 'agencies should be established to carry out the executive functions of government within a policy and resources framework set by a department' (Ibbs, 1988, p 9). This approach had to some extent been foreshadowed in the Fulton Report (1968), which had argued that certain kinds of work could appropriately be entrusted to autonomous boards or corporations that would operate outside the day-to-day control of ministers, although the scale of change proposed by Ibbs was substantial, and by 1997 three quarters of civil servants were operating within agencies. In many respects the use of agencies was intended to acknowledge the distinct and important role of delivery in achieving policy intent, but could be seen as a shift towards separating policy from delivery. This was largely based on the view that there is a reasonably clear divide between policy making by ministers and the implementation and management of those policies by civil servants. In practice, however, this division has not always been clear and the accountabilities of ministers and civil servants have been blurred. In addition, the use of these agencies, together with other quasi-governmental organisations, led to further questions about the extent to which these bodies were circumventing democratic accountability and adding to the 'democratic deficit'.

At the same time, the Conservatives were also bringing a new perspective to the idea of accountability, emphasising accountability of providers to consumers, including through parental choice of schools and the Citizen's Charters, rather than the traditional notion of accountability through elected representatives. This emphasis was also reflected in developments of consumer and user groups from the 1960s, and the increased focus on participation, particularly from the 1980s, with pressure for more user-centred and responsive services (Croft and Beresford, 1992; Bochel and Bochel, 2004). Early emphasis was on consulting users on service provision; this later developed into a concern with actually involving consumers in the early stages of policy design, giving voice to the notion of 'inclusive policy making' as typified in the 'Policy Action Team' approach adopted by the Social Exclusion Unit (for example, SEU/CMPS, 2002).

The use of audit and inspection bodies also saw a new impetus under the Conservatives, with the creation, in 1983, of the Audit Commission, initially to audit the work of local authorities in England and Wales, with its remit later being extended to cover the National Health Service (NHS), and organisations such as the Social Services Inspectorate (SSI), Ofsted and the Quality Assurance Agency (QAA) for Higher Education. Within central government, the National Audit Office scrutinises public expenditure on behalf of Parliament, with reports produced by its head, the Comptroller and Auditor General, being considered by the Public Accounts Committee.

Given the scale of change under the Conservatives, it is perhaps unsurprising that substantial elements, although far from all, of Labour's 'modernisation' programme have reflected further development of many of these ideas. Modernisation has arguably been seen by Labour as key to their attempts to improve the quality of public services. Newman (2001), however, makes a strong case for seeing New Labour's reforms in a much broader economic, social, political and ideological context. Approaching this from a somewhat different direction, others have observed that 'the idea and practice of public service and its users are significantly more complex than in the past' (Gray and Jenkins, 2002, p 252), and noted three implications that are of great relevance for the policy process: the reassertion of a beneficial role for public service in society; that from the government's perspective 'public service is no longer closely coterminate with the public sector' (p 251), and that the pattern of service provision is more varied and complex than previously; and that with the variety of service delivery there is equally a variety and complexity of relationships between users and services.

The extent of attention paid to the policy process since 1997 can be demonstrated by a brief review of some of the publications emanating from the government over that period. These are generally traced back to the White Paper, *Modernising government* (Cabinet Office, 1999), which identified problems such as fragmented approaches, incremental change and a separation between policy and delivery, and which set out three aims to ensure what it saw as inclusive and integrated government: joined-up and strategic policy making; ensuring that users, rather than providers, of public services are the focus; and delivering high quality and efficient public services. Related to these were commitments to the use of new technology to meet the needs of citizens and business, and a commitment to value public service. Some of the approaches associated with this can be seen as continuing the approaches taken by the Conservatives, such as the emphases on responsive, efficient, effective services and local freedom to manage, but it also reflects a much greater stress on the importance of the quality of policy making. The same year, as a follow-up to the White Paper, the Cabinet Office's Strategic Policy Making Team (1999) produced a report on *Professional policy making for the twenty-first century*. This recognised many of the shortcomings of idealised models of the policy process and set out instead what it termed a 'descriptive' model of policy making based on three themes (vision, effectiveness and continuous improvement) and nine core 'competencies': forward looking, outward looking, innovative and creative, using evidence, inclusive, joined up, establishes the ethical and legal base for policy, evaluates, reviews and learns lessons.

This clearly includes many of the key ideas that have been associated with the 'modernisation' of the policy process. In 2000, the Performance and Innovation Unit's report, *Adding it up* (2000a), which was seeking to examine some of the implications of *Professional policy making for the twenty-first century* (Cabinet Office Strategic Policy Making Team, 1999), to some extent echoed parts of the Fulton Report (1968), making the point that if policy was to be based on evidence, then that evidence had to be of good quality, and that analysts and policy makers would have to work differently. It emphasised the need for analysis and modelling to be more embedded in central government, suggesting that there needed to be a '*fundamental change in culture* to place good analysis at the heart of policy making' (PIU, 2000a, p 1; original emphasis). It also stressed the need for evidence-based policy while recognising the differing pressures and constraints (including political pressures). In 2001 the Centre for Management and Policy Studies produced *Better policy making* (Bullock et al, 2001) in an attempt to generate examples of good practice. In addition, it suggested that policy makers believed that 'new, professional and innovative approaches to policy making … were resulting in better policy and improved delivery' (p 5), but its emphasis, based on the responses of government departments, was on documenting examples of change, rather than demonstrating to what extent this policy making was 'new' or 'better' in terms of policy outcomes, or the extent to which the practice was common across government. The same year the National Audit Office produced *Modern policy making* (NAO, 2001a), focusing on a number of stages of the policy process: design, implementation and maintenance (including evaluation). As with *Professional policy making for the twenty-first century* (Cabinet Office Strategic Policy Making Team, 1999), it recognised the complexity of policy making and the range of factors and risks that could influence the success or failure of a policy and set out a series of recommendations for the policy process. Like *Better policy making* it included examples of policies that are deemed to demonstrate good practice. In addition, the Performance and Innovation Unit (Mulgan and Lee, 2001) produced *Better policy delivery and design*, a discussion paper that suggested that under New Labour 'a more sophisticated approach to performance management is taking shape' (Mulgan and Lee, 2001, p 9) around clearer expectations of performance, better monitoring machinery enabling more rapid adjustment of priorities, resources and targets, regular spending and policy reviews, other changes around cross-cutting issues, evidence and knowledge and the involvement of outsiders and practitioners, and greater investment in evaluation to analyse policy successes and failures. This emphasis on performance management was reflected in the establishment of Public Service Agreements (PSAs) for government departments and the setting up in 2001 of the Prime Minister's Delivery Unit to closely monitor delivery of the government's key priorities. The Performance and Innovation Unit report identified nine 'general conclusions' supporting the importance of knowledge and evidence, the benefits of involving practitioners, economy and prioritisation in policy goals and initiatives, the importance of monitoring and evaluation, a need to tackle problems associated with information technology (IT), and the potential for task forces to play a role in overseeing delivery as well as policy development.

The emphasis on policy making as a skill, indeed the 'professionalisation' of policy making, has also been given new emphasis in recent years, through the Professional Skills for Government programme (Civil Service Management Board, 2005), covering all government departments and agencies, which sets out the skills required of civil servants within three career groupings: operational delivery, policy delivery and corporate services delivery. The core skills identified for senior civil servants, in addition to professional expertise and broader experience, are leadership, analysis and use of evidence, financial management, people management, project and programme management, communications and marketing and strategic thinking. These clearly relate to the perceived requirements of professional policy making.

Mechanisms of modernisation

In terms of what might loosely be called the 'mechanisms' of the policy process, there have been so many changes over the past few years that can be associated with the 'modernisation' agenda that it is impossible to cover them in a short chapter, but there is perhaps a value in revisiting briefly some of the main areas of change that have been highlighted by New Labour's approach.

Performance measurement, audit and inspection

The use of performance measures was widely encouraged by the Conservatives from 1979 to 1997, including their use in 'league tables', such as those for schools and universities. As noted above, the Conservatives also made extensive use of audit and inspection, including through the Audit Commission and the creation of bodies such as Ofsted.

Labour governments have maintained this approach, with performance measures being applied to virtually all public services, although under Labour this has been accompanied by a greater emphasis on setting targets. In addition, there has been an increased role for mechanisms of audit and inspection to ensure that services are meeting their objectives, providing efficient and effective services and offering value for money. While under the Conservatives much of the emphasis was on making information available, under Labour there has arguably been an attempt to make more decisive judgements over 'quality', whether defining certain organisations as 'failing' or in the use of star systems as applied to local authorities and hospitals.

In recent years the extent of criticism of the government's use of performance measures and targets, and to some extent of inspection, has grown, with critics noting that while targets can help establish priorities and enable measurement of performance against them, too many targets and insufficient funding can create problems (Appleby and Coote, 2002), and that organisations will be affected by the need to meet the requirements of these activities (Clarke et al, 2002; Clarke, 2004). A discussion paper from the Prime Minister's Strategy Unit (2006) noted that while performance management has its strengths, it could also create problems, such as stifling innovation and creating perverse incentives. In July 2006 the new Secretary of State for Communities and Local Government, Ruth Kelly, effectively recognised this and pledged to reduce the burden of inspection and performance measurement on local authorities (Kelly, 2006).

Another development since 1997, driven in large part by HM Treasury and linked to the Comprehensive Spending Reviews, has been the establishment of PSAs, including delivery targets, with a department's performance against the PSA targets being monitored by the Treasury and the Prime Minister's Delivery Unit and made public in departmental reports.

Collaboration and partnership

Since 1979 both Conservative and Labour governments have seen a significant role for the private and not-for-profit sectors in the delivery of services. Under the Conservatives this was largely driven by a commitment to competition and the market, and a belief that such providers would be more flexible and innovative than those from the public sector. Rather than competition, partnership and collaboration have been a key part of Labour's approach to policy making and delivery. This may in part be a response to the complexity that arose from fragmentation of welfare provision in the Conservative years; in part due to a view that more holistic and comprehensive responses are needed to many policy problems; and in part due to a view that the whole policy process is more integrated and dynamic and that 'joined-upness' is a means by which governments can more successfully respond. It also reflects the view that in this complex society public sector bodies find it difficult to deliver their responsibilities without collaborating not only with other parts of the public sector but also private and voluntary agencies (Rouse and Smith, 2002); indeed for New Labour the entire concept of partnership has implied a significant role for the non-state sector. However, it might also be possible to suggest that there is also some underlying notion of seeking to empower citizens and involving people in developing responses to social problems. During the third Labour term, while the emphasis on partnership, and the role of the 'third sector', remained, there seemed to be emerging a renewed stress on meeting the needs of individual users, with the Minister for the Third Sector, Ed Miliband, arguing that 'The third sector is uniquely positioned to make sure that local users experience public services that are specifically tailored to meet their needs. The role of the Government will be to enable voluntary organisations to deliver services in partnership with the public and private sectors ...' (Miliband, 2006).

Partnership has also been seen as of importance in many of the government's initiatives aimed at tackling multiple deprivation and social exclusion, such as Sure Start and the New Deal for Communities. These have sought to place considerable emphasis on the involvement of community and voluntary organisations as partners to the public and private sectors, and to develop the skills of local people to produce more long-term, sustainable outcomes. Area-based initiatives have been widely used by the New Labour governments to involve community and voluntary organisations in responding to the problems and aspirations of their districts, with ideas of partnership and collaboration being seen as a central feature of these.

While collaboration and partnership have therefore been a key theme under New Labour (Glendinning et al, 2002), there has also been a strong view from government that these were not sufficient in themselves and that many organisations require a significant degree of direction to ensure that they achieve this (for example, NAO, 2001b). At the level of central government, new mechanisms, such as PSAs, have been introduced to attempt to identify specific government departments as responsible for the achievement of policy goals, but they have also been intended to encourage cooperation and coordination through recognition of the role of other departments. Similarly, some saw the plethora of directives and targets emanating from Whitehall during the early years of the New Labour government as reflecting a lack of faith in local-level agencies. The Conservatives' development of performance measurement has therefore been utilised to attempt to drive forward partnership and cooperation in policy making and implementation, including initiatives at central and sub-central government levels. Similarly, the introduction of Best Value, replacing the system of compulsory competitive tendering (CCT) under the Conservatives, was intended to emphasise responsiveness to consumers and accountability to the local community, rather than simply to be concerned with the cost of a service.

However, as Newman (2001) has argued, Labour's attempts to encourage collaborative forms of governance have been restricted by the same government's attempts to centralise and manage through the use of goals, targets, performance measurement and audit and inspection. These, Newman suggests, inevitably create constraints on the ability to successfully draw on more bottom-up initiatives, including participation and collaboration (Rouse and Smith, 2002). As Newman et al (2004) point out, there are in turn potentially conflicting imperatives for those at the local level: they must seek to encourage participation but at the same time have to deliver on the targets that are imposed by the centre.

E-government

In November 1996 the Green Paper *government.direct* (Cabinet Office, 1996) was published, setting out a prospectus for the electronic delivery of government services, with a vision of direct, one-stop, access to public services. Given Labour's emphasis on 'modernisation' it was not surprising that the incoming government also identified 'e-government' as an area that could alter the relationship between citizens and government, for example through allowing online access to information services 24 hours a day, seven days a week, and was committed to having all government services available electronically (primarily via the internet but also through telephone call centres, digital television or other means) initially by 2005, later changed to 2008. The overall strategy was based on a vision about 'better using technology to deliver public services and policy outcomes that have an impact on citizens' daily lives' (Chief Information Officer, 2005, p 3). One of the new developments in relation to transactional services was the launch of the Directgov website (www.direct.gov.uk) in 2004, designed to provide 'joined-up' information on and access to government services through one site. However, e-government is also clearly seen by government as potentially freeing up resources, challenging existing models of service delivery, improving policy outcomes and helping citizens feel more engaged with the processes of democratic government (Chief Information Officer, 2005).

The scale of change foreseen as arising from the use of technology in government is great: the government spends around £14 billion a year on IT and directly employs around 50,000 professionals (Chief Information Officer, 2005), and existing programmes, including Connecting for Health, reform of the criminal justice system and the Harnessing Technology strategy in education, are being joined by new developments such as the 2012 Olympics and the introduction of identity cards. However, while the greater use of technology may offer such potential improvements, progress towards this goal has not been as rapid or as smooth as the government had hoped (NAO, 2002; Margetts, 2006), while demand in the UK appears relatively low compared with some other countries (Margetts, 2006). In addition, the potential for using e-government to remodel the power relationship between citizens and the state has been much less discussed by the government, and at the same time there remain significant questions about equality of access through such means for different social groups (Bovaird, 2003).

Arm's-length agencies

The Ibbs report (1988), recommending the creation of executive agencies, argued that although 95 per cent of civil servants worked in service delivery or executive positions, there was insufficient focus on delivery of government services, that there was a shortage of management skills and experience of working in service delivery among senior civil servants, that short-term political priorities tended to take precedence over long-term planning, and that there was an emphasis on spending money rather than getting results. It argued that there was a need to focus on the delivery of services and on the needs of the customers of those services.

Following the Conservatives' approach, New Labour's 'Third Way' has affected the nature and the shape of the state through their use of arm's-length organisations and the increase in power and responsibility of such bodies. Both Conservatives and Labour have used these bodies as part of their mechanism of governance – they have been seen as a way of offering direction and control, bringing a more customer-focused approach, and, at the same time, of bringing public and private sectors together.

Arguably the Conservatives used these as they viewed state bureaucracies as inefficient, self-interested and unresponsive. They also saw central government bureaucracy as unlikely to deliver government goals, while believing that agencies could improve this situation by separating delivery from policy, including the use of targets for delivery. In contrast, under New Labour, at least in the early years, there was a view that (central) government action could be effective in delivering desired social and economic outcomes, reflected in further strengthening of control and coordination mechanisms. To some extent, therefore, agencies have been brought back into line with government departments, being directed towards corporate goals and managed through the same mechanisms of PSAs and targets (Gains, 2003). Bache and Flinders (2004) have argued that for New Labour's particular vision of reformed social democracy the use of such bodies is a particularly useful governance mechanism.

Multi-level governance

Multi-level governance is concerned with the spread of decision making across multiple territorial levels. Initially it was taken largely to refer to the EU, but it has become widely used to refer to the increased vertical independence of actors operating at different territorial levels. However, the *governance* part of the concept is problematic, implying a changing role for governments – towards coordination rather than policy control ('steering' rather than 'rowing') – in a more complex society. Nevertheless, the creation of devolved administrations in Scotland, Wales and Northern Ireland, albeit facing different challenges and with differing roles (see, for example, Parry, 2005), together with a gradually increasing role for the EU, does mean that we have to recognise that whatever we might think of 'governance', we do have to consider the implications of multiple levels for the policy process, including the potential for increasingly varied approaches to policy making and implementation and greater policy divergence.

At a regional level in England, there has also been significant change, despite the failure of a referendum to introduce elected regional government to the North East of England in 2004. In 1994 the Conservatives brought together some of the responsibilities of the then Departments of Employment, the Environment, Transport, and Trade and Industry into Government Offices for the Regions. Labour have built on this so that, now representing 10 government departments, these Offices are now significant players in delivering government policies at a regional level, being responsible for expenditure of over £9 billion in 2004/05. In addition, in 1999 the government created regional development agencies (RDAs), based on the Government Offices for the Regions (GOs), to help encourage regional economic development and competitiveness.

There have also been attempts to 'modernise' the policy process in local government. Under the Conservatives there was an attempt to both centralise and decentralise and to recognise and control complexity (Newman, 2001). However, central control did not achieve the aims of the government and the exclusion of key actors and the public from some aspects of the policy process led not only to problems with policy implementation but also to questions of legitimacy and accusations by some that the reduction in local government control of services contributed to a democratic deficit.

Labour set out their thinking in the Green Paper *Modernising local government: Local democracy and community leadership* (DETR, 1998a) and the White Paper *Modern local government: In touch with the people* (DETR, 1998b), which argued that councils were not effectively engaging with their communities. Reforms have arguably been focused around electoral participation and accountability ('democratic renewal'), new decision-making structures and the introduction of Best Value, while areas such as possible reforms to loosen the constraints on local government finance have been largely neglected (for example, Game, 2002). Barnett (2003) has argued that 'New Labour's approach to local government is now consistent with a move to an "active" welfare state, in line with Third Way ideas which stress responsibilities and duty along with rights as welfare principles. These require the individual behaviour of citizens to be re-shaped and the relationship with government to be re-thought. Increasingly, however, they are being applied to public agencies on an organisation-wide scale' (p 29). However, during Labour's third term there was again greater discussion of '... a rebalancing of the relationship between central government, local government and local people' (DCLG, 2006, p 4) and the idea of 'double devolution' from Whitehall to local government and from local government to citizens and communities, with the local government White Paper (DCLG, 2006) arguing that there was now a need to 'free up' local government and empower councillors, although it retained an emphasis on leadership roles, both for and within local government.

User-led services and choice

Under the Conservative governments there was a significant emphasis on the role of users, and in particular of users as consumers of services. This was reflected in policies that sought to provide users with greater choice, such as parental choice of schools, to provide users with more information on which to make choices, such as performance indicators and league tables, and the use of customer satisfaction surveys as a means of gauging the feelings of users about services.

Under Labour this interest in the consumer has remained central, although there have been some significant differences. Since 1997 there has arguably been greater consultation with consumers, and particularly with groups, and more widespread attempts to involve consumers in policy design, such as the Policy Action Teams established by the Social Exclusion Unit and the use of a range of consultation techniques such as citizens' juries. As part of Labour's approach there has also been an emphasis on the centre setting national priorities and frameworks for accountability and inspection, and a variety of providers giving choice to users. In part these attempts to involve citizens and ascertain their views derive from a greater recognition of the role of attitudes, understanding and behaviour in making policy work. At the same time there has been a re-emergence of the Conservatives' idea that providing choice is a way of improving the quality and responsiveness of services.

In many respects the major issue here is not at all new; it is the difficulty in overcoming economic, social and political inequality – the views of the affluent and the middle class are likely to dominate while the lack of financial and political resources, and other constraints on participation, mean that the input from poorer and disadvantaged people is harder to achieve. For New Labour, therefore, the major challenge has been how to achieve the inclusive approach to policy making outlined in *Professional policy making* and to involve disadvantaged groups in decision making. A simple shift towards market-type mechanisms is insufficient to achieve this, but through the use of innovative consultation methods, a range of approaches have been developed seeking to involve socially excluded groups, children and others in shaping policy.

Evidence-based policy

For social policy perhaps one of the more problematic of the themes associated with 'modernisation' is that of evidence-based policy making (Davies et al, 2000b; Walter et al, 2005). As noted earlier in this chapter, an interest in policy making based on research and other evidence is not new; however, it has certainly received a new impetus since 1997. This is generally traced back to the *Modernising government* White Paper (Cabinet Office, 1999), although the White Paper does not actually contain such a phrase (it does say that there is a need to make better use of evidence and research). The development of this emphasis can be seen in the other papers discussed above, with *Professional policy making for the twenty-first century* (Cabinet Office Strategic Policy Making Team, 1999) recognising many of the problems associated with the aims of better and evidence-based policy making, including what constitutes 'evidence' and 'research', the variations in scientific reliability and validity of data, the lack of research in some areas, and the constraints on policy makers' access to research/evidence. The Performance and Innovation Unit's report, *Adding it up* (PIU, 2000) emphasised the need for analysis and modelling to be more embedded in central government, suggesting that there needed to be a *'fundamental change in culture* to place good analysis at the heart of policy-making' (p 5, original emphasis). It also stressed the need for evidence-based policy while again recognising the differing pressures and constraints (including political pressures).

A significant feature of 'evidence-based' policy under Labour, although already developing under the previous Conservative administrations (for example, with 'Earnings Top Up', and 'Parent Plus'), has been the use of policy pilots as a way of 'testing' policy prior to full implementation. Pilots have been used for a variety of policies including the New Deal for Lone Parents, the idea of salaried defenders (public defenders) within the criminal justice system in England, and Drug Treatment and Testing Orders (DTTOs) in Scotland.

While there may be an increasing awareness within government of a need for 'evidence-based policy', it remains unclear what that is. In addition, the approach to evidence-based policy has in the past been criticised by some for being highly positivist in nature and for making assumptions about the links between measurement and policy success or failure (that what works is largely what can be measured), as well as for ignoring questions around social construction and control. Referring to the emphasis on evidence-based policy, Parsons (2002) notes that things are more complex: '"What works" is about: what works, for whom, when and how?; or what kind of evidence works for what kind of problem/policy in what context, and for whom' (2002, p 57). He also argues that if we are to move to a form of policy making that is more influenced by evidence, we will have to tackle the difficult questions of 'who gets what, when and how' (Lasswell, 1958). He notes a significant contrast in what he sees as Labour's primarily managerialist approach, to Lasswell's view that the policy sciences should be concerned with reinvigorating democracy (perhaps, ironically, another, but often separate, concern of New Labour) and that improving the relationship between knowledge and power was essentially a political and democratic task.

However, as Duncan and Harrop (2006) suggest, it is clearly desirable for researchers to consider the views of the users of research, including the contexts in which research could and should be used. Research users also need to enable adequate networking and communication with researchers. And 'Policy makers and practitioners, if they are truly committed to using research evidence, must be prepared to engage; to plan ahead; to understand the complexities and limitations of research' (Duncan and Harrop, 2006, p 172).

This discussion is far from exhaustive – to it could be added the role of HM Treasury, policy transfer, policy networks and more – but it is certainly illustrative of changes and emphases in the policy process under New Labour, and as such provides us with a basis for further consideration of this. It is also important to note that, as with other elements of policy making, there has continued to be discussion and refinement of what was arguably a rather ill-defined concept, for example around whether policy should be 'evidence based', 'evidence informed' or 'evidence inspired', with the latter, in particular, drawing on a recognition that policy making is essentially a creative process.

International context

Since the 1980s there have been many changes in government and policy making across the industrialised world. While it is not possible to easily identify coherent themes and developments, some consideration of the international context could help to understand the emphasis on the policy process in the UK.

During the 1980s, many countries faced substantial budget deficits, a situation which, together with the emergence of New Right ideas, encouraged in some states at least (with Australia, New Zealand and the UK frequently having been seen as to the fore) responses such as privatisation, emphases on efficiency and effectiveness, and managerialist approaches to the public sector and to public policy more generally. Many of these developments have been referred to as the 'new public management' (Hood, 1991). The extent to which this was accepted worldwide has been a matter for continued debate (for example, Hughes, 2003), but there have been arguments, for example, about the Labour Party's acceptance of the new public management following the examples of Labor governments in Australia and New Zealand and the Clinton administration in the US (Borins, 2002; Carroll and Steane, 2002).

More recently new and additional pressures have emerged. For example, Bovaird and Löffler (2003) list almost 30 'external factors' that they see as driving public policy reforms, including political, economic/financial, social, technological, environmental and legal/legislative dimensions. They suggest that many of these factors have served to push governments in similar directions, such as global warming and other environmental concerns, child poverty, and, particularly in the industrialised world, the ageing society and the consequent pressures on pensions. Such pressures do not relate solely to policies, and whether or not there is convergence, but also to the more central concerns of this book, policy making and implementation, although in these instances 'internal' factors mean that there may be less uniformity of direction. However, they suggest that there are concerns about, for example, how service design and delivery is shaped by the needs of all stakeholders, and that 'concerns about fragmented and disjointed public policies and governmental structures ... have encouraged governments to find more mechanisms for co-ordination and integration, but in different ways in different countries' (Bovaird and Löffler, 2003, p 17).

During the 1990s the idea that there had been a 'hollowing-out' of the state, with a shift towards governance, rather than government, increased use of market mechanisms, and privatisation and contracting out, came to prominence in some fields. The perceived transfer of power to international organisations such as the EU added to a concern for some that the role of the state was being minimised in some countries. More recently the dominant view appears to be rather that there are a variety of roles that the state may play, and that different countries may choose different approaches over time.

Debates about globalisation have also been interpreted as having implications for institutions of government and governance. Although there may be no consensus on globalisation and its impacts, it is often seen as potentially affecting many of the key institutions of social and political life, changing the nature of existing relationships and the ways in which power is exercised, with some supporters of the globalisation thesis suggesting that it will lead to the decline of the nation-state as the primary context within which agendas and policy are formulated. On the other hand, it is also possible to argue that just because problems or issues may be seen as global or international, it is not necessarily the case that policy making will take place at that level.

However, it remains the case that there is a much greater awareness of the concept of multi-level governance than was the case a decade or so ago. Not only is there a level of politics that takes place at the global level, largely focused on issues of security and trade, but increasingly also including environmental concerns. There are also supranational organisations such as the EU, which now plays a significant role in the making and implementation of some areas of policy for its member states (although it too has seen it as appropriate to consider reform of its governance, including in relation to involvement in policy making, flexibility and policy coherence: CEC, 2001), and the Organisation for Economic Co-operation and Development (OECD), which has frequently encouraged its particular view of reforms and 'modernisation' (for example, OECD, 2004a, 2004b, 2005a, 2005b). Government at the national level clearly remains of central importance, being the arena in which for virtually all states the most important decisions continue to be taken. While there have long been regional politics in many states, in some countries, such as Spain and the UK, recent reforms have provided new representative fora in which they can be played out; and while in many countries local government may be less important than it once was, it frequently retains a role in interpreting and delivering policies determined at other levels of government.

Of course, it is also true that governments have increasingly been seeking to 'learn lessons' from other states, with both Conservative and Labour administrations having adapted policies and practices from other countries. Indeed, *Modernising government* argues that becoming more forward and outward looking involves '... learning lessons from other countries; and integrating the European Union and international dimension into our policy making' (Cabinet Office, 1999, p 16). This in turn may influence the extent to which there are trends in policy making, as *Modernising government* again suggests: 'We are exchanging ideas with other countries on policy making, on delivering services and on using information technology in new and innovative ways. We are learning from each other' (Cabinet Office, 1999, p 12). Any such impacts may in turn be mitigated by national cultures and differing internal pressures, making it difficult to assess whether or not there are more or less common patterns in approaches to and mechanisms of policy making and implementation across states.

Why these nine principles?

It is clear that one of the major developments in government since 1997 has been the development and publication of guidance and information on the policy process on a scale that has not previously been seen in the UK. This renewed government interest in the processes and practice of policy making and implementation emerges in part from a rationalistic view that better policy making can lead to better policies and to better outcomes. It also reflects the belief that the world today is more complex, uncertain and unpredictable, and that for governments to respond quickly and appropriately in a manner that suits the expectations of the public, this requires a different approach to policy making. The *Modernising government* White Paper (Cabinet Office, 1999) suggested that little attention had been paid to the policy process in recent years and argued for a focus on outcomes, greater inclusivity, wider involvement of people from outside government, more forward-looking and outward-looking approaches, and the need to learn from experience. Similarly, ideas such as the need to understand and manage risk, and to undertake 'horizon scanning' to anticipate and prepare for future challenges and opportunities, add to the perceived need for improved approaches to policy making.

A further driver for change has been the perceived need to improve capacity and capability within government to enable the state to respond rapidly to new challenges and to the expectations of the public. In addition to initiatives such as the 'professionalisation' and 'joining up' of policy making, a new system of departmental Capability Reviews was introduced in 2006 with the aim of assessing departments' capability to meet future challenges, examining how well departments focus on outcomes, whether decisions are based on evidence and whether there is a common purpose within the organisation. The initial reports were generally positive but among the needs identified were the need to improve the human resources (HR) function (and through them the availability of appropriate skills) within departments, to improve management capability and to improve operational delivery of public services (Capability Reviews Team, 2006a), and the need for a framework of effective cross-departmental working and better strategic leadership (Capability Reviews Team, 2006b). In addition the Civil Service Steering Board and the Permanent Secretaries' Management Group now seek to take a corporate view of common challenges, including those related to capability issues.

In terms of New Labour's approach to modernisation and 'better' policy making, critics might argue that, while demonstrating an awareness of the complexity of policy making and implementation, it is grounded in the type of view associated with writers such as Lasswell (1958) and Simon (1945/57), with a view that better policy making can be achieved by improvements in instrumental rationality. In considering some of the developments under Labour it can be suggested that there has been a shift to what may appear to be a more 'technocratic' approach to the policy process. However, this raises some important questions, including, where is the role for values? And is there a danger that, like the Conservatives' use of markets, a 'modernised' policy process risks legitimating government decisions and the existing distribution of resources, in other words, effectively depoliticising decisions about policies and about resource allocation? Yet, at the same time, there has been a greater opportunity than for many years for policy analysts to engage with government and for their research to have some input into the policy process. While criticism of the government may be entirely appropriate, and while there is a genuine need for external analysts to reflect on the weaknesses of various parts of the 'modernisation' agenda, at the same time there may also be a need for them to consider where they stand in relation to many of the issues associated with 'better' policy making.

The remainder of the chapters of this book are structured around the nine principles, or 'competencies', set out by the Cabinet Office's Strategic Policy

—

Making Team (1999) in *Professional policy making for the twenty-first century*, which it identified as key features of 'modern policy making'. There is a real attempt to analyse the policy process, from the perspective of policy makers. The nine features can therefore be seen as focusing on some important elements of the complex and dynamic policy process, to understand and to explain to policy makers and practitioners how policy making might be improved. While recognising the shortcomings of this model, this book sets out to explore the approach and to measure it against both academic and 'real-world' ideas in order to further refine our understanding of the process; to learn from experience of putting the nine principles into practice; and to develop our understanding of 'what works' in policy making.

Chapter Two, by Hugh Bochel and Louise Shaxson, considers the extent to which policy makers are taking a long-term strategic perspective (defined as at least five years in the future, but often substantially longer) to policy making and the information sources and mechanisms that are being used, including in relation to economic, political and social changes, and the likely impact of policies. Chapter Three, by Edward C. Page and Jane Mark-Lawson, focuses primarily on international factors and influences, and in particular on the ways in which the experiences of other countries are used by policy makers to inform policy within the UK, including the ways in which organisations such as the EU impact on UK policy.

The primary concern of Chapter Four, by Andrew Massey and Jamie Rentoul, is the extent to which policy makers and practitioners are willing to challenge established thinking and ways of working and to develop and utilise new and flexible ideas and approaches, including drawing on inputs from people outside the traditional arenas of policy making.

Chapters Five to Eight are concerned with some of the areas of the policy process that have perhaps received the greatest attention in recent years. While the idea of 'evidence-based' policy has been widely discussed, Chapter Five, by Martin Bulmer, Elizabeth Coates and Louise Dominian, examines the ways and extent to which policy makers are informed by good quality evidence, including from a variety of stakeholders. Similarly, Chapter Six, by Catherine Bochel and Angela Evans, again focuses on a topical area – 'inclusive' policy making – and the ways in which policy making takes account of the views and needs of those people likely to be affected by policies, and the extent to which there is the opportunity for direct involvement in and influence on the policy-making process. Chapter Seven, by Richard Parry and Marion Kerr, considers the degree to which a 'joined-up' approach has permeated across policy making and implementation. It includes a discussion of the extent to which cross-cutting planning and objective setting have been achieved, the success or failure of joint working, collaboration and partnership arrangements, and the extent to which these have become a normal part of the policy process. And Chapter Eight, by Martin Powell and Warwick Maynard, focuses on 'review' to consider different approaches to reviewing key areas of policy and delivery, how evidence and opinion are sought, how stakeholders are involved, and how this feeds back into policy and legislative change.

The primary focus of Chapter Nine, by Robert Walker and Sue Duncan, is on the ways in which evaluation mechanisms are or are not built into the policy-making and delivery processes. It analyses the widespread use of targets, different models of evaluation, piloting policies, the extent to which criteria for success are clear and transparent, the means used to evaluate success or failure of policies, and the ways in which programmes and policies are or are not modified as a result of evaluations. While Chapter Three concentrates on the international dimension and Chapter Nine on evaluation, Chapter Ten, by John Hudson, is concerned with the extent to which policy makers learn from experiences of what works and what does not.

Finally, Chapter Eleven, by Hugh Bochel and Sue Duncan, considers the current status of 'modern policy making', highlighting areas where there has been progress and areas where there remain significant barriers.

TWO

Forward-looking policy making

Hugh Bochel and Louise Shaxson

This chapter focuses on the development of forward-looking policy making, where the emphasis lies beyond the short term, extending perhaps 10–25 years into the future. In doing this it:

- examines the use and development of futures work within British government and the increasing attention paid to it from the 1990s;
- discusses traditional techniques and outlines those that are being developed to improve the evidence base for forward-looking policy making;
- outlines some key initiatives that have contributed to the firmer establishment of futures work in at least some parts of government; and
- considers a variety of issues associated with attempts to explore the future and to embed these in the policy process.

We can either stumble into the future and hope it turns out alright or we can try and shape it. To shape it, the first step is to work out what it might look like. (Stephen Ladyman MP, Minister for Transport, speech at the Foresight Intelligent Systems Infrastructure Launch Event, Institute of Engineers, 26 January 2006)

Policy makers work in the future, setting the parameters of the society we will become. Of course they need to look ahead. (Defra, 2007, p 8)

While policy makers may often, and inevitably, be concerned with short-term goals, such as improving the standards or efficiency of a service, or responding to an immediate problem, it is the case that many of the aims, effects and outcomes from policy making are, equally inevitably, long term. Pensions reform, green taxes and hospital building programmes are examples of policies whose full effects are not seen until many years after their implementation. As the House of Commons Public Administration Select Committee notes, 'Governing for the future is both important and difficult. Important because it means getting to grips with the long-term issues that will shape the lives of future generations; difficult because it rubs up against the short-termism that is inherent in the politics of the electoral cycle' (2007, p 5). The role of the forward-looking policy maker is to negotiate this tension: to ensure that decisions taken today are informed by robust evidence of their likely future outcomes, and to balance our uncertainties about what the future holds with politicians' desire to effect definite change.

Policies are developed within the context of particular economic, political and social conditions, and these involve major decisions, including prioritising across competing needs and policy areas, the distribution of resources and the need to be in a position to respond to future developments, problems and challenges. This prioritisation depends on our current understanding of what is likely to affect the future policy environment, and this in turn helps shape the strategic goals that governments set for departments (such as Public Service Agreement [PSA] targets). Because such targets then define departmental priorities for policy development, the government is itself playing a significant role in shaping the future. Lord Birt (quoted in Public Administration Select Committee, 2007, p 10) observed that, 'policy is a subset of strategy' (see Figure 2.1), and there is a clear link between the 'big picture' that any government aspires to (strategy), the more detailed intentions it sets out (policy formulation), the actions that are taken to fulfil those intentions (policy delivery) and the consequences of those actions (effects).

Pulling it all together into a coherent storyline is a formidable task, and questions then arise from this: what information do policy makers need to ensure that there is a clear line of sight between long-term strategic goals, intermediate targets that may be set in response to short-term political pressures, and current policy development processes? And how should policy makers prioritise between developing a good understanding of what different futures might hold, and addressing current issues?

The importance of forward-looking approaches to policy making derives considerable support from rationalistic approaches to the policy process that see forecasting and evaluation as important in helping decision makers to choose the 'best' options, but even more incrementalist approaches are likely to identify some potential advantages in having greater awareness of potential challenges and opportunities. The impact of policy failures, such as the Child Support Agency,

Figure 2.1: The relationship between strategy and policy

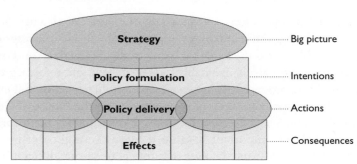

problems with Railtrack, and unanticipated crises, such as foot and mouth and BSE (bovine spongiform encephalopathy), and the recommendations of subsequent reports (for example, Social Security Committee, 1999; Work and Pensions Committee, 2005) and inquiries (for example, Phillips, 2000), have also served to encourage governments to be more forward looking and to seek to identify problems before they develop.

The assessment and management of risk has also been a significant driver for futures thinking, with the Treasury in particular having increasingly addressed issues of risk and uncertainty from the late 1980s. The Phillips Report on BSE (Phillips, 2000) identified two broad trends here: the first was the growing recognition that there were appropriate techniques available for the consideration of options and problems around which there were uncertainties; the second arose from the awareness that the public's perception of risks was often at variance with scientific evidence, and has involved attempts to try and understand the values that individuals bring to decisions about risk (for example, HM Treasury, 2005). In addition, policy makers have increasingly been seeking to make 'evidence-based' decisions, even when faced with short-term problems or incremental policy change. However, as is reflected elsewhere in this book, the extent to which decisions are informed, and the quality of those decisions, is highly dependent on the quality of information available.

Gavigan and Scapolo (1999) point out that over the past 30 years worldwide there has been a considerable amount of futures work, including strategy and policy planning, in a structured way. They argue that more recently this has been increasing in the public sector, particularly in the technology field, with this growth driven by the spread of technology and its importance for economic growth and prosperity; the growing importance of decentralised decision making, alliances and networks and the development of shared views; changes in the knowledge production system; and pressures on public expenditure, including science and technology budgets.

Professional policy making for the twenty-first century (Cabinet Office Strategic Policy Making Team, 1999) identified a number of issues around long-term thinking, including the electoral pressures on ministers that could lead to an emphasis on short-term measures to achieve immediate results, and scepticism among policy makers about their abilities to look ahead more than three to five years. It also suggested that while there had been some growth in forward thinking in many government departments, it was less clear that this was feeding into policy making. The document also touched on the question of the techniques that are used in futures work, and, as discussed later in this chapter, the type and status of many of these techniques are both new and still developing, so that not only is there greater uncertainty about which approaches to use for which purposes, but the newness of the general approach and the methods themselves means that they may be less likely to be embedded across government than those of longer standing.

However, if many of the aims of *Modernising government* (Cabinet Office, 1999) and *Professional policy making for the twenty-first century* (Cabinet Office Strategic

Policy Making Team, 1999) are to be achieved, and if policy making is indeed to be led, or even informed, by evidence, then it is necessary, particularly in the context of what many argue is a faster-changing, more complex and more uncertain world, that policy goals and decisions are set in the economic and social context, and that properly informed and scoped futures work is accepted and embedded as a central feature within the policy process. This chapter considers how forward-looking approaches have developed within government in the UK, the links, or otherwise, with policy making, the techniques that may be appropriate and how best use could be made of them.

Development of futures work

> Governments have always been concerned about the future. It is the extent to which this concern has resulted in systematic, open and effective long-term thinking which has changed. (Public Administration Select Committee, 2007, p 6)

The relationship between knowledge and policy making has been a significant issue for many years, and perhaps in particular from the 1950s and 1960s, with attempts to make policy making 'better' through greater use of 'rational' techniques to improve both policy-making processes and policies themselves, from problem definition through analysing options to implementation and evaluation. Similarly, there has always been strategic planning in government, and the 1960s and 1970s saw attempts to improve this in many areas of government, with the creation of the Central Policy Review Staff to provide strategic advice to the Cabinet, and many departments establishing their own planning units as part of the reforms that followed the Fulton Committee's (1968) recommendations. However, as Parsons (2004) notes, by the 1980s, with the influence of 'public choice' critiques and the growth of the new public management, the emphasis was largely on government 'allowing *market* and *business* rationality to operate as effectively in the public interest as it did in securing private interests' (p 43, original emphasis).

Yet, clearly, attempts to identify future possibilities are necessary for public policy. As Hogwood and Gunn put it with regard to forecasting:

> The choices we make now affect the future, and the outcome of those choices is affected by events in the future. In making choices we are implicitly or explicitly making assumptions about the future. Forecasting involves making those assumptions explicitly and rigorously, the assumption being that the resulting choices will in some sense be 'better'. (1984, p 128)

It is perhaps unsurprising, therefore, that from the mid-1990s there has been a new concern with the policy-making and strategic capacities of governments (as indeed is reflected in the production of this book). However, as Parsons (2004) suggests, the concern was now less with rational policy making than with improving the ability and capacity of governments to understand and manage complex realities and to steer strategically.

Looking ahead further than the immediate future is necessary, not only because the process of policy development can be slow, but because the full effects of policies frequently take time to be felt, with, for example, many of the potential impacts of a programme such as Sure Start, aimed at supporting families with young children, not being visible or measurable for many years following its introduction. This means that policy makers need to look at future trends and drivers to ensure that even the most focused policies are well placed to deliver, over time, in a changing society. For example, predictions on demographic trends will have major implications for policies on education, healthcare and pensions, with an ageing population implying very different policy responses and directions from those arising from a high birth rate, while those concerned with environmental change may have wide implications across a range of economic and social fields. However, in recent times the perceived need for future planning, and at the same time increased concerns over the knowledge base required for this, have received added impetus due to greater (public) awareness of the complexities, uncertainties and risks of the contemporary world.

Clearly, attempts to predict the future are fraught with difficulties: we are often uncertain about what is going on in the present, let alone the future; information may be old (for example, in relation to population planning, the Census only takes place every 10 years); it may be subject to revision; data may not exist; we are uncertain of cause and effect in many areas of economic and social policy; and forecasting may be time consuming and expensive, when decision makers may be under pressure to make rapid decisions and to minimise costs. In these respects there are clear links and overlaps with other chapters, perhaps in particular those dealing with evidence-based policy and with evaluation and review, but this chapter seeks, particularly in the latter stages, to draw out ideas and lessons that may help to improve engagement with and the production of forward-looking policies.

While forward-looking policies may be desirable, and forecasting can undoubtedly be important in policy making, as Hogwood and Gunn (1984) pointed out, it can be used, abused and ignored by decision makers. Much policy making is highly political and there are a wide variety of ideological and value-based influences that can have major consequences for the ways in which forecasts are interpreted and used. Indeed forecasts and predictions can themselves embody particular assumptions about the desirability or undesirability of particular economic, political and social ideas, and may therefore serve to reinforce particular beliefs and values. They can also embody assumptions about the appropriateness or otherwise of particular measurements. Unless care is taken to unpack them, both types of assumption can be compounded along the policy-making process: what may seem like a sensible course of action can, in fact, be fraught with risks and uncertainties.

Forecasting

Forecasting has been one of the principal approaches used to inform policy making. There are two broad categories of forecast: projections, extrapolations from current trends; and judgements about the future, or predictions (for example, Spicker, 2006).

Projections

Among the approaches that have been widely used are:

- *Extrapolation:* indicators may be used to plot trends, for example in levels of smoking, the age of populations, carbon emissions and so on. Using past and present data it is possible to seek to forecast future developments. However, trends are difficult to predict, and Parsons (1995) gives the example of five different trends (exponential, linear, discontinuous, cyclical and S-curve), each of which is upwards over a period of time, but the shape and trajectories of which might have very different implications for policy making. Further, the trends that are plotted are likely to be affected by both the measures used and the time period over which they are based.
- *Modelling,* including economic modelling, such as that used by HM Treasury to model the potential response of the UK economy to changes such as rises or falls in interest rates. In the case of the economy there are now many other similar models, including those used by large financial institutions, which seek to perform similar functions. Models such as these set out a series of assumptions derived from existing information and theoretical judgements. The model itself consists of estimated paramters and, often complex, interrelationships that act on the exogenous variables, some of which may be available as policy instruments, to determine the endogenous variables which are the forecasts. This allows a variety of options to be developed and compared. Among the types of impacts that might be modelled are changes in levels of public expenditure and their effects on the economy in terms of growth, or levels of employment and unemployment. They have significant advantages in that they allow a variety of 'what if' options to be tested and can allow investigation of what sort of changes may cause particular effects (and of what size). However, while modelling is increasingly widely used, many people remain concerned about the accuracy of the outputs and their cost-effectiveness, given that complex questions demand increasingly complex, and costly, modelling approaches. Perhaps even more importantly, policy decisions, although potentially informed by models, remain subject to the influence of political factors, and to bureaucratic and other pressures.

While some projections are quite sophisticated and seek to take account of a range of factors, it is incumbent on policy makers and their advisers to ensure that they are set in context, as many tend to reflect assumptions about exogenous conditions that are then subject to unanticipated change. So, for example, projections of migration into the UK made during the late 1990s might not have been designed to take into account the consequences of the enlargement of the European Union (EU) in Eastern Europe. Even sophisticated models, such as the Treasury model of the UK economy, are modelling relationships that are themselves evolving over time, and are frequently amended as new measures emerge or new theoretical developments inform the operation of the model. Most projections will be strengthened by sensitivity analyses that test these assumptions, showing what happens to the end result when key variables are changed. This helps decision makers to gauge the level of uncertainty and risk associated with each assumption, and to examine how other forms of evidence could be used to strengthen the analysis.

Judgemental techniques

While projection tends to be widely used in areas such as economic and population forecasting, which lend themselves to largely quantitative techniques, other policy areas, such as many associated with social policy, are perhaps more suited to judgemental approaches. These might include:

- *Scenario writing*, with the development of logical or plausible descriptions of possible future conditions, often in order to provide a clearer understanding of possible futures and the potential consequences of different choices and actions.
- *Delphi analysis*, drawing on a group of anonymous experts who are not normally in direct contact with each other, but who communicate through some form of intermediary, such as a steering group, which distributes their responses to other members of the group to produce a process of questions, responses and feedback, and following these exchanges of information and analysis the steering group produces a judgement. This is an approach that strongly emphasises the role of experts and the capacity of the steering group to reach a consensus, but which consequently may suffer from any flaws in these areas.
- *Cross-impact analysis*, involving the development of a list of events, possible impacts and outcomes, which are placed before a panel who then assess the likely impacts in terms of what might happen and in what sequence. It is therefore useful as an approach that may show how one situation may impact on another.

In addition, there have been a number of approaches developed that have sought to move away from these 'traditionalist' rational approaches to analysis, such as Strategic Options Development and Analysis (SODA) and Soft Systems Methodology (SSM). These tend to accept that analysis and decision making take place in a complex world and in the context of incomplete knowledge, and are intended to help contribute to the understanding of problems.

Generally, one of the major problems with the use of judgemental techniques is that there is no way of estimating their likely accuracy. However, they can undoubtedly have value, for example in helping to explore relationships or developments that may not be considered by more numerically based approaches. While similar criticisms about accuracy can also be made about numerical approaches, and particularly over the quality of some of the data that can inform them, they do frequently allow for some level of consideration of the possible internal margin for error. Indeed, perhaps one of the weaknesses that has affected many previous, and indeed current, approaches to looking to the future, has been that they have frequently been uni-dimensional and based on projections from current trends. Despite the increasing sophistication of both predictive and judgemental techniques there remain limitations to both, and in reality no method, and particularly no single approach, can ever guarantee accurate predictions about the future. This means that it is often necessary to consider the use of a combination of techniques that are suited to the needs of each particular situation. For example, quantitative, trend-based projections could be used to find issues that could be investigated in greater depth by focus group-type activities, or a deliberative process might be used to set the scene for more in-depth modelling work.

It is perhaps worth noting that, despite the increasing sophistication of the Bank of England and Treasury's models of the economy, the setting of major economic variables, such as interest rates, through the Monetary Policy Committee (a panel of experts), effectively combines elements of both judgemental and modelling techniques. The Stern review of the economics of climate change similarly combined extremely complex modelling work to assess the risks, uncertainties and equity issues associated with anthropogenic climate change, with a recognition that policy responses must necessarily be 'judgemental' in nature (Stern, 2007).

In addition, there has been a growing realisation that the process of thinking about the future can be of equal importance and benefit as the answers that emerge from considering what the future might look like. Among the reasons that are given for this are that it can develop new skills and perspectives, that it can improve the ability to respond to uncertainty and to changing circumstances, and, as noted above, thinking about the future can help governments consider how they might shape the future. From another perspective, Schultz (2006) has argued that '... government agencies in the UK produce solidly researched policy papers and research monographs on particular issues, but that draws primarily on past data and present trends, rarely addressing the issue of how change itself will change over time. They assemble the evidence describing the issue at the moment, as if it were frozen in time' (p 3). The challenges of considering change in greater depth can therefore add significantly to the benefits of the process.

Given this variety of ideas and influences, it is perhaps unsurprising that over the past half-century, there has been something of an emergence of futures thinking as a discipline in its own right, developing its own ideas and with its own range of techniques.

Modern policy making: forward looking?

Despite what many people saw as ideologically or market-driven approaches to wide areas of policy making during the 1980s and 1990s, a greater emphasis on forward-looking policy development was evident under the Conservative governments of the time, particularly in relation to science and technology, as was evidenced with the creation of the Foresight programme in 1994, as discussed later in this chapter.

The past two decades have, however, seen new impetuses for more forward-thinking approaches to policy making, perhaps in particular arising from concerns over the capacity of governments to determine and implement courses of action and increased awareness of 'risk' and uncertainty. With regard to the latter, recent years have seen considerable debate over scientific advances such as cloning, genetic manipulation and nanotechnology. While government and business have generally sought to portray developments such as these as matters of science, with safety limits that can be calculated through scientific trials, public, media and pressure group concerns, arguably reinforced by perceived policy failures, such as over BSE, have focused on the problems in calculating risks, the difficulty of being aware of potential problems until it is too late, and a distrust of 'experts' (see, for example, Jasanoff, 2005). In a world that is increasingly seen as complex and uncertain, this greater awareness of risk poses challenges for policy makers in their attempts to identify new challenges and opportunities, and to reassure the public about their ability to identify and to tackle these. A greater emphasis on improving the policy-making and strategic capacities of government has also been apparent, arising in part from the concerns over risk and uncertainty, but also encouraged by the shift from government to governance (from 'rowing' to 'steering'). A number of aspects of this concern to build or rebuild 'capacity' have underpinned the emphasis on attempts to 'improve' the policy process, particularly under New Labour since 1997, of which 'modern policy making' and the 'forward-looking' aspects of it have been a significant part. As Moore (1995) put it:

> If public managers are to create value over the long run, then an important part of their job consists of strengthening the policies that are sold to their authorisers. Specifically, the policies that guide an organisation's activities must reflect the proper interests and concerns of the citizens and their representatives; the story about the value to be produced must be rooted in accurate reasoning and real experience; and the real operating experience of the organisation must be available to the political overseers.... Otherwise the strengths of the political process will not be exploited, the knowledge and experience of the operating managers will not be utilised, and the acknowledged

weaknesses of the process will not be challenged. (Moore, 1995, p 55)

Professional policy making for the twenty-first century (Cabinet Office Strategic Policy Making Team, 1999) found that there were real obstacles to policy making for the long term, including ministers' desire to see measures that produce short-term results to meet the pressures of the electoral cycle, and scepticism among policy makers about their ability to look more than three to five years ahead. It highlighted as positive progress the work of the Department of Trade and Industry's Future Unit, the Department of Health's use of scenarios to look up to 20 years ahead, the Ministry of Agriculture, Fisheries and Food's Economic Research Division's 10- to 15-year forecasts, and the UK Foresight programme for its attempts to look at future developments as far ahead as 2040.

To underpin the propositions set out in *Professional policy making for the twenty-first century* (Cabinet Office Strategic Policy Making Team, 1999) and *Better policy making* (Bullock et al, 2001), Mulgan and Lee (2001) provided a number of examples of 'forward-looking' activities by a number of departments. These included the National Beds Inquiry, an attempt to determine the number of hospital beds required over the next 10-20 years, which drew on historical analysis of major drivers of demand for beds, examination of expected future trends in those drivers, such as technological change, patient preferences and public expectations, a study of different approaches and trends in other countries, and analysis of variations between health authorities in England. From these, three scenarios for the next 20 years were developed for possible patterns of services for older people, who are the largest users of hospital beds. The Inquiry was seen as having produced an analytical report that was not only forward looking but also outward looking and also founded on a strong evidence base. *Better policy making* (Bullock et al, 2001) also included another example, Transport 2010, which again drew on extrapolations for current trends and the development of illustrative scenarios.

Also, following the *Modernising government* White Paper (Cabinet Office, 1999), within the Performance and Innovation Unit a 'strategic challenges' team was created in 1999, superseded in 2000 by a 'strategic futures' team. The former was founded on a belief that government policy should be based on a consistent long-term strategy, and that at the same time it should be prepared for new problems and able to take new opportunities and that in order to achieve these things it was necessary to identify some of the key challenges that the government was likely to encounter over the next 10-20 years. Drawing on the many forecasts produced by both public and private sectors, six key forces were identified in *The future and how to think about it* as driving change: demographics, science and technology, global environment, attitudes and values, economic globalisation and political institutions (PIU, 1999). It concluded with a consideration of the role of government, suggesting that the process of thinking about the future might be more important than the result; that looking at challenges in the context of government, politics and society is quite different from seeking to project economic or technological trends; and that institutional and organisational issues are as important as specific policy challenges as they are often the source of policy failure, and that what government may actually require the most is generic skills and qualities to be able to respond rapidly and effectively in an uncertain world. This conclusion has since been reflected in the establishment of the Office for Science and Innovation within the Department of Trade and Industry and of horizon-scanning units in a number of other departments.

In addition, the Prime Minister's Strategy Unit (PMSU) has produced a number of other documents and guidance. A report commissioned for the Performance and Innovation Unit (now the PMSU) by the Henley Centre (2001), *Understanding best practice in strategic futures work*, sought to benchmark work in both public and private sectors in the UK against other countries. As one of its key findings the report suggested that:

> ... the most important issue for organisations is to ensure that the objectives, output, and methodology of the strategic futures work is aligned at the start with the audiences for the work, the needs of the organisation and its culture. Furthermore, the same organisation may choose to adopt different approaches and different techniques at different times to reach different ends. One size does not fit all. The question to ask is not simply 'does it work?', or even 'will it work for us?', but '*how* will it work for us?'. (Henley Centre, 2001, p 1)

The need to consider these questions has also been identified by Schultz (2006), who argues that horizon scanning is most effective when it is used to identify and monitor change within an integrated foresight process (see also Table 2.1).

The Henley Centre report found that there was a similarity between the language, structures and practices of academia and those of best practice strategic futures organisations. These included flat organisational structures, research that was valued and sometimes undertaken for its own sake, rather than for specific end products or users, diversity of staff, wide intellectual exchange with other organisations and effective networks. In terms of the methodological approaches, the report suggested five guidelines for organisations:

1. Ensure that there is clarity about the resource requirements of the work – this may be highly resource intensive.
2. Ensure that the process is inclusive – methods that take on knowledge from within organisations are likely to find higher levels of acceptance within organisations, while it is also essential to take on board divergent and minority opinions.
3. Ensure that people understand and trust the processes being used – transparent processes and methodologies are more likely to be successful than those that are less clear or hidden.

4. Understand the limitations as well as the opportunities offered by strategic futures thinking – while such thinking can help organisations test their assumptions about the present and the future, it will not resolve cultural or institutional issues within an organisation.
5. Understand that the process will take time to deliver benefits – work tends to be continuous rather than short-term, project-based, and it takes time to deliver results.

For all tiers of government it is also necessary to have a clear link between futures work and the policy-making process, likely through the development of departmental strategies. The PMSU's *Strategy survival guide* (2004) notes that '... as a rule, the best strategies in governments and public services are [among other things] clear about objectives, relative priorities and trade-offs [and] underpinned by a rich understanding of causes, trends, opportunities, threats and possible futures' (p 5). While good strategies will therefore incorporate possible futures, where strategy is lacking, or is short term or produced without a rigorous analysis of the potential opportunities and risks from future trends and drivers, there is a greater likelihood of failing to both reflect the future policy environment and of taking the opportunity to shape it.

Foresight

One of the most notable initiatives in the UK has been the development of the Foresight programme. In 1993 the Conservative Chancellor of the Duchy of Lancaster, William Waldegrave, launched the White Paper, *Realising our potential: A strategy for science, engineering and technology* (Chancellor of the Duchy of Lancaster, 1993). Emphasising the importance of science, engineering and technology to wealth creation and the quality of life, the White Paper indicated that the government would launch a technology Foresight programme to be led by the Chief Scientific Adviser and designed to encourage closer interaction between scientists, industry and government, and to identify future opportunities and threats for science, engineering and technology. There have so far been three rounds of the Foresight programme, generally involving panels seeking to look ahead over a 10- to 20-year period. In 2000, the Science Minister, Lord Sainsbury, announced a review of the programme that recommended that the programme should be more flexible to enable it to respond to new developments, and that it should focus resources on where they would have greatest value. The review also found that it was unclear the extent to which the Foresight programme had impacted on policy and recommended that Foresight panels should place greater emphasis on identifying action points in order to ensure outcomes.

A second review in 2006 found a significant degree of success for Foresight in achieving the objectives of identifying ways in which future science and technology could address future challenges for society and identifying potential opportunities. Unlike the 2001 review it concluded that 'Foresight has directly informed national policies and programmes' (PREST, 2006, p 3). The House of Commons Public Administration Select Committee also commended the Foresight programme, noting that it 'is recognised as a world leader in its field' (2007, p 13).

The PREST (2006) report also usefully provides short accounts of a number of third-round Foresight projects, including their aims and objectives, the processes adopted in each case, the outputs, the immediate and longer-term impacts, appropriateness and value for money. These help to illustrate the range of approaches that could be used in such initiatives with some, such as the Cognitive Systems project, drawing primarily on the generation and discussion of expert views, while others, such as the Cyber Trust and Crime Prevention project, used a combination of expert workshops and the production of models and scenarios. However, Scott (2003) noted that the extent to which departments have supported research areas that have been identified by horizon scanning has been unclear, but that the Department for Environment, Food and Rural Affairs (Defra), which he identified as particularly bruised by BSE and other food and agricultural crises, 'seems to be a leader among departments' (Scott, 2003, p 31) (see Case study 2.1).

Case study 2.1: Horizon Scanning and Futures work in the Department for Environment, Food and Rural Affairs

The Department for Environment, Food and Rural Affairs (Defra) Horizon Scanning and Futures programme was a direct response to external drivers, including the government's response to the BSE inquiry, the Office of Science and Innovation's (OSI's) Guidelines 2002, a Strategy Unit report on risk and uncertainty, and Treasury interest in the concept of horizon scanning as a priority for Defra. This was the first time a dedicated horizon-scanning programme had been developed by a government department.

Work began with an extensive consultation process to elicit ideas for research. The work programme for 2002-05 was developed from this consultation phase and included research on environmental constraints, coping with threats, future landscapes, meeting people's future needs and rethinking the food economy. Research projects or 'thought pieces' were commissioned against each theme, and a 'baseline scan' identified over 300 emerging trends relevant to the Defra agenda.

The challenge was to incorporate these research-driven outputs into ongoing policy and strategy development processes, given they were not specified against a clear policy goal. Because of the inherent uncertainty of future work and the constantly changing near-term needs of the policy process, Defra's approach from 2005 onwards re-emphasised the 'policy pull' nature of horizon scanning, commissioning short pieces focused on the specific needs of individual policy areas, and providing training in futures techniques to embed futures skills widely in the organisation.

> The programme was reviewed in 2006 and a strategy for futures work was developed to help 'Defra to be anticipatory, to manage risk and exploit opportunity and to be an efficient, proactive organisation able to build robust and resilient policy'. Defra's Horizon Scanning and Futures team plans on working on 'continuous horizon scanning, occasional large-scale futures investigations and systematic capacity-building within the department' (Defra, 2007, p 1).
>
> See: http://horizonscanning.Defra.gov.uk/default.aspx?menu=menu& module=Home (2011/2006).

Foresight projects are based on literature reviews and horizon scanning, while seeking to take into account economic and social trends (see, for example, King, 2006). There is considerable emphasis on the inclusion of a range of stakeholders and experts to work with the project teams. As noted above, they generally seek to make use of a variety of techniques to seek to take account of future developments and to ensure that there is not simply the projection forward of continuations of current trends and technologies. These have included scenario planning (for example, the Cyber Trust and Crime Prevention project and the Tackling Obesities project) and gaming (the Cyber Trust and Crime Prevention project), as well as discussion of expert views (the Cognitive Systems project) (see www.foresight.gov.uk). Foresight projects also frequently include international perspectives, as was the case with the Infectious Diseases project. The intention of these approaches is to enable the project teams to develop a range of possible paths and to use these to help shed light on how actions in the present might contribute to determining possible future outcomes.

Given the intended focus of the programme, it is unsurprising that Foresight projects have inevitably been primarily based on science and technology, although some, such as the Flood and Coastal Defence project, used inputs from different socioeconomic scenarios to affect their thinking, while others, such as the Age Shift project and the Tackling Obesities project, may have social implications. However, while it was clearly intended that the Foresight programme be focused on science and technology, it is also true that the bulk of futures work in UK public policy has been around such areas, while by comparison social issues have received less attention.

It is important to note that, in line which much 'futures thinking', Foresight projects are not seeking to predict the future. Instead, they aim to identify a range of possible outcomes based on an in-depth understanding and analysis of the topic, with the goal of assisting policy makers to understand how their decisions might affect the future; and to broaden the range of decisions that they might need to consider in light of the variety of possible future impacts.

Other developments in futures work

As is clear from much of the preceding discussion, over the past decade or so government departments have been encouraged to develop processes to enable them to anticipate future challenges, to be 'forward looking'. This has frequently been interpreted as or termed 'horizon scanning', although it is important to realise that horizon scanning is in reality a particular technique, one of many that could be used for futures work (see Box 2.1).

Box 2.1: Horizon scanning

The OSI Horizon Scanning Centre defines horizon scanning as:

> Looking ahead (beyond usual timescales), and looking across (beyond usual sources): *looking beyond a single future to the implications for today's decisions.* (Horizon Scanning Centre, personal communication; see also www.foresight.gov.uk/horizonscanning/)

This makes two points: first, that the sources of evidence for horizon scanning are likely to be outside the mainstream; and second, that the purpose of horizon scanning is to envision a set of different possible futures, and track backwards from those to understand how current decisions could affect the possible paths policy might take. A complementary definition puts more emphasis on the systematic nature of the approach:

> The systematic examination of potential threats, opportunities and likely future developments which are at the margins of current thinking and planning. Horizon scanning may explore novel and unexpected issues, as well as persistent problems or trends. (www.foresight.gov.uk/horizon_scanning_centre/FANclub/Index.htm)

A third definition brings out the scanning nature of the approach:

> Horizon scanning is a 'knowledge radar' that scans for clues and suggestions at the outer periphery of what is known and understood and gives advance warning of the opportunities and threats that lie just out of sight. (Defra, 2007, p 1)

As discussed elsewhere, horizon scanning is only part of the futures toolkit and will not, on its own, deliver forward-looking policy making. However, it is an important part of the process of improving the resilience and adaptability of departmental strategic plans and priorities, using evidence and analysis to test strategic assumptions, identify priority uncertainties, and rigorously analyse what is thought to be certain about the future. The tools that are used are designed to create 'safe, neutral spaces' for discussion, and are heavily dependent on creative, workshop-based approaches. Modelling and other predictive techniques can be used as evidence for horizon scanning, but are unlikely to form the core of horizon-scanning activities.

Given the relative newness of horizon scanning and futures work across government, it is perhaps unsurprising that previous (mainly research-driven) horizon scanning undertaken by individual departments took a variety of approaches with mixed results. The creation of the Office of Science and Innovation's (OSI's) Horizon Scanning Centre has done much to systematise approaches and spread best practice. As well as promoting best practice in the use of horizon scanning and futures techniques, it conducts regular cross-government strategy horizon scans, which underpin existing horizon scanning and inform cross-government priorities. The team also supports specific project work with departmental stakeholders (singly or in groups of departments) that helps ensure that the policy clients for the outputs of the projects are involved in the process and thus become more likely to understand the implications of the results, and use them, as they emerge.

The Treasury, too, has been encouraging greater forward thinking, including through the Comprehensive Spending Reviews, in part by providing expenditure plans for spending departments over a three-year period, but also, for example, requiring longer-term thinking and consideration of trends and future challenges as part of the process, including through the production of a report, *Opportunities and challenges for the UK: Analysis for the 2007 Comprehensive Spending Review* (HM Treasury, 2006), designed to inform the 2007 review process, which sets out to examine possible developments arising from demographic and socioeconomic change, globalisation, technological changes and pressures on natural resources and climate change over a 10-year period.

However, it is not only government departments that have been using futures techniques. In recent years governments have increasingly used reviews and enquiries to develop strategic thinking. The Pensions Commission, for example, sought to produce 'an integrated set of policies to create a new pension settlement for the 21st century' (Pensions Commission, 2006, p 10). One of the key elements of its approach was an examination of trends in pension provision and pension saving, for example from the Family Resources Survey and the Employers' Pension Provision Survey, and to model from these up to as far as 2050. However, in producing its proposals it also sought to incorporate a number of criteria and assumptions, including that there should be strong encouragement for individuals to save for earnings-related pensions through automatic enrolment, and that there was a role for the state where there was not good employer-sponsored provision. It is also worth noting that the Commission stated that:

> ... over the long term the likelihood that consensus can be maintained, and that the inevitable adjustments to policy can be made with continued cross-party support, could be improved if debates on pension policy were informed by independent analysis of key trends in demography and pension provision ... [and that] a permanent Pensions Advisory Commission should be created, charged with monitoring developments and laying before Parliament every three to four years a

report describing relevant trends and spelling out the inevitable trade-offs which result. (Pensions Commission, 2006, p 44)

Other major reviews have included the Wanless (2003) review of health trends, Lord Leitch's (2006) review of skills and the Barker (2006) review of land use planning, each of which was required to take a long-term view. In evidence to the Public Administration Select Committee inquiry into *Governing the future* (2007), Lord Turner, chair of the Pensions Commission, suggested that commissions such as his bring benefits, for example in 'Blue Sky thinking free from short term Civil Service constraints, but in the public arena rather than privately' (Public Administration Select Committee, 2006), and that it had allowed a 'process of political management' of the pensions issue that enabled the political parties to move towards consensus in a way that would have been difficult in the normal arena of party politics. Futures thinking to shape government policy is not, therefore, the sole remit of government departments: for long-term and complex issues such as pensions and climate change, it does appear also to be potentially useful to have high-level independent advice that can be subsequently embedded deep within the ongoing political dialogue.

In addition other tiers of government undertake some work that seeks to identify future trends and their implications, with areas such as population and transport being of major strategic interest because of their implications for services such as education, health and social care and their impact on the economy.

In other areas work has been undertaken that spans a number of tiers of government. The ESPACE (European Spatial Planning: Adapting to Climate Events) initiative (Case study 2.2) is both multi-national and multi-level in approach.

Case study 2.2: ESPACE (European Spatial Planning: Adapting to Climate Events): future-proofing planning policy against the effects of global warming

Work over the past few decades has tended to focus on mitigating the effects of climate change (for example, the Intergovernmental Panel on Climate Change and the Kyoto Protocol). The ESPACE project – a collaborative four-country effort led by Hampshire County Council and funded through the EU Interreg IIIB North West Europe Programme – set out to work out how to future-proof spatial planning policy against the uncertain effects of global warming.

While a national strategy to adapt to climate change is led by Defra; the ESPACE project has adopted a multi-level, evidence-based approach to developing and testing guidance for planners and regional policy makers, ensuring that climate change will become a major consideration in planning decisions and processes. A focus on water management issues allows planners to consider the effects of climate change on issues such as the use of water

---

as a resource to people and industry, likely future flood problems, the role of water in maintaining wildlife habitats, and its contribution to land use management issues in both rural and urban areas.

As well as contributing to regional climate change adaptation policy, ESPACE has focused on important local issues, for example a statutory regional framework for development in South East England to 2026. It supports local decision processes and ensures that central planning policies are informed by 'what works' on the ground.

The ESPACE partners have relied on modelling to test existing policies for resilience to climate change, presenting results to stakeholders – such as the FloodRanger© mapping tool, which illustrates different flood management options in the Thames estuary in an accessible way. Other outputs include a decision support tool for planners, to help them take account of climate change; and helping ensure that local risk management bodies consider long-term risks.

Extensive stakeholder consultation at individual, local and regional levels has informed work on stimulating behaviour change – awareness raising; improving decision making in ESPACE partner organisations; supporting local policy-making processes by developing future-proofed guidance; and providing robust evidence and analysis to central government policy makers to support and inform national strategies for climate change.

See www.espace-project.org

Taking a forward look at forward-looking policy making

It is apparent from the discussion so far that futures thinking is an area that is still being developed, both in terms of identifying and embedding its role in the policy-making process and in terms of the techniques used. However, the range of developments and initiatives make it appropriate to consider these here.

Futures techniques

Approaches to systematically exploring the future were first developed by the American military and moved into the business world after Shell successfully adopted scenario planning in the 1970s (Schwartz, 1996). Their ability to enable people to make better decisions about the future led to interest from many fields – including government, other practitioners and academics. However, the development of techniques has taken time, not least perhaps because much of the academic work done in this area has been of a critical nature, with theoretical approaches only rarely being translated into tools and techniques that can be costed, used in policy making, evaluated and subsequently improved. Arguably, too, there have been shifts in techniques as awareness has grown of the different approaches, with a shift away from straightforward attempts to focus on what the future might be to attempts to explore diversity and to recognise that the future can be shaped (Slaughter, 2002).

Compared to the established academic disciplines, futures research is relatively new, and it has different goals and methods, but this does not mean that it should be any less rigorous:

> ... imagine that futures work makes predictions, produces models and tells you what's going to happen. It doesn't. In reality, futures work is just another strategic tool. It won't tell you what's going to happen in twenty years' time, or even five, but it will show you a picture of a world that plausibly could happen, and challenge you to think about what that would mean, whether it should be welcomed, how it might be avoided. Sometimes the picture is a very broad and hazy one, sometimes narrow and precisely drawn. It all depends on the questions you choose and the techniques you use to address them. It doesn't aim to converge on a single authoritative view of one reality, but to spread out and examine the range of possible futures ... noting and combining the faint signals that might mark the start of something important, or the point at which action is decisive. (Defra, 2007, p 2)

There are many different techniques on offer: as part of an integrated programme of policy development work they have a key role to play in describing possible contexts for future policy impacts, examining what might happen and what the preferred outcome would be, and planning policies to deliver the needed changes. While the basket of futures activities to be utilised will change depending on the question that is asked and the time and resources available, Table 2.1 summarises a selection and their uses.

Futures methodologies arguably work best when they are allowed to evolve, when the users remain open to the alternatives and make judgements about the best way of getting results based on what comes out of each stage of the enquiry. As noted in Defra (2007), 'The ideal model for futures research is more radial than linear, featuring iterative loops of investigation and product development, a work in progress continually adjusted through experimentation and conversation, always useful and controversial, and always stimulating debate' (p 8). Adopting a forward-looking approach to policy making arguably therefore relies less on trying to assimilate expert judgements on single issues, and more on adopting an enquiring approach to each stage of the process of developing policies. Equally, in relation to any particular futures project, the scoping phase is likely to require clarity about what is being sought from it, and this in turn will inform decisions about which techniques can be used cost-effectively.

Table 2.1: Five key activities of integrated foresight: description and example-related methods (indicative, not exhaustive, examples)

Key activity	Identify and monitor change: looking for challenges and opportunities	Assess and critique impacts	Imagine alternative outcomes	Envision preferred futures	Plan and implement change
Activity description	Identify patterns of change: trends in chosen variables, changes in cycles and emerging issues	Examine primary, secondary, tertiary impacts; inequities in impacts, differential access, etc	Identify, analyse and build alternative images of the future, or 'scenarios'	Identify, analyse and articulate images of preferred futures, or 'visions'	Identify stakeholders and resources, clarify goals, design strategies, organise action and create change
Examples of related research methods	Horizon scanning, survey research, focus groups, leading indicator analysis, cohort analysis, citizen panels, STEEP analysis, trend/driver analysis	Causal layered analysis, focus groups, cross-impact analysis, futures wheels, systems models and causal loop analysis	Content analysis, econometric models, systems dynamic models, scenario building, cross-impact analysis, Delphi consultations	Future search, future workshops, community visioning, fluent visioning, simulation gaming, modelling	Backcasting, SSM and rich pictures, joint problem solving, SWOT analysis, strategic choice, PERT and Gantt charting, road mapping, relevance trees, morphological analysis, wind tunnelling and wildcards

Source: Adapted from Schultz (2006); OSI (nd); Defra (2007)
Notes: STEEP = Sociological, Technical, Economic, Environmental, Political; SWOT = Strengths, Weaknesses, Opportunities, Threats; PERT = Programme Evaluation and Review Technique.

Futures work and policy making

In considering how to integrate this enquiring approach at all levels in a policy-making organisation, it is useful to consider exactly what is meant by strategy, policy development and policy delivery. A useful encapsulation is provided by Defra (nd), which underscores the need for thinking ahead in order to provide decision makers with policy options that are not viewed in the context of a static policy arena, but rather are framed by an understanding of how their context may change in the future.

- Strategy – setting the direction of travel by understanding and scoping existing and future context and challenges and developing capability and capacity to deliver desired outcomes.
- Policy development – structuring choice for decision makers that is based on robust evidence.
- Policy delivery – implementing policies with stakeholders to deliver measurable outputs.

These definitions also make the point that an important part of forward-looking policy making is to understand the capacity to deliver change, to involve stakeholders in working out how to measure progress in delivering it, and to understand governments' role in fostering innovation. In this respect innovation is no longer seen as 'invention in search of a purpose' (IBM, 2006, p 3), rather it is now more broadly defined as 'the successful exploitation of new ideas' (DTI, 2003, p 8), ideas that may encompass technological, social and institutional issues and both incremental and radical (or 'step') change and which is increasingly global, multi-disciplinary, collaborative and open. In general, there is not yet a well-developed understanding of how to incorporate and address innovation and the role that horizon scanning and futures has to play in the policy-making process, although Defra (2006) notes that 'horizon scanning and futures research has a critical role to play ... as an appreciation of possible futures will provide intelligence for understanding the context for long-term innovation and the opportunities presented by emerging technologies' (pp 16-17). Harrison (2006) presents a useful way of thinking about how to structure future evidence needs, and the types of evidence that could be procured, asking: 'where are we?'; 'where are we going?'; 'where do we want to be?'; 'how do we get there?'; and, making the point that evaluation is as much part of the policy-making process as forward-looking approaches, 'how well did we do?'.

Given the long-term nature of policy goals, particularly in the context of rapid global change and greater public uncertainty, horizon scanning and futures work is as important as other elements in helping to inform policy makers' choices and the direction of policy initiatives. However, the nature of the evidence is inherently uncertain and more open to challenge and alternative interpretation over time, as policy impacts and other developments unfold. But building an evidence base can be a powerful policy instrument in its own right (see also Chapter Five, this volume), because of its role, for example, in developing a critical mass of people to foster and enable change. Thus forward-looking approaches help set the context and shape of the evidence base on which future policies will be constructed. Given that policy making is a deliberative process supported by evidence (rather than the other way round), it follows that the more forward looking the policy, the more it needs to be based on processes that rely on judgement and deliberation of multiple possible futures, and less on uni-dimensional predictions.

However, while there are many increasingly well-established tools for generating horizon scanning and futures evidence, there are few that can successfully deliver 'rigorous dialogue' at the interface between horizon scanning and futures work and policy. It can certainly be argued that a greater and more rigorous focus on long-term issues can bring greater rigour to the policy process, but this idea does need to gain a firmer foothold both in the policy process (for example, through the inclusion of futures work as a routine part of the scoping phase of strategy and policy work, in the same way that evaluation has become more mainstream over time [see Chapter Nine, this volume], and among evidence providers including academia and think-tanks (to produce evidence where the primary criterion is policy relevance rather than interesting researchable questions). It is not clear that the current mix of disciplines in the policy process can deliver the tools for rigorous dialogue that see stakeholder engagement as an essential part of scoping the evidence base for future policy options. They are, perhaps, as likely to emerge from fields such as knowledge management, which, in terms of policy making, combines an understanding of how to involve many different types of stakeholder in generating evidence with an appreciation of the organisational issues that need to be addressed to ensure cost-effective delivery of policy options.

There are also a variety of other issues and areas of debate associated with the development of forward-looking policy. One of these is the applicability and use of futures work across different areas of government and different policy arenas. While it may be the case that it is equally necessary and appropriate in different spheres of government activity, in the UK government has arguably paid the greatest attention to explicit future planning in those fields which, on the face of it, appear more measurable, such as science and technology and some areas of demography, although bodies such as the Strategy Unit and the Social Exclusion Unit have produced analyses and proposed solutions on a wide range of social issues. There may be a variety of possible explanations for this. For example, some subject areas that make greater use of quantitative and numerically led techniques might appear to policy makers to be more amenable to futures work, while, in contrast, 'soft' policy areas, or those where values or attitudes appear more important, might appear more problematic, although in reality neither of these necessarily hold true (and see Loveridge and Street, 2003). Alternatively there may simply be greater uncertainty among decision makers and their advisers about the techniques to be used when seeking to assess possible futures in fields such as welfare provision, where patterns and trends in human behaviour may appear more difficult to predict. Or it may simply be that in some areas government has felt a greater need or willingness to learn for the future, with the BSE and foot and mouth disease crises making Defra a prime candidate for attempts to introduce futures thinking. Whatever the explanation, and in spite of the OSI's central function as promoter of best practice in futures techniques, it does remain the case that the interest in and take-up of futures work is highly varied across both central government and different tiers of government.

Conclusions

Clearly attempts to look into the future have long played a significant role in policy making, but, equally, recent years have seen a much greater focus on futures thinking and increased attempts to draw it into the mainstream of the policy process, at least in some areas of government. Given experience over the past two decades it is perhaps possible to conclude the following:

- The idea of forward-looking policy making is now well established in concept and attempts to undertake long-term planning are apparent across the work of government departments (with some extending well into the future, with Defra's sustainable development and climate change policy having the longest target of any department, 2050), even if it is clear that there is no standard approach to embedding futures work in departmental activities or across tiers of government, while the greatest visibility remains in areas such as science and technology, economic policy and population and demographic studies.
- A standard approach is likely to be inappropriate. For example, for some areas of activity the OSI will continue to provide 'big picture' evidence on large cross-cutting issues, but how these are taken up and made operational within departments will and must depend on how they approach their long-term policy goals. Given that many departments have relatively short-term targets, including those embedded in PSAs, and also have to respond to short-term political pressures, their enthusiasm for and ability to devote scarce resources to developing better framings for their policies may be questionable.
- A major barrier to the successful adoption of a forward-looking approach to policy making arguably relates to the lack of established 'futures' expertise throughout government, and the competition it faces with existing disciplines, including in relation to both time and resource constraints on policy makers. If 'forward looking' is to become as important a component of policy making as any other of the nine principles, it will be necessary to develop structural solutions that can cope with these opposing pressures.
- As in many areas of policy and policy making, the government's role in fostering innovation is important – not only in the instances of science and technology innovation, but also in the ways in which goals are set, targets are defined and policies are developed and delivered, and in terms of its dealings with stakeholders and the public.

- As with other shortcomings in the policy process, poor forecasting can lead to wasteful provision, or services that are inadequately or inappropriately prepared for demands in terms of the levels or configuration of provision available, and can lead to delays and dissatisfaction among stakeholders and the public; it is therefore as necessary as with other areas to ensure that the evidence base is as robust as possible and to develop tools that deliver a rigorous dialogue with stakeholders and a well-structured evidence base that helps to understand what constitutes cost-effectiveness in the long term.
- Forward-looking policy making is made even more difficult for policy makers and practitioners as contexts within which policies operate and judgements of what constitute success or failure are likely to change over time. This may require even greater emphasis on the maintenance of a continual dialogue around issues, even when a policy has been implemented.
- While it is important to realise that the great majority of important decisions are likely to be primarily political rather than technocratic, one of the major arguments for policy being forward looking (as with many of the other characteristics of 'modern policy making') is that the decisions of policy makers can usefully be informed by a greater awareness of the context within which decisions are made. In addition, in some instances, politicians actively seek evidence, and this, as may be the case with the report of the Pensions Commission and the Stern review on *The economics of climate change* (2007), can impact on political considerations. Crucially, evidence is every bit as necessary for longer-term strategy and policy development as it is for more immediate and time-sensitive requirements (Shaxson, 2005). The calls in the Public Administration Committee's (2007) report, *Governing the future*, for continued transparency with regard to background evidence, analysis and uncertainty, and for a role for Parliament in considering long-term issues, reflect a desire to enable parliamentary and public scrutiny.
- Returning to the quote from Moore (1995), the concept of delivering value for public money can only be understood by holding wide-ranging discussions of what that 'value' might look like, and to whom, and how it might change over time.

Further reading

Defra (Department for Environment, Food and Rural Affairs) (2007) *Looking back at looking forwards: Next steps for Horizon Scanning and Futures*, London: Defra – a detailed review and analysis of Defra's horizon-scanning programme activities, with useful pointers for those implementing futures projects and programmes in government.

Henley Centre (2001) *Understanding best practice in strategic futures work: A report for the Performance and Innovation Unit*, London: Henley Centre – outlines some of the uses and methodological approaches for futures work, together with some recommendations for best practice.

Pensions Commission (2004) *Pensions: Challenges and choices: The first report of the Pensions Commission*, London: The Stationery Office – a thorough and detailed report that draws on a variety of techniques to raise a number of issues that were considered in the Commission's subsequent reports and policy recommendations.

PIU (Performance and Innovation Unit) (1999) *The future and how to think about it*, London: PIU – explores 'six key drivers for change' (p 1) likely to impact on government in the coming decades.

Public Administration Select Committee (2007) *Governing the future*, London: The Stationery Office – a broad review of the role of futures thinking and analysis in government.

Schwartz, P. (1996) *The art of the long view: Planning for the future in an uncertain world*, New York, NY: Currency Doubleday – a relatively early contribution to futures thinking drawing on experience when working for Shell.

Useful websites

www.foresight.gov.uk/ – Foresight at OSI provides access to information on the Foresight programme and its reports

www.foresight.gov.uk/HORIZON_SCANNING_CENTRE/Good_Practice/Toolkit/Toolkit.html – this provides guidance on a range of possible techniques.

http://horizonscanning.Defra.gov.uk/ – Defra's horizon-scanning site gives information on Defra's horizon-scanning strategy and its programme of work.

www.policyhub.gov.uk/better_policy_making/forward_looking.asp – the forward-looking section of the Policy Hub website provides links to a range of advice and reports, and has the virtue of being continually updated.

www.oecd.org/department/0,2688,en_2649_33707_1_1_1_1_1,00.html – on an international level the OECD's International Futures programme uses a variety of tools in its attempt to provide early warning of emerging issues and to highlight major developments.

THREE

Outward-looking policy making

Edward C. Page and Jane Mark-Lawson[1]

Travel broadens the mind. Thus the appeal of looking at how problems are addressed in other jurisdictions is that it allows the development of policies, procedures, practices or organisational structures that would not have been developed if inspiration or advice had simply been sought from close to home. When setting up a new form of regulation for, say, telecommunications, you do not have to confine yourself to looking at how telecommunications were regulated in the past, or seek to draw lessons from how water or electricity are regulated, you could also draw ideas from how telecommunications regulation is handled in other jurisdictions. It is, of course, also common for jurisdictions to learn from other jurisdictions operating within the same polity: local authorities and health authorities can learn from each other, as can Whitehall ministries and devolved administrations. However, the concern of this chapter is with *international* comparisons. The chapter therefore:

- outlines the attractions of this approach to policy makers;
- examines the constraints and obstacles to good-quality 'lesson learning'; and
- considers how this approach generally works in practice and what can be understood and learnt from this.

The use of international models and practices is especially relevant for a discussion of the modernisation of policy making under New Labour as the use of comparative cross-national experience has become a conventional part of the evidence base on which policy should be developed. The importance of such evidence was underlined in the early years after 1997 by a series of central policy initiatives inspired by international evidence, including the development of labour market and social policies in part modelled on US 'workfare' initiatives (King and Wickham-Jones, 1999), the 'National Literacy Strategy' introduced in schools after 1998 (Beard, 2000; see Case study 3.1), and a series of law and order policies, including 'three strikes and you're out' and 'zero tolerance policing' (Jones and Newburn, 2007). It is possible to find examples of the explicit use of the policy experiences of other countries under previous governments – the Conservative government's introduction of the Child Support Agency, for example, in 1993, was based in part on an analysis of similar institutions in Australia and the US. However, after 1997 the notion that international examples could help improve policy making was given significantly greater emphasis in the New Labour modernisation agenda than it had ever been given before. Moreover, as we shall discuss below, there is evidence that institutions that sought to shape government from the inside (such as the Prime Minister's Strategy Unit [PMSU] or HM Treasury) or from the outside (such as think-tanks including Demos and the Institute for Public Policy Research) increasingly visibly developed their ideas in the light of cross-national experience.

Case study 3.1: Introduction of the National Literacy Strategy: drawing on international research

The National Literacy Strategy (later part of the Primary Framework for Literacy and Numeracy) was introduced in 1998 to raise levels of literacy among primary school children. The National Literacy Project, piloted in 15 local education authorities (LEAs) under the Conservative government in 1996, helped shape the subsequent Labour initiative, but within Labour work began on the strategy while the party was in opposition in 1996 when David Blunkett set up the National Literacy Task Force. Its reports in 1997 formed the basis for the introduction of a literacy strategy aimed at ensuring that 80 per cent of children would be reading at their reading age by 2001 compared with 57 per cent in 1996. The framework set out teaching objectives to help improve literacy; strongly encouraged and gave guidance on the development of a 'literacy hour', during which primary schools would concentrate on reading skills; and set out strategies for achieving greater literacy, especially through an approach known as 'synthetic phonics'.

The strategy was developed using educational and psychological research from other countries, above all the US and Australia, including psychological research on children's phonological development, shared reading and guided writing and research from the US and Australia on the use of phonics and systems of guided reading. Thinking about how the strategy was to be implemented in schools also reflected the influence of US experience. The international character of the policy deliberations was underlined by the presence and influence of Bob Slavin, a US education researcher, from the very early years of the development of the initiative.

The full account is given in Beard (1999, 2000). See also House of Commons Education and Skills Committee (2005) and Rose (2006), and for a range of materials on literacy in schools see www.standards.dfes.gov. uk/primaryframeworks/literacy/ and www.literacytrust.org.uk/.

There are many attractions to such use of foreign experience. The idea that policies developed in one country should provide models for the development of public policies in another is in part a matter of common sense. Rather than trying to envisage how a policy works, you can see it in action somewhere else; you can learn from any mistakes that the other jurisdiction may have made, or even plan improvements safe in the knowledge that the proposals are being based on a real operating model rather than abstract theory; and many of the details – how much a programme is likely to cost, whether it has any unintended consequences – can be identified. The development of the National Literacy Strategy could thus build on the wealth of educational and policy research generated through schemes and initiatives tested in Australia and North America.

In addition to its practical attractions, cross-national policy learning has also generated considerable academic social science attention. In perhaps the most cited article on the subject, DiMaggio and Powell (1983) argue that 'isomorphism', the processes of emulation by which the policies in one jurisdiction come to resemble those found in others, is on the increase. As decision makers and citizens become increasingly aware of the apparent benefits provided by the way programmes are delivered elsewhere, the pressures to imitate the policies of other countries become extremely powerful, irresistible if not automatic, and thus different polities increasingly come to resemble each other.

This perceived tendency is often discussed under the heading of 'policy transfer' (see Evans, 2004). The term policy *transfer* might, however, be somewhat misleading. Like heat transfer, or even the transfer of money from one bank account to another, the word suggests that the process is straightforward if not involuntary. It implies the simple movement of a set of policies from one place to another with no (or limited) change of state, as the policy can be clearly recognised as an import from another jurisdiction. However, policy transfer in this sense is rather rare because borrowing a policy from another jurisdiction is not straightforward. Policies borrowed from one country have to be adapted to a greater or lesser degree to the conditions of the importing country. Moreover, just because a policy has been borrowed from elsewhere does not mean it can bypass the complexities of policy making – including the need for policy makers to mobilise political support for it and make compromises with affected interests.

The use of foreign examples to shape domestic policy is thus invariably a matter of policy *learning* rather than policy transfer. Richard Rose's (1993, 2001, 2005) work sets out the steps that need to be followed to draw valid lessons from cross-national policy comparisons. These are discussed later in this chapter, but these steps are systematic and rigorous, but practically doable. To the possible challenge that different national experiences – cultures, legal systems and so on – make cross-national lesson drawing impossible, he replies that 'the critical issues of lesson-drawing are not whether we can learn anything elsewhere, but when, where and how we learn' (Rose, 1993, p 157).

Given its undoubted attractions, it might appear surprising that systematic lesson drawing is a relatively uncommon activity. The next section of this chapter seeks to justify this apparently pessimistic conclusion and goes on to discuss why this should be the case. There are intellectual as well as political limits to systematic lesson drawing. Intellectual limits refer, above all, to the high level of knowledge and understanding about the policy from which lessons may be drawn, the context to which the lessons will be applied, and the constraints associated with applying them, including the time needed to develop and process this knowledge. Political limits refer above all to the difficulties of ensuring that the entire policy is shaped – from inception through developing the necessary legislation and securing funding to implementation – by the concept that has been derived from the intellectual process of drawing a lesson.

However, these limitations are not discussed to show how international experience cannot be used to shape public policies. Such a conclusion would fly in the face of the evidence – the international diffusion of policies; the development of freedom of information and data protection legislation (Bennett, 1997; Kelemen and Sibbitt, 2004); new public management (Pollitt and Bouckaert, 2004); 'new' environmental policy instruments (Jordan et al, 2003); value for money audits (Pollitt et al, 1999); and the development of workfare policies (Dolowitz, 1998), these are but a few of the most obvious recent examples of policy areas where it appears that countries looked at and learned from the experience of others. Rather the purpose is to show that while policy learning in anything like a pure lesson-drawing form might be rare because of the intellectual and political constraints, awareness of these constraints helps understand what type of cross-national policy learning is possible within them. The chapter goes on to look at how policy learning takes place under the pressure of these constraints – how experience and ideas drawn from looking at how policies work in other countries is *actually used* to shape policy. It argues that 'inspiration', elaborating 'policy labels', 'demonstration' and 'smart ideas' are common methods of cross-national policy learning. Such borrowing can be understood as the result of policy makers employing a range of shortcuts or 'heuristics'. In its conclusion this chapter discusses how, where systematic lesson drawing is not possible and the yardstick of analytical rigour cannot apply, the quality of learning can be assessed and the contribution that cross-national experience can make to the development of policy could be increased without losing sight of the constraints that make lesson drawing difficult.

Constraints on lesson drawing

How common is systematic lesson drawing?

Several authors have suggested that cross-national policy learning has become increasingly common (for example, Dolowitz and Marsh, 1996). Yet it is extraordinarily difficult to demonstrate that this is the case. It is remarkable how a variety of major institutions appear to have developed in similar ways at approximately the same time for the last millennium across large parts of Europe, from the development of feudalism, the separation of church from state authority, the development of national legal systems to the growth of constitutionalism, the nationalisation (and later denationalisation) of industry and the expansion of the welfare state. Several recent developments point to the growth in cross-national policy learning. The development of international forms of governance and regulation, whether through international regimes (see Held, 2003) governing, for example, air travel, banking and money laundering and the internet, as well as the growing role of the European Union (EU) in shaping public policies. Such developments suggest that public policies are increasingly coming to resemble each other and that the policies pursued by the government of any one country are shaped by policies and decisions taken outside its borders.

Moreover, in many countries it has become increasingly accepted as a virtue that policy makers should look outside their boundaries for ways of dealing with policy problems. In the UK the use of international evidence was a dominant theme of the New Labour approach to policy making as set out in, for example, its White Paper on *Modernising government* (Cabinet Office, 1999), which argued that policy making needs to be 'more forward- and outward-looking. This means learning to look beyond what government is doing now; improving and extending our contingency planning, learning lessons from other countries; and integrating the European Union and international dimension into our policy making' (p 16). This was certainly not empty rhetoric: for example, substantial effort was made by bodies such as the PMSU to include foreign evidence in developing proposals for policies such as adoption and drug dealing (Performance and Innovation Unit, 2000d, 2000e), and the National Health Service (NHS) Modernisation Agency (Department of Health, 2002) developed its agenda with a significant focus on international experience, a feature that is continued in the work of the NHS Institute for Innovation and Improvement (2006) that replaced it.

However, while there is evidence to support the view that policy makers as well as service deliverers have become increasingly sensitive to understanding how services and policies are developed and delivered elsewhere, the degree of actual *cross-national policy learning* that this has involved can be questioned. As Rose (1993, 2005) points out, policy learning involves a rigorous set of procedures that include: scanning alternatives and deciding where to look for lessons, learning how the programme works in situ, abstracting a generalised model of how the foreign programme works, developing the model for the national context in which one wishes to apply it and 'prospectively evaluating' the policy before adopting the lesson. It is difficult to prove that policy learning has taken place in this way. However, two types of evidence can be used to highlight why policy learning of this sort might be a rare phenomenon.

First, in cases where there is prima facie strong evidence that policies have been substantially influenced by those from another jurisdiction, closer inspection shows that the influence of foreign experience is limited and does not appear to have been based on any such direct lessons. The 'New York Miracle' – the apparently sharp drop in crime in New York City in the 1990s – was drawn on in both the UK and Australia for anti-crime strategies. However, in the UK, the changes in *sentencing* and *criminal law* associated with 'zero tolerance' bore little direct resemblance to the *policing* reforms introduced by Police Commissioner Bill Bratton (see Case study 3.2). Even in Australia, where arguably even greater efforts were made to imitate Bratton's policing reforms, Dixon and Maher (2005) show that 'the crucial transfer may be not so much of particular policies, but rather of less specific perceptions and attitudes, in this case a confidence in the ability of police to reduce crime' (p 126).

Case study 3.2: Zero tolerance policing and the 'New York Miracle': borrowing and adapting experience abroad

'Zero tolerance' is now in common usage to convey the idea that minor transgressions of any kind should be met with a firm response. It was originally associated with drug abuse and violence against women and later with policing, especially under New Labour. Local experiments in 'zero tolerance policing' emerged in the UK in the early 1990s. Although some were apparently domestically inspired, others were informed by the success of the 'New York Miracle'. Under Mayor Giuliani, crime rates in New York City had fallen sharply in the early 1990s. While there was Conservative government interest in how the 'miracle' was achieved, the term became a central part of New Labour's thinking about being 'tough on crime' in the run-up to the 1997 election.

New Labour politicians, advisers and think-tanks examined New York policing in the 1990s, and a variety of 'policy entrepreneurs', including New York Police Commissioner Bill Bratton, and a number of seminal texts, notably Wilson and Kelling's (1982) 'Broken windows', helped spread what appeared to be a successful North American approach to crime control. However, what the UK actually 'borrowed' from the US experience, apart from a general predisposition that policing should help 'nip things in the bud' by targeting disorderly conduct and other 'quality of life' offences, was rather limited. The core of the Bratton and Giuliani approach had also included police use of civil law as a means of combating crime; the development of a system for monitoring crime at the precinct level, used to hold precinct commanders accountable; and targetting of high-visibility crime reduction strategies through the Street Crimes Unit.

The core elements of the New York approach did not fundamentally shape policing in the UK, where chief police officers, with a surviving tradition of independence from political control, resisted them in part because of fears of the impact on relations with minority ethnic groups and in part because of a reluctance to devote substantially increased resources to minor crimes. The general 'broken windows' approach did, however, exert a significant impact on New Labour's wider law and order agenda, most obviously through the development of policies against anti-social behaviour, above all through the creation of Anti-Social Behaviour Orders (ASBOs).

For a full account see Jones and Newburn (2007).

In a similar manner, the 'workfare' reforms in many US states, such as Wisconsin, conducted and evaluated as social experiments, attracted UK policy makers in the 1990s. However, while it is possible to demonstrate that some specific aspects of the UK New Deal were influenced by US experiences, Walker and Wiseman (2001) suggest that the most noticeable impact of the US experience was at the level of 'rhetoric' and 'strategy'. As Cebulla (2005, p 47) comments, 'the evidence that has informed policy debate in Britain has been based on the results of individual studies, site visits, anecdote and selective, narrative reviews of the experimental results. While the experiments themselves may have been rigorous, surpassing in quality most of the policy evaluations conducted in Britain and continental Europe, lesson-learning has been at best casual'. Similar evidence of apparent lesson drawing that fades away on closer inspection can be found in areas such as the development of regulatory agencies (Humphreys and Padgett, 2006) and Enterprise Zones (Mossberger, 2000). While in all of these cases there may have been some cross-national influence on domestic policy making, this generally falls far short of the process of lesson drawing outlined by Rose (1993, 2001, 2005).

Second, where the most determined efforts have been made to create the conditions for cross-jurisdictional policy learning, the results have been very modest. The EU has, since 2000, promoted the idea of an 'open method of coordination' (Chalmers and Lodge, 2003), which sought to develop practices of cross-national networking and peer review to bring about a convergence of national social policies through 'benchmarking' best practice. Casey and Gold's (2005) study has shown in the case of the European Employment Strategy, part of which was a scheme designed to produce National Action Plans for employment in each member state based on a series of visits by national policy officials to other member states to learn from practices elsewhere and, where appropriate, shape the policies of their hosts, that the result of this scheme was modest from the point of view of cross-national lesson drawing: there was relatively little 'real' learning going on, and the 'peer review procedure has tended to be exclusive, involving a narrow "epistemic community" ... and has had scarcely any impact upon either the Commission or the governments of the member states' (Casey and Gold, 2005, p 24). A different example of a determination to create the conditions for transfer having modest results in producing policies that closely resemble those of the jurisdiction from which they are borrowed is provided by the Austrian experience of university reform (Pratt, 2004; Mayer and Lassnigg, 2006). While close involvement of UK experts on the Council for National Academic Awards (CNAA) in the process of policy making was a distinctive feature of the development of the Austrian 'accreditation model', the transfer that took place was as much of ideas and buzzwords as a particular policy or institution, with the role of the British model being as much about 'inspiration' as 'emulation' (Rose, 1993). This point is illustrated by the fact that the key Austrian actors based their decisions on misapprehensions and misunderstandings about the nature and function of the CNAA, and these misunderstandings even helped ensure that the CNAA model shaped the Austrian reform (Pratt, 2004).

—

Why lesson drawing is difficult

Why does lesson drawing involving the analytical steps outlined by Rose (2001) appear to be so difficult? Each of the major analytical stages he sets out is demanding in terms of intellectual effort, information required, time or resources. *Identifying the policy and country from which lessons are to be drawn* implies, as with 'rational' approaches to policy making (Lindblom, 1959; Parsons, 2002), a high degree of clarity about objectives. The 'rational shopper' is one metaphor used by some analysts (see Mossberger, 2000) to describe the activity of looking for policies from which lessons are to be sought. The rational shopper starts out with a clear idea of what s/he is after and then can evaluate what is on offer. Moreover, as the degree of 'rationality' in decision making is argued to increase with the number of policy alternatives considered, so too the rationality of cross-national policy shopping increases with the number of countries whose policies are examined for possible emulation.

The choice of countries is not only shaped by political choice, a feature of decision making perfectly commensurate with the notion of a 'rational shopper', but by the availability of information about a sufficient range of countries to allow an enlightened choice. The simple fact is that it is not easy to find out about how any particular country deals with a particular policy problem. Compendia of practice in some countries might be available for some policies, such as drugs policies (EMCDDA, 2001) or education systems, but such sources tend to lack the details describing and evaluating how a policy works in a way that can inform policy development. Such guides can serve as a means of identifying countries that might be of interest, but finding out how policies work elsewhere – through methods such as study visits and direct contact with experts – is a time-consuming enterprise that is not cost free. It is not surprising, then, to observe that choices of which country to look at for lessons tend to be made following a limited number of comparisons, if any at all.

However, even with time and resources, *finding out how policies work* in a foreign country is not always straightforward. Even with well-documented policies, as with the US welfare-to-work programmes, there was limited understanding of 'what works' within the US itself, even though, thanks to the way federal funding was organised, rigorous evaluation of these programmes was mandatory (Walker and Wiseman, 2001; Cebulla, 2005). Travel to the country is an important means of finding out how programmes work (see Rose, 2005). However, study trips themselves can have important drawbacks. Little is understood about how such visits work and how much can be learned from them, but the available evidence suggests that the host–guest relationship between the visitor and the host might both inhibit frank questioning of the merits of the programme being visited and/or lead to the host presenting the programme in the best possible light for both domestic and international consumption (Page et al, 2005).

Deriving lessons from the observations – getting to the heart of what makes the programme work in such a way that these lessons can be adapted and applied to the 'importing' jurisdiction – requires a close link between policy analysts and policy makers. It is not enough to visit other countries and draw lessons from how things work there; the lesson has to be communicated and taken seriously by policy makers. While we know little about the dissemination of lessons drawn from policy visits, the evidence from Casey and Gold (2005) suggests that officials looking for better practices elsewhere do not automatically gain the ear of those in a position to make changes. In fact, the relationship between analytical policy advice and policy practice, while improving in the UK, is notoriously weak in general: policy makers tend not to make much direct use of research whether in national government (Cabinet Office, 2003) or local government (Percy Smith et al, 2001). The role of analytical policy analysis has been likened to that of the surfer, in Kingdon's (1984) famous analogy: policy analysts cannot expect their findings to be taken up by policy makers because the availability of analytical advice often does not coincide with the political 'windows of opportunity' to shape policy. Thus policy analysts have to have their policies ready and wait for the right political opportunities to persuade policy makers that the time is right for a new policy, much as surfers have to have their boards waxed and ready for when a good wave comes along.

Assuming that policy makers do listen to analytical policy advice based on cross-national comparison, the application of that advice in *developing a new programme* is also problematic. Like any other process of policy making, developing policy using foreign experience is a political process. To develop a policy based on a consistent and methodological understanding of the experiences of another country requires an ability to sustain the concept derived from the intellectual process of policy learning over the entire policy-making process; it requires a significant degree of control: over the agenda of policy making, so that the proposed policy has a chance of receiving the legal, financial and human resources required to put it into effect; over the decision-making process, so that opposition to the concept, as well as counter-proposals that serve to dilute or wreck it, can be avoided; as well as over the implementation of the programme, to ensure that those who actually administer or deliver the programme follow the model developed from international experience.

It is generally rare in modern democracies for any one body to have sufficient power and internal unanimity to sustain a single vision for a policy, as derived from systematic lesson drawing, across the whole policy process, from agenda setting to implementation. The implementation of lessons drawn from foreign experience appears to have had the support of the state in Meiji Japan in the fields of the police service (where those developing the policy looked to France as a model), the postal service (the UK) and press reform (the US) (Westney, 1987), but in modern democracies, even those governed by single parties in an executive-dominated system, the need for political support, even intra-party support, makes systematic lesson drawing problematic. Even where the imperatives to follow a foreign model are strong, democracies find it difficult to sustain a single externally defined model in the face of demands from domestic groups and politicians.

Jacoby's (2000) study of postwar West Germany showed that the reform of the German education system, although under strong pressure from the occupying forces, above all the US, to follow a North American schooling model, reflected more strongly domestic views and interests in the education system.

Cross-national policy learning under pressure

Forms of policy learning

Cross-national lesson drawing is an intellectually demanding enterprise. The constraints of modern policy making also mean it is difficult to secure political and administrative support for the policy based on the lesson. Such support for a vision of policy derived from the cross-national lesson would need to be mobilised and sustained over an extended period; in practice it is extremely difficult to maintain alongside an open democratic process of discussion and compromise. Moreover, these two types of constraints interact with each other: cross-national research, like any other kind of research, takes time, and windows of opportunity for policy change do not stay open for ever. If policy proposals based on the evaluation of cross-national evidence are not already available when the policy hits the political agenda, the political enthusiasm and support cannot be expected to persist while a policy response is researched. The National Literacy Strategy (see Case study 3.1), even though it arguably did not exactly follow Rose's lesson-drawing pattern, could build on a wealth of academic and policy evaluation evidence that had already been developed, and could do so in the context of a political agenda in which the issue of school education remained at or near the top for several years, including the last years of the Conservative administration. However, such conditions are not common and it is thus not surprising that it is extraordinarily rare to find examples of policies that follow the rigours of lesson drawing.

This finding certainly does not suggest that the role of international experience has been small, but rather that this experience cannot work exclusively or even frequently through a process of lesson drawing involving an analytical look at how policies work elsewhere, followed by a systematic extraction of a lesson, its application to a new environment and the 'prospective evaluation' of the policy thus derived.

So how are cross-national policy comparisons used to shape domestic policies if not through the formal stages of policy learning? We leave aside the symbolic uses of foreign examples, where decision makers seek to make their policies more acceptable by aligning them with those of another country (see Bennett, 1997), as well as the mandating of policies, some of which may be based on the programmes of one member state, on all member states within the EU (as, for example, with the development of emissions trading; see Wurzel, 2000). Such influence through international organisations has been described as 'uploading' national practices into a mandate or soft law, which individual states then 'download' as national policy (Bulmer and Padgett, 2004). While mandated policies might involve some form of lesson drawing within the international institution 'uploading' the policy (although it is not necessarily any more likely to do so than it is in individual member states), our concern in this chapter is with the ability of *domestic* policy makers to learn lessons from other countries.

With these qualifications, the most common use of cross-national policy examples is *inspiration*. To be inspired by a foreign experience is to take a basic idea, possibly even loosely defined, and develop a form or version of it more or less independently of the original model from which the idea was drawn. For example, the New Labour approach to Working Families Tax Credit was developed with the explicit aim of drawing from the experience of the US. The Chancellor, Gordon Brown asked the chair of the task force chosen to review the tax and benefits system, Martin Taylor, to look at the North American Earned Income Tax Credit (EITC) system (see Walker and Wiseman, 1997). However, Taylor identified substantial differences between the UK and US systems and the resulting system of Working Families Tax Credit introduced in the UK, although 'obviously based on the same concept as the EITC, in that it is a tax credit – it either reduces the tax bill or is paid to the family if it exceeds the tax liability … owes much more of its detailed structure to [UK] Family Credit than to the American system' (Strickland, 1998, p 10).

Inspiration is the kind of policy learning, for example, that corresponds to Mossberger's (2000) description of the importance of 'policy labels' in the international diffusion of ideas. Mossberger's study shows how the UK experience of 'enterprise zones' (EZs), itself influenced by the experience of Hong Kong as a 'freeport', was taken up by US states. The UK version introduced under the Thatcher administration in the early 1980s fell far short of a freeport, but allowed some tax exemptions and streamlined planning conditions for firms locating within them. The UK idea found advocates in the US and by 1993 forty US states had EZ programmes. However, Mossberger's detailed study of five of these state schemes showed that the process of learning included little systematic observation of the UK model on which it was to be based (as set out in Rose's definition of the term). 'State decision makers did not know whether the enterprise zones policy was successful in other places. The idea diffused to many states long before there were any answers to this question, even anecdotal ones' (Mossberger, 2000, p 202). Moreover, the five states had substantially different schemes that had little in common with each other, or the UK, apart from the label 'enterprise zones'. Mossberger concludes that what actually travelled across the Atlantic in this case was a policy label, 'an ambiguous and loosely bundled idea' (2000, p 194).

The notion that broader ideas travel more easily than more complex analytical blueprints for policies is suggested by the attraction of 'new public management' initiatives in the industrialised (Pollitt and Bouckaert, 2004) and the industrialising world (Sutton, 2006). As Argyriades (2006) puts it, 'The way the prescriptive tenets and underlying assumptions of the New Public Management [hardly a self-contained, coherent, and solid set of principles] gained currency over the years attests to the influence of international agencies and consulting corporations and the effectiveness of packaging in the promotion of policy transfers' (p 281). Similar forms of inspiration can be found in the Japanese debate about the reform of the Japanese civil service following the UK model of Next Steps agencies, but 'the idea of agencification represented two different things in the two countries' as the Japanese 'reinterpreted and redefined it' (Nakano, 2004, p 186). Walt and her colleagues (2004) show how complex procedures and routines developed for treating tuberculosis in Africa successfully 'spread' only after they had been simplified as a marketable policy – DOTS (directly observed treatment, short course). Countries adopting DOTS programmes subsequently had to develop their own detailed versions of the scheme.

Demonstration is another form of influence. By observing policies in other countries it can be demonstrated that courses of action are possible. It has already been remarked how the New York experience was used, above all in Australia, to demonstrate that police reform could cut down on crime. The US experience was also used by privatisation advocates to demonstrate that a bold and radical step in the Thatcher administration's pursuit of privatisation policy was possible by extending it to prisons – an area that was once considered essentially a state service and not privatisable (see Jones and Newburn, 2002).

Smaller-scale practices or 'tricks' can be borrowed, quite often without any of the analytical procedures that accompany lesson drawing. *Using smart ideas* is a form of policy learning that was used effectively in 1996 to set up the negotiations that produced the Good Friday Agreement over Northern Ireland when Dick Spring proposed the idea of 'proximity talks', as set out in newspaper discussions about the Dayton peace negotiations over the Bosnian question as a means of getting hostile groups involved in a common round of negotiations. On a somewhat more modest level, those framing UK legislation seeking to use civil law to seize criminal assets in the 2002 Proceeds of Crime Act sent copies of the Irish legislation doing the same to the parliamentary drafters to give some ideas about how such matters could be handled within a common law jurisdiction.

Using cross-national experience without drawing lessons

If the use of policies developed in other jurisdictions is not developed according to principles of lesson drawing, two questions need to be asked. First, what shapes the process of these forms of policy learning if it is not a systematic comparison of evidence? If prevalent forms of policy learning from other countries do not conform to a lesson-drawing model, to what do they conform? The second question follows on from this. With analytical lesson drawing we may judge its rigour by the degree to which it conforms to social scientific norms of adequacy – the evidence available, how that evidence is assessed and what conclusions were drawn from it. Thus with less rigorous forms of policy learning – such as inspiration, demonstration and 'smart practices' – we must ask: how does one assess whether less rigorous forms of policy learning improve the policy-making process? In other words, how do we judge whether policy learning, in the forms in which it is most commonly practised, is being done well and how might it be done better?

With regard to the first question – what it is policy makers do when they use foreign examples – as Weyland (2004) points out in his discussion of social reform in Latin America, because analytical lesson drawing is so demanding, above all in terms of time and resources, decision makers use 'heuristics' or short cuts. Instead of going through the stages of lesson drawing, policy makers use quick guides to action. Understanding the nature of the heuristics employed by decision makers helps explain why some policies seem to serve as the inspiration for reforms along similar lines in many other countries without any lesson drawing of the kind identified by Rose. Moreover, understanding the heuristics also helps one to understand why particular policy makers appear to seek out one model rather than another.

Weyland (2005) shows that decision makers in Bolivia were attracted to the Chilean experience of pension reform, and paid little attention to other Latin American countries that had already started to develop (Chilean-influenced) pension reforms of their own. One reason for this was the *availability heuristic*. Bolivian decision makers did not have to seek out information on pension reform; Chilean consultants were available to explain how the system worked and how it could be adapted to Bolivia's conditions, and reformers were 'fixated' on Chile to the exclusion of other countries. The *representativeness heuristic* was a short cut to reaching conclusions about the success of the Chilean model: while it is costly and demanding to try and conduct a rigorous cost–benefit analysis of the Chilean system, even more so in relation to other types of reform, this was avoided by highlighting a narrow range of indicators of success – above all the annual return on investment by Chilean pension managers in one particularly good year. The *anchoring heuristic* was the answer to the question of how the policy should be adapted to Bolivian circumstances: broadly this involved no systematic consideration of how to change the Chilean model but an adherence to the model until the legislative phase of policy development, when political pressures within the Bolivian political system forced some deviations from the Chilean model. In this case the deviations concerned 'peripheral aspects' of the reform rather than its core, although there is no necessary reason to expect the democratic policy process only to affect peripheral aspects of borrowed policies.

It is thus possible to have imitation without any lesson drawing: a variety of heuristics can be used to shape policy, which means that the foreign example can have a profound influence. Perhaps the most important heuristic from the point of view of whether the policy is 'inspired by' or imitates more or less closely that of the other country is the anchoring heuristic: Weyland (2005) is here suggesting that domestic modifications made to a foreign programme that has served as a model depend on how far key policy makers insist on keeping the original features and how much the domestic political process makes changes to it.

Weyland does not claim his discussion of heuristics is exhaustive. One additional heuristic that is worth particular mention is a *trust heuristic*. In their study of local regeneration partnerships Wolman and Page (2000) show that policy makers tend to use the experience of other partnerships and local authorities – mainly domestic but some foreign. Faced with a large number of models that are put forward as offering good practice from which they can learn, policy makers tend to look seriously at those models they can trust. The trust can derive from the source – possibly a trusted organisation or a person whose advice is trusted – or from the ability of the policy makers to see things for themselves. In the latter case being influenced by a neighbouring partnership or authority is a common expression of this trust heuristic as the policy makers knew the conditions, background and people in the neighbouring authority well and could 'see things for themselves'.

Similar trust heuristics seem to be employed frequently in government. Thus, as discussed above, it appeared to be the advice of the person entrusted with developing thinking about reform that ended with Working Families Tax Credit, Martin Taylor, that led the Treasury away from a close reliance on the US model. Policy advisers tend to shape policy makers' views less because they have conducted or can interpret research with a direct bearing on the issue in question, than because their judgement is trusted. This means it is possible to have expert advice about policies that are found in other jurisdictions that are not based on the kind of rigorous examination of a programme as set out in a model of lesson drawing. Thus, for example, the cross-national evidence used by the Performance and Innovation Unit in the deliberations that led to the 2002 Proceeds of Crime Act had a steering panel of international scholars and consulted authorities with agencies that sought to use civil law to seize money from suspected criminals, although the evidence that such schemes should be emulated did not extend much beyond judgements that criminals did not like having money taken away and the presentation of a few headline figures on amounts ordered to be seized (not actual seizures; Performance and Innovation Unit, 2000e). Evidence that might offer, for example, evaluations of the cost of enforcement or the impact on other anti-crime or money laundering legislation was unavailable and not therefore considered.

Conclusions

The discussions in this chapter make clear that the practice of looking abroad for 'lessons' in policy making is long-standing and widespread, and the commitment in the modernisation process makes it increasingly likely that policy makers will use such techniques. That said, there are a number of important conclusions that can be drawn:

- While the methodology of drawing lessons is well understood and clearly set out by Rose, much of what appears to be a use of international experience falls well short of an analytical process of lesson drawing. This is quite understandable if we consider the intellectual and political difficulties involved in the process, and the problems of making the timetables of the political and intellectual processes coincide in such a way as to create a 'window of opportunity' for proposals for policy change derived from analytical lesson drawing. A more usual form of influence of international models comes in forms such as inspiration, picking up 'labels', 'smart ideas' and demonstrating the possibilities of policy change. Such forms of influence, and adaptation of international examples to domestic circumstances, can be achieved without the policy 'borrowed' being subjected to any substantial or rigorous lesson-drawing analysis.

- Not subjecting policies in this way to rigorous lesson-drawing analysis does not guarantee, or even necessarily indicate, that the policy will 'fail' any more than subjecting such policies to such analysis guarantees 'success'. As Bolivian pensions policy and Austrian university reform have shown, reforms enjoying, apparently, some degree of success, can be based on uncritical or even mistaken perceptions of international examples. The difference between lesson drawing and other ways of using international experiences is rather that analytical processes allow one to learn more: more about, for example, how well a programme works, what makes it work, what is needed to make it work elsewhere, what its costs, benefits, strengths and weaknesses are and what unintended consequences it might have. Thus a central purpose of policy learning is precisely to learn – to generate information, insight and share experience – and uncritical imitation does not fill this purpose.

- However, to suggest that all international policy learning should be analytical lesson drawing means effectively ruling out the way most such learning actually takes place – through a variety of heuristics or short cuts that allow international models to shape domestic policies without lesson drawing's essential components: rigorous evidence and analysis, the time to develop and apply it and control of the policy-making process. But, simply to say that proper lesson drawing is difficult and people 'learn' in other ways does not answer the question of how properly to use international evidence. The issue here is, as James and Lodge (2001) point out, rather analogous to the debate about 'rational policy making' and 'bounded rationality' arising from the work of authors such as Lindblom (1959) and Simon (1945/57) (see also Weyland, 2004). 'Pure rationality' in decision making, involving the systematic investigation of a full range of alternatives when developing a policy, is rarely feasible if ever possible. Instead decisions are taken using a variety of non-analytical techniques or through distant approximations of 'rational' techniques, and a similar process holds true for lesson drawing.

- Suggesting that cross-national policy learning should be more analytical and seek to follow lesson-drawing techniques as closely as possible is one answer both to the question of how to judge the quality of policy learning and to the question of how cross-national policy learning can be made more effective. Yet much of the time this is likely to be difficult. Thus, such an injunction, if ever it were able to be followed, would serve to limit international policy learning to a trickle. Not only is the advice to follow a true path unlikely to be followed, it would also have the result of cutting off a source of policy ideas that has proved extremely rich. As with the debate about 'rational' policy-making techniques generally, the two most obvious alternatives – becoming more rational, or accepting that 'anything goes', surrendering all decisions to the short-term vicissitudes of politics and the policy process – are not very attractive.

• When we think of much cross-national policy learning as the application of a variety of heuristics – short cuts to facilitate policy making – one important option is to be *critical about these heuristics as a means of gaining more from the cross-national comparison*. While this might not lead straight back to the true path of lesson drawing it does allow a form of interrogation of cross-national experience likely to enrich the policy-making process – one of the main benefits of policy learning under pressure. Thus questioning the availability heuristic could open up the possibility that one or many more appropriate models are out there; looking more closely at the representative heuristic might lead to a greater understanding of the likely payoffs and costs of a policy; taking a serious look at how such a policy should be anchored and how much altered in the pre-legislative design stage forces a form of 'prospective evaluation' and an understanding of the differences between the exporting and host jurisdiction; and looking more critically at the views of those you trust might encourage advisers to look harder to justify their advice. None of these requires the aerodynamics of the policy process to change – the intellectual and political costs of such an approach need not be high – but rather would require a more critical approach to learning from foreign lessons than is commonly found.

Note

[1] Some of the work for this chapter was conducted for the Economic and Social Research Council's Future Governance programme (Grant L216342003).

Further reading

Heclo, H. (1974) *Modern social politics in Britain and Sweden: From relief to income maintenance*, New Haven, CT: Yale University Press – a pioneering and influential work on policy learning that remains significant.

Rose, R. (1993) *Lesson drawing in public policy. A guide to learning across time and space*, Chatham, NJ: Chatham House; and Rose, R. (2005) *Learning from comparative public policy. A practical guide*, London: Routledge – Rose's two books on lesson drawing discuss the theoretical and practical issues involved in using cross-national experiences to develop policy.

Westney, E. (1987) *Innovation and imitation: The transfer of western organizational patterns to Meiji Japan*, Cambridge, MA: Harvard University Press – this study of Meiji Japan is a readable account of a very serious attempt to learn from public policy by studying successful models from the west.

Useful websites

www.law.qmul.ac.uk/lisbon/seminars/seminars.html – on the 'open method of coordination', a useful website, containing discussion and good analysis as well as empirical analyses of how the system of policy learning and 'peer review' works in practice; this is the ESRC-funded seminar series on the Lisbon Agenda held in 2005 and 2006 at Queen Mary, University of London.

www.policyhub.gov.uk – the government publishes some guidance on cross-national policy learning on its Policy Hub website, including the Cabinet Office's 1999 'Beyond the horizon: international comparisons in policy making toolkit'.

www.futuregovernance.ac.uk – the website of the ESRC's Future Governance programme (1998-2003) contains conference papers and discussion papers on cross-national policy learning.

FOUR

Innovative, flexible and creative policy making

Andrew Massey and Jamie Rentoul

The 'innovative, flexible and creative' competency outlined in *Professional policy making for the twenty-first century* (Cabinet Office Strategic Policy Making Team, 1999) encompasses a variety of ideas and stimuli, some of which are reflected in the other competencies dealt with in this book, such as inclusiveness and being outward looking. Any analysis of this area is therefore subject to different interpretations of what 'innovative, flexible and creative' might mean. This chapter therefore takes a fairly broad view of innovative, flexible and creative policy making, examining:

- the context within which there is perceived to be a need for innovative policy making;
- the drivers for policy change; and
- the development of strategic policy-making units, in particular the role of the Prime Minister's Strategy Unit (PMSU).

This chapter explores the British government's attempts to develop policy making that may be seen as innovative, flexible and creative. There are a variety of programmes (or approaches) that have been developed over the past decade that might justifiably be seen as meeting these criteria. These include the New Deal, for jobseekers and long-term unemployed people, and the Sure Start programme, designed to deliver a comprehensive or 'joined-up' approach to developing children's potential. The latter does this by seeking to take a whole-government approach to an individual, by bringing together early education, childcare, health and family support, with the lead being taken by the Sure Start, Extended Schools and Childcare Group within the Department for Education and Skills. In this wide, yet targeted, approach it displays many of the characteristics that have been at the forefront of New Labour's reforms, an approach that seeks to use central government to coordinate a structured and strategic dynamic to modernising government through the development of higher quality citizen-responsive public services.

Alongside these broad programmes (and programmatic approaches) have come fundamental reforms that as individual policies have shaped and in many cases transformed the constitution and political life of the UK. These include statutes on devolution (1998), the Human Rights Act (1998), the Disability Discrimination Act (2005), the Age Discrimination Act (2004), the Race Relations Amendment Act (2004), and the Bank of England Act (1998). There have also been machinery of government reforms, such as a large increase in the number of independent and specialist advisers, especially in the expanded Prime Minister's Office at 10 Downing Street, and the revamped Treasury under Gordon Brown (Massey, 2005). Taken collectively the reforms have significantly restructured the way in which Britain is governed; they have left many of the old institutions in place while replacing the software that works them. An innovative and flexible approach to policy making has been one of the ways in which Labour has sought to get traction on the problems it perceives to have beset the nation, and from this strategic approach a notion of progress through reform has flowed. In this chapter we will first explore some of the background to that change, before considering the modern context to policy making and then describing the way in which the PMSU, in particular, has sought to adopt an innovative and responsive approach to making policy.

Background to change

After 18 years of opposition the Labour Party returned to power in 1997 determined to continue their Conservative predecessors' commitment to reform and intending to modernise the process of government. An essential element of this was to be a fundamental reappraisal of the way in which policy was made and implemented; a new approach that was to be an innovative, flexible and creative way of doing things in keeping with New Labour's modernising agenda. The agenda largely accepted the new public management critique of the bureaucratic structures of the postwar welfare state and sought to imbue the business of government with the managerial ethos of the private sector (Massey and Pyper, 2005). As if to prove this, powerful business leaders, such as Lord Sainsbury, were co-opted into government, demonstrating the business-friendly credentials of the party. Labour returned to power, however, unused to the ways of government, as a political generation had passed since it had last controlled the great departments of state.

The party had transformed itself politically and procedurally in the political wilderness, but it had also lost some of its institutional memory; put simply, there were few ministers in the first Blair government who had ever held high office, much less worked with senior civil servants to draft new policies (although in sensitive areas of security and defence senior frontbenchers are routinely briefed under Privy Council rules and there had been a lot of contact at workshops and seminars under 'Chatham House' rules). Although, in opposition, political parties have little choice but to seek advice from think-tanks and other organisations, the party and its new ministers had been in opposition for so long, and had so completely accepted the rhetoric of the new public management approach of Mrs Thatcher, that they had become used to contracting out for much policy advice to think-tanks and interest groups. This has proved to be a significant habit, almost a model for how the party continued to behave in power for the next 10 years, arguably making it more difficult to learn how to make best use of civil servants. In some ways policy advice, formulation and even delivery has become a market, albeit a deformed, imperfect market. To be fair, this dilution in policy-making terms of the senior civil service had begun under Mrs Thatcher. What Hood and Lodge (2006) define as 'public sector bargains' and which 'involve explicit or implicit understanding between (senior) public servants and other actors in a political system over their duties and entitlements relating to responsibility, autonomy, and political identity, and expressed in convention or formal law or a mixture of both' (2006, p 6) had been part of the new public management assault on traditional public administration. In other words, the power of ministers in the policy process had been enhanced and 'the monopoly of the civil service as advisors to ministers was challenged by the growth of "think tanks", and a new central policy unit was established to help the prime minister contest civil service advice' (Newman, 2001, p 57). Such challenges are not limited to the UK; in many jurisdictions such as Australia, New Zealand and the Netherlands politicians are still 'living together [but] growing apart' ('t Hart and Wille, 2006, p 121). Labour adapted to the free market in advice in power, just as it had done in opposition. Although we comment on these changes here as if they were entirely novel, it ought to be remembered that the wartime coalition government of Winston Churchill similarly sought policy advice from a plethora of sources in new and creative ways. So there is a precedent and in many ways the multi-faceted challenges of Europeanisation and globalisation present as comprehensive a challenge (if not threat) to the British state as the dark days of the 1940s (Smith, 1979).

The Blair government's first comprehensive attempt at modernisation of the structures of central government (other than the hastily prepared and unfinished devolution programme) was the 1999 White Paper *Modernising government* (Cabinet Office, 1999). Perhaps somewhat surprisingly, the White Paper confirmed a hierarchical approach to the process of modernisation. At about the same time a new strategic policy-making team in the Cabinet Office produced a report setting out a model for what was termed *Professional policy making for the twenty-first century* (Cabinet Office Strategic Policy Making Team, 1999). As outlined in Chapter One (this volume), the model was based on a series of core competencies linked to the policy process:

- forward looking
- outward looking
- innovative and creative
- using evidence
- inclusive
- joined up

- evaluates
- reviews
- learns lessons.

The two documents should be taken together, as they inform the policy-making approach adopted over subsequent years and affirmed a belief in the efficacy of government to deliver services to the nation in a coherent and efficient way. As such it was a perspective that was heavily criticised by, among others, Parsons, who sought a more creative approach to policy making, arguing that:

> Given that policy-making takes place in conditions of ignorance, unpredictability, uncertainty and complexity ... a strategic policy model should also aim to incorporate approaches to strategy that are more focused on these factors. (Parsons, 2003, p 184)

Parsons' critique, in essence, was that the 'new' strategic approach was far from being innovative and flexible, but was in fact rather stodgy and old-fashioned, replicating tired old textbook approaches taken straight out of (elderly) business school courses. The programmatic, rather stolid model adopted in the two papers also represents something of a paradox in that although new public management is located within the individualistic theoretical terrain of public choice and the Virginia school of economists, Labour initially sought its implementation by employing the kind of centralised and mechanistic bureaucracy emphatically opposed by the neoliberals. But then, that also had been the approach of the previous administrations (Newman, 2001).

Whatever one makes of it, *Modernising government* had three clear aims:

1. To ensure policy making became more joined up and strategic;
2. To make sure public service users became the focus;
3. To deliver public services that were of high quality and efficient;

and five key commitments:

1. Policy making will be forward looking and deliver results; it will cease reacting to short-term pressures.
2. Public services will be responsive to citizens' needs.
3. Public services will be efficient and of high quality with continuing improvement.
4. The government will use new technology to meet the needs of citizens and business and will not trail behind technological developments.
5. Public service will be valued not denigrated.

However, there is something of a confusion of dynamics at work over this period. Newman summarises it in a diagram that charts the 'dynamics of change', noting that there is:

- a self-governance model, which is based on citizen or community power and moves towards devolution, participation and sustainability;
- a hierarchy model, at the other end of the spectrum to self-governance. It is based on formal authority and moves towards control, standardisation and accountability;
- an open systems model, that is based on flows of power within networks and sees a move towards flexibility, expansion and adaptation;
- a rational goal model, that is based on managerial power and sees policy shaped by a move towards the maximisation of output and economic rationalism (Newman, 2001).

At any time and with regard to any policy area it is possible to see one or any combination of all four of the dynamics contained within these models at work. The examples quoted at the start of this chapter are an illustration, in that at the same time as the government was passing legislation on devolution and taking pains to ensure public services were more responsive to individual citizens' needs, it was passing a great ream of legislation in terms of anti-discrimination policies that were based on a hierarchical model for their structure and implementation, significantly increasing the burden of regulation on both private and public sector organisations. Neither is it clear what evidence was used to ensure the formulation and explanation for the latter series of measures, beyond broad manifesto commitments. Indeed the commitment to evidence-based policy making (see Chapter Five, this volume) made by the government appears not to have been adhered to in the case of the anti-discrimination legislation, where, not surprisingly, the dynamic was an ideological commitment. This underlines again the importance of context for policy making, the context in the case of this collection of legislative initiatives being political in its ideological sense and not an attempt to 'manage' or 'deliver' services in an improved way.

There is, however, an additional, obvious but often overlooked, reason why policy making should be innovative, flexible and creative, and that is that public policy and public services affect the lives and interests of citizens. Donahue (2005) argues that for this reason innovation in this sector is crucial. Innovation can enable new needs to be met, and old needs to be met more effectively; conversely, he suggests that a failure to innovate may result in reduced benefits for the public.

Modern context of policy making

Governance and multi-level governance

The introduction to this book (Chapter One) discusses the notions of governance and multi-level governance. An understanding of these terms is clearly one of the keys to understanding the role of policy makers in contemporary society. Given the observation at the end of the last section to this chapter, it is worth revisiting some of these points here in order to locate the issues that afflict the policy process and can inhibit it. For example, Mulgan and Albury (2003) argue there are a number of barriers to policy innovation. These include:

- reluctance to close down failing programmes or organisations
- over-reliance on high performers as sources of innovation
- technologies available but constraining cultural or organisational arrangements
- a culture of risk aversion
- delivery pressures and administrative burdens
- short-term budgets and planning horizons
- no rewards or incentives to innovate or adopt innovations
- poor skills in active risk or change management (2003, p 31; see also Koch and Hauknes, 2005).

These barriers are situated within the frameworks of governance and multi-level governance and the resulting intergovernmental relations can be part of the problem, especially in terms of a mismatch of organisational arrangements, lack of competencies or even budgetary constraints of various kinds. The different actors within the policy networks (and here we accept Rhodes et al's definition of policy networks as they apply to the civil service in the UK (2003)) will often be resistant to change for reasons of administrative culture and vested interest. However, there have been attempts to address some of the barriers identified by Newman (2001); notably the new Spending Review process, which attempted among other things to address some of the issues of short-termism, and an increased emphasis on risk (HM Treasury, 2004b, 2004c), which aimed to anticipate risk in a systematic way, rather than allowing it to act as a force to dampen innovation. Risk management is now an integrated element in government planning processes. Whether addressing these barriers has worked to encourage innovation is a moot point, but at least it has helped to create a more favourable climate.

The term 'governance' refers to the activities and processes of government and reflects the fragmentation and complexity of the modern state. One view of governance is closely linked to multi-level governance as it refers to activities simultaneously located at several different governmental levels: local, national, regional and global. The complexity of policy making may be understood with particular regard to the emergence of policy networks that have evolved around national government departments, and are now an essential prerequisite to the delivery of policy: 'they are a form of private government of public services.... Commonly, welfare state services are now delivered by packages of organisations' (Rhodes et al, 2003, pp 26-7). An example of this and its limitations in the devolved political structures of the UK may be observed in the case of Sure Start. Sure Start is a government programme aimed at alleviating the impact of social and economic disadvantage; it is designed to increase the availability of childcare provision, to improve the health and emotional development of children and to support parents in entering or re-entering the job market. But with devolution there is greater scope for differential policies, the devolved nations having responsibility for childcare issues within their jurisdiction. These arrangements again demonstrate the paradox that lies at the heart of many attempts to be innovative and creative in policy terms – the political context and ideological dynamics inherent to the policy process disgorge powerful contradictory forces from within the heart of government. While service delivery and policy formulation is thus characterised, an increasing body of both public and private sector regulation and standards accreditation further complicates the attempts of those who would be flexible and creative. Thus:

> Governance represents the differentiation of government, government functions and governmental authority; it crosses the penumbra between the state and civil society weaving a seamless web between the two. (Massey, 2005, p 3)

And in so doing often throws up unexpected barriers to effective progress. For the reasons outlined elsewhere in this book, the term 'governance' has become prominent in the political science literature and official governmental publications around the globe. Although:

> Peck, amongst others, argues the need for caution regarding the ubiquity and utility of the usage (2004), the dispersal of traditional governmental activities to the private sector and international NGOs [non-governmental organisations], has made it a useful descriptive shorthand for the way policy is made and services are delivered in a growing number of jurisdictions and across a growing number of areas such as trade, welfare, and environmental policy. (Massey, 2005, p 4)

Governance represents the inclusion of civil society and the economic, professional and social interest groups into the networks of policy formulation and delivery: that inclusion, however, is not comprehensive and neither is it on an equal basis. The Policy Action Team approach to making policy, adopted by the Social Exclusion Unit, illustrates this, and is discussed more fully in Chapter Six (this volume). Newman notes that governance, therefore, has become a somewhat promiscuous concept but is nonetheless useful as an explanation of social change as well as different approaches to understanding the policy process and institutional change (2001). Among these explanations are included the use of markets, hierarchies and networks to coordinate economic activity, responding to complexity, diversity and dynamic change and the problems of governing the nation in a period of globalisation and 'hollow state' governance. As far as the latter is concerned, it may be argued that:

> The hollowing out of the state and the differentiated nature of the polity ensures that many government policies are doomed to failure. This situation is not because of a lack of commitment on the part of public servants, but because with power and authority ebbing away from London to Brussels, the devolved countries and amorphous power-brokers within the internationalised (or globalised) economy, British national government has lost the ability to impose its will through the hierarchical institutions of command and control. The modern world is immune to several of the techniques that an old-style national government may use to modernise itself. Much change therefore is imposed from outside, or rather … it is the result of external triggers forcing governments and institutions to respond to change elsewhere by changing themselves. (Massey and Pyper, 2005, p 172)

The complexity of modern policy making ensures there has to be a new approach to the process as it is nothing short of an attempt to remake civil society, and through initiatives like Sure Start it is the politics of inclusion (Newman, 2001; see also Chapter Six, this volume). But this is an inclusion in a political context where the nation-state has less power and a declining influence on those who reside within its borders.

To take a broader view, the European Union's (EU's) White Paper on *European governance* (CEC, 2001) defines governance in its European context as:

> Rules, processes and behaviour that affect the way in which powers are exercised at European level, particularly as regards openness, participation, accountability, effectiveness and coherence. (p 8)

With few exceptions hierarchical and centralised government is no longer the dominant form of political system; a new diversity and complexity is becoming the dominant policy-making model, sometimes explained as the 'differentiated polity'. Policy makers are less able to depend on giving orders to ensure the effective implementation of their policies, but must rely instead on diplomacy and negotiation to get their way.

The differentiated polity model was first developed by Rhodes to explain the changes occurring in the UK accelerated by EU integration and evolution. It views:

- policy networks as a medium of policy making;
- a segmented and sometimes fractured executive;
- intergovernmental relations and an emphasis on diplomacy and negotiation;
- a hollowed-out state (Rhodes et al, 2003).

In other words, multi-level governance is a reality that exists in several forms in different contexts. The concept of the differentiated polity also brings into the discussion about policy making regional political organisations, devolution, federalism, professional groups, international corporations and other transnational organisations in governance. Multi-level governance reflects policy making at the supranational level, at the national level, where sovereignty remains legally located, but from which much has migrated, and at the sub-national level. This accelerating complexity of the policy content should be added to Mulgan and Albury's (2003) aforementioned list as to why there are so many barriers to policy change, and so many more to strategic, comprehensive, creative and flexible policy making.

Flexible and creative policy making in this context needs to be:

- transparent;
- accountable in terms of management, project implementation, financial management and information disclosure;
- ethical;
- concerned with equal rights and issues of diversity.

To put these into practice it is necessary for policy makers to define what is meant by some of the key phrases such as 'transparency', 'ethical' and 'accountability'. The EU's White Paper on *European governance* (CEC, 2001) goes some way towards this, arguing for:

1. Openness; with EU institutions working in an open manner communicating their activities widely throughout the EU and beyond, using language that is accessible and understandable for the general public in order to improve public confidence in complex institutions.
2. Participation; while accepting that direct democracy has a limited applicability, the Commission seeks wide participation through what it calls the policy chain – from conception to implementation, this participation relies on national governments pursuing an inclusive approach when developing and implementing EU policies.
3. Accountability; in the form of a more defined role for the legislative and executive processes with each of the EU institutions explaining what they do and taking responsibility for this area. All institutions need to develop greater clarity and responsibility.
4. Effectiveness; with policies being effective and timely, delivering what is needed, on the basis of clear objectives, with an evaluation of future impact and, where available, of past experience. Effectiveness is also seen as dependent on

implementing EU policies in a proportionate manner and on taking decisions at the most appropriate level.

5. 'Coherence' as an essential element of good governance. 'Policies and actions must be coherent and easily understood' (CEC, 2001, p 10).

It is sometimes difficult to distinguish what, if anything, is the major dynamic for policy making within this complex set of structures and motivations. Certainly some observers lament the loss of a kind of ethical ideal, almost a platonic guardian role for senior civil servants (O'Toole, 2006), but such a position of trusteeship is often incompatible with modern demands for core competencies and accountability from politicians schooled in the new economic tradition of principal and agent theory (Hood and Lodge, 2006).

There is also a strong element of isomorphism here in its normative, mimetic and coercive forms. Coercive isomorphism occurs when organisations are obliged to change and adopt certain practices and procedures. The 2000 Race Relations (Amendment) Act is an example of this, as is the regulatory regime imposed by institutions as diverse as the Quality Assurance Agency (QAA) for Higher Education, the Health and Safety Executive or the Food Standards Agency.

Mimetic isomorphism occurs when organisations voluntarily copy each other in order to be identified with prevailing norms and best practice (Newman, 2001), or as a result of some attempt to win legitimacy or acceptance, an example being the steady Europeanisation of public administrations across the continent, especially by those aspirant nations currently outside of the EU (Carr and Massey, 2006).

Normative isomorphism occurs when professions or occupations develop institutional norms of behaviour; examples may include best practice in National Health Service (NHS) hospitals (or even poor practice) or the way different groups of professionals interact in their various roles in youth offending teams (Newman, 2001). Often this isomorphism is simply a way of following prevailing managerial and administrative fashion. This is illustrated by a telling comment from a senior official, quoted by Hood and Lodge, when referring to how he saw Next Steps agencies developing after 2003. He dismissed the whole edifice as, 'Last week's salad' (Hood and Lodge, 2006, p 171). Given that when they were established following the Ibbs report in 1988, Next Steps agencies were seen as part of a spectacularly creative reform, deemed to have been responsible for delivering executive flexibility in service delivery; their transmogrification into 'leftovers' is an intriguing insight into current Whitehall practice.

Modern policy making

It is also the case that, as suggested in *Professional policy making for the twenty-first century* (Cabinet Office Strategic Policy Making Team, 1999), a number of developments associated with the other competencies outlined in this book themselves have clear implications for 'innovative, flexible and creative' policy making, and these merit some consideration here. For example, the introduction of techniques such as the use of horizon scanning, outlined in Chapter Two, is in itself to some extent innovative for the public sector, although the idea of not simply seeking to envisage possible futures, but also to shape them, is likely to entail both creativity and flexibility over sustained periods of time. As Chapter Seven (this volume) makes clear, while attempts to achieve more joined-up government have a considerable history, the scale of such initiatives (including the Social Exclusion Unit [now Task Force], the Women and Equality Unit and others, both within central government and the devolved administrations) is unprecedented, and to be successful requires a high level of flexibility from the agencies involved. In the same way, new approaches to 'inclusiveness' (Chapter Six) may be to a greater or lesser extent innovative, while truly listening to and taking on board the views of a range of stakeholders, including traditionally 'hard-to-reach' groups, requires a greater degree of flexibility in policy making than has traditionally been the case. This is perhaps even more true when combined with the arguments from Chapters Five and Nine that the role of evidence and policy evaluation has become increasingly embedded in policy making (although, as they and Chapter Eight also make clear, there remain a number of important caveats), including more widespread use of policy pilots that have not only considered the degree to which policies achieve appropriate outcomes, but also the processes of implementing policy, the mechanisms of delivery and the role of frontline staff, all of which further imply flexibility and creativeness in policy making and responding to evidence.

There is also an argument that emerges from a number of the other chapters that further emphasises creativity in policy making. This is perhaps particularly true in relation to the learning lessons, forward-looking and evidence-based competencies, which highlight the need for creativity in responding to complex problems in complex societies, the potential to seek to shape the future and the use of evidence to aid what some consider the 'art' of policy making. Taken together these can be seen as requiring policy makers to reconsider elements of their current thinking and to respond to agendas that are, at least in part, defined by others and affected by a wide range of influences.

Strategic development of policy

While regular senior civil servants largely remained policy advisers, which included the brief of speaking 'truth unto power', it was also the case that this part of their traditional public service bargain had become more problematic after 1997 (Hood and Lodge, 2006). In many cases special advisers were becoming the source of radical policy ideas, acting as challenge agents, while the impact of new public management meant that the switch from policy making to management for many senior officials made the difference to whether they were promoted or not, their seniors often expressing a preference for good managers over creative policy innovators (Hood and Lodge, 2006).

In essence, then, the nature of the senior civil service was also being reformed, perhaps not to the extent that it could be labelled the death of a paradigm, but certainly to the extent that it became one of several competing sources of new strategic policy thinking. Sometimes ministers deliberately tried to force their regular officials to come up with interesting strategic or policy ideas, but often the officials would revert to type, seeking to act as policy arbiters, choosing between options put forward by others. Ministers are reported to have found this frustrating; one, for example, viewed meetings as a kind of strategic brainstorming:

> Expecting the officials to have a fantastic chance to pour out ideas, but they would come to the meeting and say, 'What do you want, Secretary of State?' And he would say, 'I have some ideas, but aren't you guys doing any thinking?' (Hood and Lodge, 2006, p 90)

This reflects the official's traditional role as an adviser, a trustee and a guardian (of the minister if not the interests of state). Officials in a standard hierarchical relationship with ministers would advise and warn, they would take raw policy ideas and work them up into feasible strategies and deliverable policies, and then move on to the next issue. This often gave the impression that officials and career politicians cared little if anything for the outcome of many of their policies, knew nothing of the outputs and rarely, if ever, evaluated the results. New Labour sought rather more from its officials; it wanted them to think strategically, to be innovative and to follow through, including an evaluation of what they had done. It wanted them to learn the lessons of their failures as well as their successes (see Chapter Ten, this volume).

It is not surprising therefore that some of the reforms to the civil service, notably the Professional Skills for Government programme, have sought to enable shifts such as those required for 'modern policy making', including the innovative, creative and flexible policy making, for example:

> Our task in the Civil Service of supporting the Government of the day is becoming increasingly complex and demanding. In response to this we have for some time been growing the skills and expertise of our people, and bringing people in where we do not have the necessary expertise. Professional Skills for Government builds on this to apply a systematic approach which will ensure that:
>
> • the Civil Service has the right skills, expertise and experience to support the work of the Government, including delivering services to the public effectively and efficiently;
> • individuals have the opportunities to gain the necessary skills to do an excellent job and are provided with a clearer framework for career development; and

- our approach to skills and career development is more systematic and consistent.

These developments will move us right away from the old days of generalists and specialists and will equip the Service for the work Governments may ask us to do in the future, as well as meeting the needs of current priorities for public service reform. (Civil Service Management Board, 2005, p 5)

Given some of the priorities and challenges outlined above, the government established a series of strategic policy-making units both centrally and in departments, a reformulation of the old Central Policy Review Staff and other in-house think-tanks. These were staffed by a mix of high-flying career officials and an eclectic mix of co-opted 'outsiders'. As noted above, such an approach was not new and built on experience going back to that of the wartime Churchill administration. The PMSU was among this administrative collection and in 2004 produced the *Strategy survival guide*. It argued that:

Effective strategy development requires the mandate to challenge, the space to think and the commitment of stakeholders. For these, and many other reasons, strategy work is best undertaken within the context of a clearly defined project that can act as a focal point for generating momentum behind a change in conventional thinking. (2004, p 1)

This development can also be seen as reflecting the view that 'Innovation at the policy level is based on policy learning' (Koch and Hauknes, 2005, p 31), including policy makers being able to learn what is needed to change behaviour.

Although not a direct riposte to the criticisms of Parsons and others, this approach began to address some of the complaints about a rather stodgy and overly structured policy process. That said, however, Figure 4.1 does still owe more to the 1999 White Papers than, say, the work of Parsons, who argues that:

Innovation is difficult to institutionalize. As the Peer Review report of the Cabinet Office noted: 'one cannot "command" innovation or "control" creativity. Neither can one buy "breakthroughs" or "foresight"'. (Cabinet Office, 2000, para 3.5.2, quoted in Parsons, 2003, p 166)

The analysis of Parsons, therefore, could lead observers to the view that the PMSU itself was locked into the kind of overly structured formulaic approach of which he was so critical. He asks the question 'How do we know what works, works?' in that 'Policy problems and policy solutions are, of their nature highly contextual. What works is what works, when, how and for whom?' (Parsons, 2003, p 168).

Given these caveats, however, the PMSU developed the diagram in Figure 4.1 as a guide to good strategy development.

Figure 4.1: A framework for the development of strategy

Source: PMSU (2004, p 9)

Its officials noted that:

> Although the process of developing strategy is complex and often iterative in nature, strategy projects tend to naturally move through a number of phases.... The framework provides a helpful reference point but should not be interpreted as a template. In practice the phases are unlikely to be entirely discrete and sequential, tasks may actually span across phases, and phases may need to be revisited as the true complexity of the project unfolds. As the need for fresh strategic thinking starts to emerge, it is important to bring clarity to the scope, rationale and approach for the proposed work. At this early stage it is important to:
>
> • demonstrate the need for the project
> • identify and structure the issues that need to be addressed
> • plan how the project will be structured
> • pull together an appropriate team. (PMSU, 2004, p 2)

In other words, the authors of this rather old-fashioned approach were aware of its limitations and sought its use as a guide, a kind of primer, for approaching issues, rather than as a template for solving problems. A later section of the guide, however, switches into more didactic mode, perhaps reflecting the novelty of this kind of approach to policy making, arguing through a series of definitions that the:

---

terms 'strategy' and 'policy' are used in many different ways, and sometimes interchangeably.

- *Strategy* is the overall process of deciding where we want to get to and how we are going to get there.
- *Strategic direction* describes the desired future and sets out what needs to be achieved in order to bring it about. It provides the guiding principles that give context and coherence to action.
- *Policy* provides the means of moving in that direction – and often a number of policies need to work together to deliver particular strategic outcomes. Policy design work is concerned with identifying how to achieve strategic objectives, selecting the most suitable policy instruments for doing this, and detailing how these instruments will work in practice. (PMSU, 2004, p 4)

We can see here a demonstration of an attempt to encourage officials to think creatively about the policy process and to be flexible and innovative through each of its stages. But at the same time as issuing the call to be creative and innovative, the PMSU was mindful of the need to keep sight of the overall picture. Arguing strategies:

> ... help organisations think through what they want to achieve and how they will achieve it. Putting strategies into practice and acting strategically ensures that they are focused on the things that really matter – not buffeted by events or short-term distractions – and are able to allocate their resources accordingly. (PMSU, 2004, p 3)

The PMSU notes the 'huge literature on strategy in business and in warfare; strategy in government is similar, but tends to be more complex. It generally involves multiple goals rather than one single bottom line and it is implemented through a wide range of policy instruments, including laws, taxes and services' (2004, p 3). In other words, far from 'being a neat linear process, it is shaped by unexpected events and political pressures' (p 3), and in echoing the points made by the EU's White Paper on *European governance* (CEC, 2001), it 'also often needs to be more visible and accountable than strategy in other fields' (PMSU, 2004, p 3).

The PMSU's guide argues that:

> the best strategies in governments and public services are:
>
> - clear about objectives, relative priorities and trade-offs
> - underpinned by a rich understanding of causes, trends, opportunities, threats and possible futures

- based on a realistic understanding of the effectiveness of different policy instruments and the capacities of institutions (strategies that work well on paper but not in practice are of little use)
- creative – designing and discovering new possibilities
- designed with effective mechanisms for adaptability in the light of experience
- developed with, and communicated effectively to, all those with a stake in the strategy or involved in its funding or implementation. (2004, p 3)

In taking a strategic approach 'decisions on strategic direction, policy design and delivery are seen as an end-to-end process of change management, with constant testing, feedback, learning and improvement.... All strategies need to be adaptable, with quick feedback and effective information flows to respond to new information, and take account of changing circumstances or unexpected events' (PMSU, 2004, p 3). Quite how it is intended that such an approach builds in or responds to the political context and ideological drivers, such as those that shaped the equality agenda over race, disability, sexual orientation and age, is not explained. But it is addressed in terms of delivery in the diagram reproduced below.

The PMSU's new diagram (Figure 4.2), demonstrating their kind of creative thinking, includes feedback loops familiar to students of policy analysis (for example, Parsons, 1995), but nonetheless they were arguably innovative in the intentions behind their implementation.

Figure 4.2: A framework for strategic direction

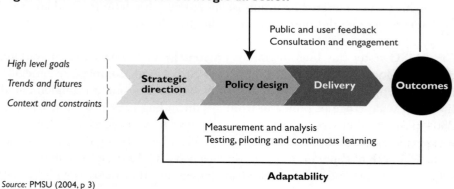

Source: PMSU (2004, p 3)

An example of this approach in action is the PMSU's project on minority ethnic groups and the labour market, replicated in Case study 4.1.

The PMSU notes that 'strategies and policies that are not deliverable are of little use. Strategy work needs to involve frontline practitioner knowledge from the outset, and proceed grounded in a realistic understanding of delivery capability. Feedback mechanisms are needed from delivery back into strategy and policy design in order to create adaptable learning systems that can evolve in the light of experience and unexpected results' (PMSU, 2004, p 5).

Case study 4.1: Strategic framework – the Prime Minister's Strategy Unit, minority ethnic groups and the labour market project

The PMSU gives this as an example of the development of a clear sense of direction, based on analysis of a range of strategic choices and their implications, drawing on: a vision (a statement of aspirations describing a desired future); aims (the outcomes needed to achieve that future); and objectives (the things that need to be achieved to realise the outcomes).

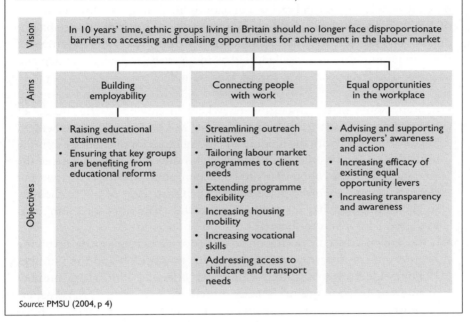

Source: PMSU (2004, p 4)

The Sure Start programme (Case study 4.2) provides an interesting example of a policy that can be argued to be, in many respects, innovative (although it draws on the Head Start initiative in the US), flexible and creative. In practice, it can also be seen to be informative, with the work of different evaluation teams confirming the importance of a national change agent (see Koch and Hauknes, 2005), for example, the Chancellor of the Exchequer; but also confirms the importance of micropolitics and the need for effective leadership and communication at local level (Bagley et al, 2004). Borins (2001) found that one of the key obstacles that attempts at innovation often fail to overcome is inadequate resources, and for Sure Start the commitment of the incoming Labour government and of the Chancellor of the Exchequer were arguably important factors. It is also an example of what Brown and Liddle (2005) refer to as an emergent 'service domain' model, built around innovative and creative service integration and complementary multi-professional partnerships for pre-school children and their families in disadvantaged communities.

Case study 4.2: Sure Start

The Sure Start initiative was targeted at young children and their parents living in the 20 per cent most disadvantaged areas, with each of the devolved administrations having responsibility for their own jurisdiction. It was intended to improve outcomes for children, parents and their local communities through an integrated approach to the delivery of Early Years services in order to promote children's development and increase parental employment.

Sure Start is not wholly novel, with uncanny echoes of its antecedence in previous official reports and recommendations (including the Plowden report of 1967), but what was arguably truly innovative is that it did not remain 'a dream', but was put together, funded and set into place. Other features of the programme can also be identified as innovative (as well as flexible and creative) to a greater or lesser extent. For example:

- Echoing some of the discussion elsewhere in this book, the success of establishing the Sure Start programme lay at least in part in its being a Treasury initiative, with the funding and momentum for the policy emerging from the most powerful of Whitehall's ministries in order to meet the commitment of the Labour Party to combating child poverty, a commitment clearly strongly supported personally by the Chancellor of the Exchequer. As such the policy had an early and powerful champion, something that was essential if it was to succeed.
- It was evidence based, drawing on an evidence-gathering process involving 11 government departments, the Social Exclusion Unit and the Number 10 Policy Unit, a steering group of ministers, meetings with a large number of relevant interest groups, service providers and service users, papers commissioned from experts, seminars and visits to projects, which offered services to young children and families (NESS, 2000).
- From the very beginning a joined-up, whole-government approach was adopted, indeed required, by the Treasury in order to reduce obstacles to the programme and seek out efficiencies and best value in terms of delivery (NESS, 2000). A new central unit was established to administer the programme, run by a ministerial steering group representing 10 government departments with an interest in children and families.
- It was also envisaged from the outset that the outcome of the policy would have wider social implications, including in relation to employment and levels of crime.
- It sought to build legitimacy and acceptance from within communities instead of (or, perhaps more accurately, as well as) imposing it from above, reflecting a belief that if communities, parents, interest groups and others 'own' a policy then it has a far greater chance of success.

Experience across the UK of the implementation has been diverse (NESS, 2000), but the policy itself remains radical, innovative and original. As noted above, it reflects the modernising agenda, and:

> This 'modernizing' agenda distinctively targets the needs of individuals, groups and communities, as opposed to the traditional approach of conceptualizing needs and service provision in terms of professional group interests and bureaucratic boundaries. Subsequently, as public services are delivered locally, so it is claimed they need to be more user-centred and focused. (Bagley et al, 2004, p 596)

The barriers to success in some of the local programmes remain those generic ones outlined earlier in this chapter, including problems of coordination, lack of sufficient numbers of trained staff, reluctance to close down 'old' ways of doing things, delivery pressures, administrative burdens and so on (NESS, 2000). For all its flexibility and innovative approaches, however, Sure Start follows on from a century or more of attempts and approaches to shape 'the poor' and make them behave in different ways in order to 'redeem' them for society (Moss, 2004).

It is clear from this that current attempts to provide innovative, flexible and creative policy making in central government recognise that the need for strategic thinking extends far beyond the realms of a formal strategy development project. At all stages of policy design and delivery, a strategic perspective is needed to ensure that government action is focused on and capable of meeting the true needs of the public. The questions posed by the three criteria of suitability, feasibility and acceptability form the basis of such a strategic perspective. However, as we noted earlier, all attempts at adopting a comprehensive, strategic (joined-up) approach can be, and often are, frustrated by the reality of the differentiated polity. There may also be a question about the use of cross-cutting units in bringing change into departments. While there is a clear rationale for such a mechanism, and drawing staff into these units to focus on a particular role may well be effective in promoting innovation and policy change, it remains a key challenge to embed these new approaches into the everyday work of departments, and the extent to which this is happening remains unclear.

Conclusions

This chapter has explored the background and dynamics to the British government's attempts over the past 10 years to develop policy-making approaches that are innovative, flexible and creative:

- There has been an attempt to locate the drivers of policy change within their immediate historical, political and administrative context and a discussion of the barriers to successful policy formulation and implementation, including the shift to governance and the increasing complexity of society, policy formulation and service delivery.

- The way in which the aims and directions of the post-1997 Labour administrations were inevitably shaped by the party's long experience in opposition has been considered, as well as how its incoming commitments have also served to structure the government's approach to policy making, positioning the policy-making machinery fully within the new public management inheritance of the Thatcher/Major years, indeed even expanding on it. This was placed within the global context of governance and the differentiated polity.

- The fact that other developments in modern policy making have implications for, and indeed perhaps require, higher levels of innovation, flexibility and creativity in policy making, for example, in responding to the needs and demands of a wide range of stakeholders and an evidence-informed agenda, has been highlighted.

- The notion of a strategic development of policy in recent years, using Hood's (2006) analysis of public sector bargains to understand how things have evolved, has been examined, before a discussion of the contribution of new strategic policy units, like the PMSU, and a case study of an innovative policy, Sure Start. It is safe to assume that there is little that in reality is entirely new, creative or innovative in British policy making. Setting aside the rhetoric, however, Sure Start is a close example if only because it has actually been established. Its success will be measured by whether child poverty remains in 2020, when it is supposed to have been eradicated. We cannot know if there will still be child poverty, but it is safe to assume that British society, like British politics, will have become further differentiated. Perhaps tilting at windmills will remain a favourite pastime for politicians and civil servants alike.

Further reading

Koch, P. and Hauknes, J. (2005) *Innovation in the public sector*, Oslo: NIFU STEP – although ranging much more widely than policy making, this report gives an extensive review of debates around innovation.

Massey, A. and Pyper, R. (2005) *Public management and modernization in Britain*, Basingstoke: Palgrave Macmillan – outlines some of the major influences on public management since the 1970s and the changes to the structure and organisation of the British state.

Mulgan, G. and Albury, D. (2003) *Innovation in the public sector*, London: Cabinet Office – sets out a range of arguments to support the spread of innovation in the public sector.

Newman, J. (2001) *Modernising governance: New Labour, policy and society*, London: Sage Publications – this book provides a thorough critique of much of New Labour's modernisation agenda, including the dynamics of institutional change and the politics of governance.

Useful websites

www.cabinetoffice.gov.uk/strategy/survivalguide/index.asp – the PMSU has continued to update its *Strategy survival guide* intended to support the development of strategic thinking across government.

www.surestart.gov.uk/ – a thorough understanding of the Sure Start initiative can be gleaned from this Sure Start website; and www.ness.bbk.ac.uk/ – the National Evaluation of Sure Start.

www.youngfoundation.org.uk – The Young Foundation seeks to encourage social innovation but also makes a number of publications and other resources available, including on aspects of government and policy making.

www.policyhub.gov.uk/better_policy_making/innovative_and_creative.asp#risk – the 'innovative and creative' area of the Policy Hub site is another useful source of information and guidance.

FIVE

Evidence-based policy making

Martin Bulmer, Elizabeth Coates and Louise Dominian

This chapter considers the emphasis on 'evidence-based' policy, noting its history and its place as a major element of the modernisation process since 1997. It therefore:

- examines the roots and development of evidence-based policy making;
- explores the ideas underpinning the emphasis on evidence under New Labour;
- considers obstacles to the implementation of evidence-based policy making; and
- suggests that while the use of evidence in decision making may have increased, evidence-based policy making remains somewhat elusive.

'Evidence-based' policy in UK central government is not a new idea but, since 1997, we have entered a new phase in the relationship between social science research and policy making. The introduction and establishment of social science research within central government is, of course, much older, and has taken different forms within departments, from separate research and analysis units to mixed disciplinary teams of analysts working alongside colleagues responsible for policy and delivery. It encompasses externally funded programmes of research and evaluation, large statistical data-gathering inquiries such as continuous surveys and the collection of administrative data. The idea of evidence-based policy is of clear appeal to policy makers, incorporating as it does an apparently 'common-sense' view that decisions should be made on the basis of evidence and at a time when the levels of information available through research and collection of data for administrative purposes appear to be ever-increasing.

The tradition of research for policy goes back half a century or more. Donald T. Campbell enunciated it clearly in his article, 'Reforms as experiments', almost half a century ago:

> The United States and other modern nations should be ready for an experimental approach to social reform, an approach in which we try out new programs designed to cure specific problems, in which we learn whether or not these programs are effective, and in which we retain, imitate, modify or discard them on the basis of their apparent

> effectiveness on the multiple imperfect criteria available. (Campbell, 1969, p 409)

The use of research and analysis in policy has also been the subject of a number of government reports (see, for example, Fulton Committee, 1968; Rothschild Report, 1971; Performance and Innovation Unit, 2000a).

In common with other parts of the 'modernisation' agenda, Campbell's (1969) statement suggests a clear link to rationalistic ideals of policy making (outlined briefly in Chapter One, this volume), where decision makers are able to make choices on the basis of the availability of good quality information, including evidence. The vogue for evidence-based policy also owes a good deal to parallel and earlier developments in the medical sciences, where the emphasis on grounding practice in the evidence, the use of research synthesis and meta-analysis and the rise of evidence-based medicine preceded by some years the development of the strengthening of the evidence base in relation to social affairs. This was symbolised by the establishment of the Cochrane Collaboration in 1993, which produces and disseminates systematic reviews of healthcare interventions, seven years before the creation of the Campbell Collaboration, which set out to address social welfare, education, and crime and justice. Sackett et al (1996) stated that '[t]he practice of evidence based medicine means integrating individual clinical expertise with the best available external clinical evidence from systematic research' (p 71), and, as such, holds much relevance to these more recent developments in policy making.

Evidence-based policy in social departments of central government acquired a new prominence from the late 1990s in the wake of Cochrane. 'Evidence-based policy' has been contrasted with 'opinion-based policy', a more traditional form of decision making in British central government, which relies on either the selective use of evidence (such as single studies, irrespective of their representativeness or quality), or on the untested views of influential individuals or groups, drawing on prejudice, ideological standpoint or speculation (Davies, 2004a). Evidence-based policy in this context has been defined as an approach that 'helps people make well informed decisions about policies, programmes and projects by putting the best available evidence from research at the heart of policy development and implementation' (Davies, 1999, cited in Davies, 2004a, p 3).

To use research, or indeed any evidence, policy makers need to be able to understand what the weight of evidence in cross-cutting areas tells them; single studies are of less value than an understanding of the overall body of evidence and, where research findings are apparently inconsistent or inconclusive, a means of judging quality, taking account of context and weighing the importance of one study against another is crucial. The attractions of systematic review techniques, as espoused by Campbell and Cochrane, are that they provide help in judging what the evidence tells us about what works in policy and practice and, equally importantly, where there are gaps in our knowledge.

In practice, however, the Cochrane tradition is only slowly taking hold in the world of social research and public policy. Completed systematic reviews are only gradually emerging from the Campbell Collaboration, although there are other initiatives, such as the work of the Institute of Education's Evidence for Policy and Practice Information and Coordinating Centre (EPPI-Centre). But there is an inherent problem in systematic review processes; although they tend to start with a map of the evidence available in a broad area, they focus down on a tightly defined question. For policy, a broader approach is often needed in order that a range of policy options can be considered. The formal techniques of systematic review do not cope well with these broader questions. Similarly, the lengthy process of 'full-blown systematic review' does not sit well with the need for quick responses to policy questions. Within government, social researchers are being trained in systematic review techniques but, in parallel, techniques of 'rapid evidence assessment' are being developed (Davies, 2004c), with the aim of identifying the main practical implications of a body of knowledge for policy. This is an example of the way techniques are evolving to respond to the increased use of research evidence in policy formulation and review, but more work is needed if government is to be able to make full use of the available evidence.

However, while it might on the face of it appear simple, the policy–research relationship is, in reality, a complex one, which defies simple description. Duncan characterises the goal of government social researchers as being:

> ... to ensure the right research and analysis is there to inform policy, and to use research knowledge to anticipate problems and issues to which policy will need to respond in future.... Other factors aside, social science evidence doesn't tend to provide the black and white answers that could potentially be useful to policy – we can't always say unequivocally 'what works'. (Duncan, 2005, p 11)

Duncan emphasises that there is not a uni-linear relationship between knowledge and policy, and that research is only one of the influences being brought to bear:

> Research which informs policy rarely if ever points to a single and unequivocal course of action – it all depends upon what policies are trying to achieve, how much money is available, which solution is workable and publicly acceptable, and how a chosen policy solution will impact upon other policy areas. Research and analysis will only ever be one of the influences upon policy. (Duncan, 2005, p 11)

In explaining the relationship between evidence and policy, Duncan likens the process of policy making to an iceberg in the sense that much of the activity goes on unseen 'below water level'. Figure 5.1 also illustrates the many influences, apart from research, on the policy process. These range from costs, to public opinion, political ideology, and the experience of practitioners, through to research data.

Figure 5.1: The policy iceberg

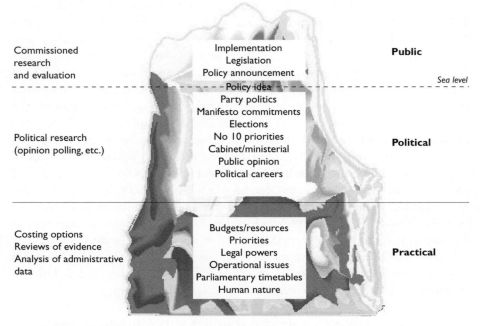

Commissioned
research
and evaluation

Implementation
Legislation
Policy announcement
Policy idea

Public

Sea level

Political research
(opinion polling, etc.)

Party politics
Manifesto commitments
Elections
No 10 priorities
Cabinet/ministerial
Public opinion
Political careers

Political

Costing options
Reviews of evidence
Analysis of administrative
data

Budgets/resources
Priorities
Legal powers
Operational issues
Parliamentary timetables
Human nature

Practical

Source: S. Duncan (2004) 'Using research in social policy', unpublished presentation to CRSP.

On this basis, the remainder of this chapter has several aims:

- to consider what a government view of evidence-based policy might be;
- to examine initiatives to support the use of analytical evidence in policy making;
- insofar as a pluralistic notion has been advocated, to outline what constitutes analytical evidence in a government context; and
- to address hindrances to the implementation of evidence-based policy.

Evidence-based modern policy making

Although not without precedent, there is a general consensus that the recent emergence of a concern with using evidence in policy making can be attributed to the election of the Blair government in 1997 (Davies et al, 2000a; Wyatt, 2002). This is because of New Labour's stated commitment to move away from politics guided by ideology and towards 'what counts is what works' (Blair, 1998), a more pragmatic and strategic way in which to make policy. This vision was clearly stated in the *Modernising government* White Paper, published in March 1999 (Cabinet Office, 1999). It set out the long-term plans for the reform of government and placed the modernisation of the policy-making process within a framework of other changes that are discussed in Chapter One of this book.

In relation to policy making, significant importance was attached to bringing the efficiency of the process into line with that of service delivery. The White Paper highlighted the centrality of reforming the policy-making process in order to facilitate the development of better public services.

Use of evidence and research is only one of nine key characteristics of modernised policy making, and the reform of this aspect of government business is but one of the changes striven for overall. Second, wider reform signified New Labour's commitment to internal change, in particular with its attention on policy making. Although in tune with the direction of previous reforms in the 1980s and 1990s, for example the Next Steps programme (Ibbs, 1988) and *The civil service: Continuity and change* (Cabinet Office, 1994), *Modernising government*, as Wyatt (2002) highlights, did represent 'a real and radical departure' (p 15) in its focus on policy. Third, the White Paper was important not only in its own right, but because it led to subsequent publications and initiatives relating to the use of evidence in government, several of which are briefly considered here.

However, while the recent emphasis on evidence-based policy may in some respects be unprecedented, it is important to recognise that past governments have also paid significant attention to research and evidence, albeit in different ways. This was particularly true during the 1960s and early 1970s, another period when rationalistic approaches to policy making were receiving attention from governments. The Heyworth Committee (1965), for example, recommended increased government support for the social sciences and the establishment of an autonomous, government-funded, Social Science Research Council (Bulmer, 1978), the forerunner of the existing Economic and Social Research Council (ESRC). The Rothschild Report (1971) examined the policy–research relationship and suggested that applied research should be done on a customer–contractor basis, resulting in new structures for commissioning and funding research across central government; it also emphasised the importance of 'science', in its broadest sense, in the policy process. From the mid-1970s, and particularly with the election of the Thatcher governments from 1979, a new ideological impetus combined with a degree of scepticism of the potential of a social engineering role for research, as seen in, for example, the work of Titmuss and Abel-Smith. In parallel, there was a growth in numbers and scope of 'think-tanks' (Nutley and Webb, 2000), which brought about a considerable diminution of the research–policy linkage.

Evidence-based policy: a governmental view

Modernising government (Cabinet Office, 1999) was followed up six months later by a report from the Cabinet Office Strategic Policy Making Team (1999). Taking direction from the White Paper, *Professional policy making for the twenty-first century* consolidated the vision of policy making by producing the nine core principles to which government was to aspire, each of which is considered in a separate chapter in this book. With respect to the use of evidence, *Professional policy making for the twenty-first century* provided useful clarification on the meaning of this in a government context, something that had not previously been articulated (Wyatt, 2002). It stated that:

> The raw ingredient of evidence is information. Good quality policy making depends on high quality information, derived from a variety of sources – expert knowledge, existing domestic and international research; existing statistics; stakeholder consultation; evaluation of previous policies; new research, if appropriate; or secondary sources, including the internet. Evidence can also include analysis of the outcome of consultation, costings of policy options and the results of economic or statistical modelling. (Cabinet Office Strategic Policy Making Team, 1999, p 31)

This broad definition is expanded later in the report, where it is suggested that, although evidence is sometimes conceived of as coming from large-scale research, the information and insight that can be gathered from service users and providers can sometimes be collected more easily and quickly than, and have as much relevance to a policy problem as, research. One might argue that such an exhaustive definition is appropriate given the varied informational demands of different policy areas (Davies et al, 1999). Indeed, this was demonstrated by the review conducted as part of the *Professional policy making for the twenty-first century* report, which found that the types of evidence used varied according to policy area.

A similar review of senior civil servants was conducted by Bullock et al (2001), which advanced previous work by examining the practice of modernised policy making since the publication of *Modernising government* and *Professional policy making for the twenty-first century*. Based on information from 27 departments it generated 130 good practice examples. At this point, the greatest achievements were identified in policy making that was 'inclusive' and that 'used evidence', while fewer examples of being 'forward' or 'outward looking' were identified.

Again, building on the vision set by the earlier Cabinet Office publications (Cabinet Office, 1999; Cabinet Office Strategic Policy Making Team, 1999), Bullock et al (2001) summarised the meaning of the evidence-based competency in policy making. Key points of an evidence-based approach to policy making include 'reviews existing research, commissions new research; consults relevant experts and/or uses internal and external consultants; considers a range of properly costed and appraised options' (Bullock et al, 2001, p 14). The good practice examples centred around the use of evidenc: (a) to identify a need for policy reform and help to inform its development; (b) to inform the understanding of policy areas and contexts in their broadest sense; and (c) where forecasting had been used, to facilitate the implementation of policy. In addition to this, examples of the use of evaluation of either existing or proposed policies prior to their roll-out were also given.

Although sensibly mindful of the different roles that research evidence can play in the policy process, it is difficult to ignore Wyatt's (2002) suggestion that despite the overall positive tone of the report, it is hard to determine the extent to which these examples actually represented change. This probably reflects the point, made earlier, that 'evidence-based policy making' symbolised an increased emphasis on an existing practice, rather than a new venture. The report itself highlighted that although there are some examples of good practice in the use of evidence, these are equalled by examples where evidence was not mentioned, and where the extent to which it had played a part was not apparent. This, in part, reflects the way evidence and policy interact.

There have been a number of attempts to analyse the way evidence and policy interact; perhaps the most useful in this context is the work of Davies et al (2000a). They describe four key ways in which evidence can have an influence, with research leading directly to a policy decision – 'instrumental' evidence in Davies et al's terminology – being just one source; although the most easily recognisable form, it is probably the least common. Another means of influence is termed 'conceptual', describing circumstances where research leads to changes in knowledge, understanding or attitude; this type of influence tends to be gradual. A third form, 'mobilisation', is where evidence stimulates policy action, for example an influential media story or event that catches the public imagination. Finally, they cite 'wider influence', where evidence leads to large-scale shifts in thinking, usually in policy areas such as poverty, ageing and so on. So the links between policy and evidence are often slow to have an impact, leading to gradual changes in approach, rather than direct policy innovation.

More recently, the Capability Reviews (see Case study 5.1) have suggested that practice in the use of evidence is still variable in government departments. The Select Committee on Science and Technology report (2006a), discussed further later in this chapter, also makes a similar point, while also noting that some of its witnesses identified areas where evidence may not support existing government policy.

Government initiatives to support the use of evidence

The role of government-based analysts in working towards evidence-based policy making was emphasised in both the Cabinet Office Strategic Policy Making Team report (1999) and Bullock et al's (2001) report. One of the problems identified in the former was the capacity for and quality of microeconomic modelling in government departments, which was the focus of a subsequent publication, *Adding it up* (PIU, 2000a). Although the focus was initially on economists, the work of other analytical specialists (such as statisticians, operational researchers and social researchers) was also addressed. In practice the different analytical specialisms now tend to work closely together in government, recognising that the combined perspectives of the social sciences provide more powerful insights than the individual disciplines alone; much research and analysis in government is now a 'combined effort'. The majority of issues discussed and recommendations made by *Adding it up* were applicable to the analytical community in government as a whole.

The *Adding it up* report made several recommendations. These included: the need to engage and train ministers and civil servants in order to strive for stronger leadership on the use of analysis; and the requirement to improve the analytical planning strategies in all departments by subjecting these to peer review and publication, and building this into the Comprehensive Spending Review process. It also identified a need for improvements to the system of recruiting and retaining high quality analytical staff, for example, with respect to increasing pay and offering more varied and attractive career options in the civil service. In addition to these, the report recommended that the quality and quantity of, and access to and use of, data needed to be improved. This ranged from the greater employment of simple statistics and administrative data, to the provision of more complex sources such as longitudinal studies. A need to make greater use of pilot studies prior to the national implementation of a policy was also echoed here (see also Chapter Nine, this volume). A series of further recommendations centred on the need to integrate policy and analysis, and this was proposed in one of three ways. First, through the provision of training for both analysts and policy makers. Second, through improvements to interdisciplinary working between analytical groups, at both an individual and cross-government departmental level. And third, the report discussed the opportunities presented by the 'bedding out' of analytical teams either organisationally, into policy directorates under the same management structures, or by creating mixed policy and analytical teams. This recommendation has been widely adopted across government and the monolithic units of organisationally separate analysts are now relatively rare. It is also possible to see the implications of these recommendations in some of the more recent initiatives in government: for example, Professional Skills for Government, which seeks to enhance capability and capacity within the civil service.

Professional Skills for Government

In line with the modernisation agenda already outlined, and reflecting wider civil service reform, Professional Skills for Government was launched by the Cabinet Office in 2004 (see Case study 5.1), with the aim being to 'give professional recognition to those skills and experiences of staff formerly thought of as "generalists" and "specialists"' (Civil Service Management Board, 2005, p 3). In this way, it provides a framework that recognises the skills and expertise of both the 'generalist' (policy) and 'specialist' (analytical, and others, such as lawyers, scientists and so on) arms, in order to facilitate professional development and progression through the civil service. Professional Skills for Government is relevant here insofar as 'analysis and use of evidence' is listed as a core skill for all civil servants. Other core skills include people, financial and programme or project management; the importance of leadership is also recognised. Professional Skills for Government also distinguishes three work streams, which are operational, corporate services and policy delivery, and it is noteworthy that the role of analysts falls within other work streams, rather than existing as a stream in its own right. This very much reflects the more integrated approach to analysis for policy operating currently.

Case study 5.1: From *Adding it up* to Capability Reviews: reviewing use of evidence in government

Adding it up (Cabinet Office, 2000a) concluded that more needed to be done to increase the demand and supply of high quality analysis within Whitehall. An increased emphasis on performance management, scrutiny of public investment and policy implementation has further emphasised data quality and departments' capacity to use it. The Cabinet Office initiated departmental Capability Reviews in 2006 to provide a transparent set of assessments of the relative capabilities of departments to meet the demands of the future. They explicitly included an assessment of use of evidence and analytical skills, placing integration of evidence as a clear element of successful performance.

Reviews to date have found some examples of strong performance in use of evidence, for example the Department for Education and Skills (DfES) and the Department for Work and Pensions (DWP). The DWP Review noted 'the Department has a strong evidence and analysis base, which it uses in strategy and policy formation. It routinely pilots and evaluates new approaches and actively looks for good practice overseas' (Capability Reviews Team, 2006c, p 16). In others, for example the Home Office and Department for Communities and Local Government (DCLG), reviews found that performance in this area required strengthening. Even those with a relatively well-developed evidence base were not always using it to best advantage to support difficult decision making.

Departments draw up action plans in response to Capability Reviews. Specific actions include improvement and use of the evidence base. The DCLG is committed to 'enhancing the knowledge base of the Department and increasing the number and profile of economists, scientists and other analysts over the next twelve months' (Capability Reviews Team, 2006b, p 19). In the Home Office, key reform projects include improving information quality and improving the policy-making approach. The DfES action plan includes 'setting up arrangements within 12 months to collect and act upon fast and effective feedback of data and intelligence from partners, providers, employers and users on what is happening at local level, what works and what is getting in the way' (Capability Reviews Team, 2006a, p 11).

A pluralistic notion of evidence?

The definition of evidence-based policy outlined in the documents above provides a pluralistic notion of what constitutes evidence, and research evidence, in a government context. In order to support the production of high quality social research and, thus, advice to policy makers, the Government Social Research Unit (GSRU), the professional support unit for the Government Social Research Service (GSR), provides training courses on research evaluation and the use of research and analysis in policy and delivery. It has also produced a guidance manual, *The magenta book* (PMSU, 2003), which is available through the Policy Hub website (www.policyhub.gov.uk/) and provides guidance on policy evaluation complementing HM Treasury's *The green book* on policy appraisal (2003). *The magenta book* contains chapters on a broad range of methodological elements of policy evaluation, systematic reviews and meta-analysis, statistical analysis, sampling, survey and qualitative data collection, as well as experimental and quasi-experimental design. The strong emphasis on professional training is mirrored elsewhere in the civil service; in the case of research and analysis it is recognised that if policy is to be evidence based, it needs to be good evidence.

In addition to and in support of this more general advisory publication, the GSRU has been engaged in work related to more specific research methods. For example, the National Centre for Social Research was commissioned by the GSRU to develop the *Quality in qualitative evaluation: A framework for assessing research evidence* (Spencer et al, 2003). This involved a review of methodological literature, interviews and a consensus workshop to help develop guidelines for effective utilisation of qualitiative research in government and more widely.

One very clear expression of an increased interest in evidence for policy was the growth in the use of policy pilots (Sanderson, 2002). Although these had occasionally been used before, they came into their own under the New Labour government and were a very literal response to the manifesto assertion that 'what counts is what works' (Blair, 1998). Evaluating a policy experiment was seen as a route to establishing whether a policy 'worked' in terms of both policy outcome and delivery mechanism, before full roll out. This new approach took time to bed in and early policy pilots were not without problems; for policy makers and evaluators there was a steep learning curve in order to maximise the insights that policy pilots had to offer. The problems of best use of pilots for policy making were addressed in *Trying it out* (Cabinet Office, 2003), which aimed to raise awareness of, provide guidance on and stimulate discussion about the use of piloting in government. *Trying it out* also responded to the encouragement in *Adding it up* (Cabinet Office, 2000a) to make more use of pilots in policy evaluation and the recognition that there was a need for development of techniques and a wider understanding of their value (see also Chapter Nine, this volume).

Davies (2004a) highlights the various types of research evidence that can be used in policy making according to differing policy questions. These are evidence of:

- *impact:* the impact of policy on outcomes;
- *implementation:* the effectiveness of the implementation and delivery of policies, programmes and projects;
- *descriptive analytical:* evidence drawn from descriptive surveys and administrative data;
- *public attitudes and understanding:* evidence on the values, attitudes and understanding of citizens;
- *statistical modelling:* methods based on statistical models and assumptions about policy scenarios;
- *economic:* such as cost, cost–benefit and cost–effectiveness of policies;
- *ethical:* decisions frequently affect the distribution of resources or services between different groups of people, requiring evidence such as relative cost, relative effectiveness and of social justice and ethics.

Similarly, on the grounds that the breadth of knowledge available for informing policy making has increased, Mulgan (2005a) also suggests that social research needs to be considered within a broader framework of knowledge used by policy makers. His typology contains some of the same forms of evidence but develops it further:

- statistical knowledge, for example, of population size and migration;
- policy knowledge, for example, on what works in reducing reoffending;
- scientific knowledge, for example, on climate change;
- professional knowledge, often informed by rigorous testing, for example, on the impact of vaccination;
- public opinion, for example, quantitative poll data and qualitative data;
- practitioner views and insights, for example, police experience in handling organised crime;
- political knowledge, for example, the balance of opinion in the ruling party;
- economic knowledge, for example, on which sectors are likely to grow or contract;
- classic intelligence, for example, on the capabilities and intentions of hostile states or terrorist networks.

Case study 5.2 considers the former Social Exclusion Unit (since 2006 the Social Exclusion Task Force) to illustrate the uses to which a varied evidence base can be put. This is an empirical case of a policy domain, looking at the extent to which evidence has been used in framing policy initiatives.

Case study 5.2: The Social Exclusion Unit: a broad evidence base for cross-cutting policy

The Social Exclusion Unit was set up in 1997 to produce joined-up solutions to complex social exclusion issues that fell between government departments. It was unable to draw on well-established government or academic research for policy development since the necessary joined-up information often simply did not exist. The tight timescale for producing reports also precluded commissioning any major new pieces of work.

The Unit adopted a wide-ranging approach that included many of the usual approaches for evidence gathering but also included a specific focus on evidence from users and practitioners and on looking across the usual professional and service delivery boundaries.

Meta-analysis was used, for example, to answer key policy questions on effects of sex education on young people's sexual behaviour. Re-analysis of existing data was commissioned, in particular cohort studies, to examine longer-term outcomes for young people out of education, training or employment and on the impact of having a baby on teenage mothers. Local data and evaluations were used where national data were not available, for example in the project on reducing reoffending. Local area studies were sometimes commissioned, for example, to inform the access to transport study.

The Unit also drew on the combined skills of departmental analysts and academics, often from a wide range of disciplines. Working groups of these experts provided both advice and challenge to the Social Exclusion Unit in their use of research evidence, with the aim of enhancing the authority of the Unit's work. Every project had a wide consultation phase with written and face-to-face consultation to flush out evidence and good practice, locally and nationally. Policy Action Teams were set up to generate recommendations; for example, the project on neighbourhood renewal drew together people living and working in deprived areas, voluntary groups, practitioners, the private sector, academics and civil servants. Within the Unit, teams working on projects had a mix of civil servants from different departments and external secondees, including frontline deliverers, users and researchers – all aimed at increasing the depth and breadth of evidence collection and policy generation. Finally, international comparisons and evidence were used to benchmark performance and evaluate different approaches. Projects reviewed lessons learned on successful evidence collection and these were fed into other projects.

Obstacles to the implementation of evidence-based policy

The numerous influences on the policy-making process have been widely identified in the literature, and a brief summary is all that space allows for here. In a liberal democracy, government analysts work in a political environment in which ministers are in charge of departments and dictate the priorities and policies to be followed, even if they are only involved personally in a very small proportion of day-to-day decision making, confining themselves either to broad policy framing or high level decision making about the most prominent issues. It is possible to exaggerate the possibility of ministerial involvement, which in practice is quite limited, but in a fundamental sense, British central government is inevitably subject to political direction, and ultimately to political control.

Values, too, play a most important role in policy. In an area such as criminal justice policy, the values held by the public, political beliefs and ideology play an important role, which policy analysts can ignore at their peril. There is bound to be tension between values and ideology on the one hand, and evidence from social research on the other. This is clearly recognised by politicians who acknowledge the value of evidence, but assert that it is the responsibility of ministers, and ultimately Parliament, to decide on policy. For example, attitudes to punishment will inevitably be affected by social and ethical judgements, regardless of what evidence might tell us about the success or failure of different approaches. Indeed, some have argued that the vogue for evidence-based policy is itself a political ideology, elevating empirical demonstration on a par with political discourse and prescription, while others will note that much of the concern with the 'modernisation' of government is itself based on a belief in rational models of policy making that have themselves been subject to extensive critique (Newman, 2001). It is partly for this reason that there has been so much debate about the term 'evidence-based policy making', many preferring to reframe it as 'evidence-informed policy making', reflecting the wider influence on the policy process.

Despite the strong political influence on policy, many of those who have studied the policy-making process put as much emphasis on the experience, expertise and judgement of decision makers. Traditionally, in the UK system senior administrators, whose expertise lay in long acquaintance with the system, deployed a collegiate and consultative way of working within a small hierarchical inner group, and used their cumulative knowledge as a way of judging what decisions to take. Nowadays, when senior civil servants change jobs every few years and experts, who are not career civil servants, are regularly brought into government, the situation is somewhat different. Nevertheless, civil servants still emphasise the importance of political judgement in the policy-making process (GSRU, 2007). One issue to explore in relation to evidence-based policy is the extent to which external evidence can be integrated with such experience, expertise and judgement exercised by those who are not professional analysts. This is not easy and logically demands policy makers to weigh different sources of evidence against each other; this is part of the skill of the experienced policy maker. It is a challenging task but one whose importance is recognised in making 'analysis and use of evidence' a core skill for the civil service. The idea, embodied in Professional Skills for Government, that different skills should be equally valued, reflects an attempt to move away from a situation where the analytical skills are seen as subservient to policy skills.

Social science researchers may not be expert in making choices between the use of resources for competing ends (a definition that some favour for the discipline of economics). The existence of finite and sometimes declining resources within government is an inescapable part of the policy-making process. Making research-based policy decisions has to be set in the context of the resources available for a course to be pursued. Another scarce resource in the political system is time, particularly if legislation is required to follow a particular course of action. The limits that time can play on the scope for governmental action are not always considered, but are often considerable, both in terms of the ability to fit legislation into the parliamentary timetable, and the pressure on politicians to deliver results, or at least to be seen to be taking action, within the electoral cycle.

Habit, tradition and culture often also form a basis for action (or inaction) within government, and ritual and ceremonial procedures often form part of the political fabric. The recent attempts to change the role of the Law Lords, and to remove them from the House of Lords into a new Supreme Court, is one illustration of the problems that there can be in trying to devise a more rational structure for government. Traditions within particular government departments are often observed to exercise a strong influence on the course of policy, whatever evidence may suggest about the direction in which to move.

In the Westminster and Whitehall arenas, other actors who can play an important role include lobbyists, pressure groups and consultants. The presence in the British system of both 'interest' and 'issue' pressure groups is well established, and in some arenas (for example, farming policy and policy for rural areas) may play a major role. The 2004 legislation to ban fox hunting provided a vivid instance of the ways in which such pressures may be exerted, both for and against a particular course of action. Such groups may make use of evidence, but its use is generally less systematic and more selective than the proponents of evidence-based policy might like.

Evidence-based policy is a strategic as well as an operational activity, but it can be challenged by events (famously summed up by the former Conservative Prime Minister, Harold Macmillan, as 'Events, dear boy, events'). For instance, the Fuel Crisis of 2000, the foot and mouth outbreak of 2001 and the BSE (bovine spongiform encephalopathy) crisis all posed challenges to government in responding to unanticipated events where the research base available to mount a response was variable, while fears of potential future events, such as the risk of the H5N1 strain of bird flu in the winter of 2006-07, can also impact on policy. Such contingencies are inevitably part and parcel of the business of government.

The House of Commons Select Committee on Science and Technology (2006a) tackled the issue of evidence-based policy and noted how during its inquiry 'various witnesses queried whether evidence based policy making was in fact feasible, given political and other constraints' (p 45). Submissions to this inquiry provided mixed verdicts on the government's ability to practice evidence-based policy; with critics highlighting the lack of evidence to support policy direction and even the most positive accounts tended to recognise that there was progress to be made. On this basis, the Committee's report acknowledged that there would be many policies that were driven by other factors than evidence and agreed that this practice was necessary. However, it provides a balanced recommendation on how to proceed, calling for greater openness regarding the basis of decision making, thus:

> We have detected little evidence of an appetite for open departure from the mantra of evidence based policy making. It would be more honest and accurate to acknowledge the fact that while evidence plays a key role in informing policy, decisions are ultimately based on a number of factors — including political expediency. Where policy decisions are based on other such factors and do not flow from the evidence or scientific advice, this should be made clear. (Select Committee on Science and Technology, 2006a, p 47)

Evidence-based or evidence-informed policy?

> Governments have become ravenous for information and evidence. A few may still rely on gut instincts, astrological charts or focus groups to guide their decisions, but most recognise that their success, in the sense of achieving objectives and retaining the confidence of the public, now depends on a much more systematic use of knowledge than in the past. (Mulgan, 2005a, p 216)

This may be an accurate statement of the role of knowledge in the modern policy-making process, but it does not follow that 'evidence-based policy' rules the roost. There are many considerations that lead to the intrusion of other influences, one of them political. Mulgan again puts this rather nicely:

> It is not necessary to accept Renan's definition of nations as forged by the things they forget in order to recognise that all societies are held together by accepted ambiguities and silences. In politics, as in personal life, full revelation is nice in theory but can be deeply destabilising and destructive of self- and mutual respect. Where different groups have diametrically opposed views or interests, the assertion of rationality and evidence may have little impact, and good politicians understand this often much better than academics. (2005a, p 224)

The vogue for evidence-based policy has clearly had important influences on the role of social research in government, for example in promoting experimental evaluations of social policy initiatives such as that undertaken about Educational Maintenance Allowances for 16- to 18-year-olds (Middleton et al, 2005; Rennison et al, 2005). Some of these developments were touched on by evidence from Norman Glass and William Solesbury, both former civil servants turned independent researchers, to the Select Committee on Science and Technology, discussed earlier. (Select Committee on Science and Technology, 2005b).

Nevertheless, the balance of evidence 10 years after the arrival of 'evidence-based policy' is arguably that 'evidence-informed policy' would be a more accurate description of the reality of policy making within central government. This is in line with Young and colleagues' notion of an 'evidence-informed society' (2002, p 223) and Duncan's recommendation of 'evidence inspired policymaking' (2005, p 11). Evidence-based policy appears to offer more than it can deliver. Obstructions to its successful implementation include inherent obstacles in the policy-making process that inhibit its full use. Some of these stem from democracy, including what may sometimes be a justifiable scepticism on the part of politicians that 'expert' knowledge is an unerring guide to correct action. Consider, for example, vogues in medical treatment for particular conditions. Basing policy solely on what the medical profession consider the correct policy line at a particular date may be of doubtful usefulness as a guide to action.

High-pressured decision making in government also militates against careful testing and evaluation. Quick judgements in conditions of uncertainty are at a premium. Tacit, craft knowledge of how the world works is at least as important as formal, explicit knowledge in operating under these circumstances. Moreover, social knowledge, by its very nature, is reflexive; actors act in the light of available knowledge, and this limits the capacity of governments to influence the behaviour of others. Much social science knowledge is historically contingent, and there needs to be healthy scepticism about the universality and permanence of research findings. Living with this uncertainty is hard, both for the policy makers and for the social researchers and analysts who advise them. The lack of fit between the problem-based preoccupations of government and the discipline-based orientation of academic researchers is another issue that gets in the way of driving policy purely on the basis of evidence.

For all these reasons, it is perhaps more plausible to argue for evidence-informed policy than for evidence-based policy.

Conclusions

While policy makers have frequently sought evidence, either to assist them in decision making, or to support decisions made, the extent to which it has become part of the mantra of modernisation since 1997 is unprecedented, and is perhaps even more striking when compared with the more overtly ideologically driven policy making of the preceding years. However, when reflecting on the experiences of the past decade a number of points can be derived:

• The idea of using evidence to assist in policy making is arguably widely accepted, but there are a wide range of other influences that impact to a greater and lesser extent on the decision-making process.

- While it is possible to identify many examples of good practice across a range of government departments and tiers of government, there are also many examples where there is little clear link between evidence and decisions.
- While it is clearly unnecessary and undesirable to have a fixed approach, the very idea of 'evidence' is subject to interpretation, ranging across a variety of approaches, methods and techniques, and from very small-scale to very large-scale projects.
- There are a variety of obstacles to the more complete operationalisation of evidence-based policy making, including the capability of government departments, the impact of values, attitudes and ideology among decision makers and the general public, and the many other pressures on policy making in liberal democracies.
- Overall, the extent to which policy making is evidence driven, or even evidence based, remains highly contestable, so that the situation may be more appropriately characterised as 'evidence informed', rather than 'evidence based'.

Further reading

Davies, H. T. O., Nutley, S.M. and Smith, P.C. (eds) (2000b) *What works? Evidence-based policy and practice in public services*, Bristol: The Policy Press – an early but still valuable examination of evidence-based policy.

Duncan, S. and Harrop, A. (2006) 'A user perspective on research quality' *International Journal of Social Research Methodology*, vol 9, no 2, April, pp 159-74 – a useful discussion of the needs of users of research and the ways in which funders, researchers, policy makers and practitioners seek to engage more completely with each other.

Nutley, S.M., Walter, I. and Davies, H. T. O. (2007) *Using evidence: How research can inform public services*, Bristol: The Policy Press – a complimentary book to *What works?*, considering the ways in which research is used and how it could have a greater impact within and on public services.

Useful websites

www.campbellcollaboration.org – the Campbell Collaboration, an attempt to develop for the social sciences a resource similar to the Cochrane Collaboration (see below).

www.cochrane.org/index.htm – the Cochrane Collaboration, founded in 1993 and named after the British epidemiologist Archie Cochrane, this promotes the use of evidence in healthcare and makes available worldwide systematic reviews of healthcare interventions.

www.gsr.gov.uk – the website of the Government Social Research Unit contains articles of general interest about the use of evidence in policy and related issues.

SIX

Inclusive policy making

Catherine Bochel and Angela Evans

This chapter examines 'modern', 'inclusive' approaches to policy making, considering in particular what is embraced by these concepts, the degree to which they are significantly different from previous approaches to policy making, and the extent to which it is possible to identify impacts on policy making and policy outcomes. It does this through:

- a consideration of the main types/methods of policy making that government have identified as being associated with 'inclusiveness';
- an examination of who these methods are 'inclusive' of; and
- a discussion of how 'inclusive' policy making is developing.

As with many of the terms associated with 'modern' policy making, it is not necessarily immediately apparent what 'inclusive' policy making might be, nor how it should be interpreted. At its most basic, it could be said that 'inclusion' is about being able to participate in society, having the opportunity to be involved, and being able to undertake activities regarded as 'normal'. From the perspective of policy making, this might be operationalised through a whole variety of different methods, such as joining in activities in the community, having a say in how the country is run at local and national levels through voting in elections, or having input through a variety of mechanisms such as attending meetings, providing feedback on existing services and facilities, joining pressure groups, campaigning, responding to consultations, becoming members of user forums or citizens' panels, or volunteering.

As 'inclusiveness' relates to modern policy making, *Professional policy making for the twenty-first century* (Cabinet Office Strategic Policy Making Team, 1999) suggests that an inclusive approach, as initially outlined in the *Modernising government* White Paper (Cabinet Office, 1999), is 'concerned with ensuring that policy makers take as full account as possible of the impact the policy will have on different groups – families, businesses, ethnic minorities, older people, the disabled, women – who are affected by the policy', and that it might be achieved by involving relevant '... service delivers/implementers, academics, and voluntary organisations – in the policy process' (Cabinet Office Strategic Policy Making Team, 1999, para 8.1). There is therefore a concern with the extent to which there are opportunities for individuals, organisations and groups to get involved in and influence the policy process. However, this interpretation extends the notion of 'inclusive' policy making beyond the involvement and participation of people in the community, to others who are involved in the different 'elements' of the policy process, such as implementation, feedback and evaluation. This is indicative of a shift towards a broader interpretation of 'inclusion' in the policy-making process than that which can be identified in most previous attempts at involvement, which tended to focus largely on 'user' or 'citizen' involvement, as well as to one that emphasises inclusion across the policy process. In turn this arguably reflects a view within government that policy making can be improved through the earlier involvement of key stakeholders and that this will, in turn, lead to better policies.

In terms of which tools and approaches should be used to pursue inclusive policy making, *Modernising government* (Cabinet Office, 1999) refers to a variety of methods, including central government initiatives such as the People's Panel, the Listening to Women exercise and the Home Secretary's Race Relations Forum, and local initiatives such as 'citizens' juries, community fora and focus groups' (Cabinet Office, 1999, p 25), while *Professional policy making for the twenty-first century* (Cabinet Office Strategic Policy Making Team, 1999) refers to the means of achieving inclusiveness only in general terms, such as 'consultation', 'involvement' and 'impact assessment'. *Better policy making* (Bullock et al, 2001) is similarly general in its treatment of the idea, saying that 'Departments seem to be using an array of consultative techniques, combining more targeted and direct consultation with key stakeholders with more traditional types of written consultation' (p 42), although it gives examples ranging from issuing consultation documents to the use of pilot projects and involving groups of independent experts. This is a broad canvas, and for the purpose of this chapter it is necessary to narrow our focus slightly to consider the key areas of participation and consultation, and the perhaps less familiar, but potentially important, impact assessment.

It is possible to see a number of advantages that could emerge from an inclusive approach to policy making, and publications such as *Modernising government* (Cabinet Office, 1999), *Professional policy making for the twenty-first century* (Cabinet Office Strategic Policy Making Team, 1999) and *Better policy making* (Bullock et al, 2001) clearly identify potential benefits in relation to 'improvements' in the formulation of policies and in ensuring that policies achieve their intended consequences, for example in relation to identifying potential problems with implementation and assessing the likely impact on those affected by policies. For services to be provided that best meet the needs of citizens, the participation of key stakeholders in the policy process is seen to be helpful. Stakeholder involvement in these processes has the potential to improve not only the ways in which policies are formulated and implemented, but also policy outcomes. Involvement in these processes might also enable service providers to claim that consumers bear some responsibility for the actual services provided, or that their involvement helps legitimise the service.

In addition, there may also be potential wider social benefits from an inclusive approach to modern policy making. Involvement may help people feel that they are more a part of society. Participation can bring opportunities to learn more about the society we live in, to learn more about ourselves and to develop new skills through working with others. More generally, there are also other potential spin-offs, for example in terms of generating social capital, with, for example, Putnam (2000) arguing that involvement in many kinds of associations, including social movements and apolitical groups, encourages the development of both generalised reciprocity and social capital more generally.

As is apparent from discussion elsewhere in this book, it is important to recognise that there are close links and, indeed, overlaps between the nine core competencies as set out in both *Better policy making* (Bullock et al, 2001) and *Professional policy making for the twenty-first century* (Cabinet Office Strategic Policy Making Team, 1999). Arguably those that are most closely linked to an inclusive approach to modern policy making include evidence-based review and evaluation (see Chapters Five, Eight and Nine, this volume), and for an 'innovative, flexible and creative' approach (Chapter Four). Research and evaluation is an important part of the policy process and relates directly to elements of participation and consultation, as well as to impact assessment. Appropriate evaluation can enable feedback from those who are affected by particular policies as well as those who are responsible for implementing them, and feedback and review can continue on a regular basis. For inclusive policy making, questions that arise from this include: to what extent have the comments and views of those affected by the policy been taken into account, and where their suggestions have been discounted, why were these decisions taken? This information also needs to be fed back to all of those involved. To aid this dynamic and circular process, policy makers need to work in an environment where the culture is receptive to research and evaluation and where it is seen as an integral part of the policy process. This is also about learning lessons about 'what works' (Davies et al, 2000b; see also Chapters Five and Ten, this volume), highlighting links with the 'evidence-based' and 'learning lessons' competencies.

While the potential of inclusive approaches can clearly be seen to have an appeal for governments, as Chapter One points out, recent years have seen some concern with the capacity and capability within government to successfully implement such initiatives. Central government has seen the introduction of Professional Skills for Government, designed to ensure that civil servants have 'the right mix of skills and expertise to enable ... [them to] ... deliver effective services' (http://psg.civilservice.gov.uk), including 'analysis and the use of evidence'. One important feature of this is the extent to which there are attempts to ensure that the importance of using evidence, including the views of users, citizens and other stakeholders, is being embedded into the policy process.

However, despite the potential for improvements to policies and their implementation there remain areas of concern. Indeed, *Professional policy making for the twenty-first century* (Cabinet Office Strategic Policy Making Team, 1999) recognises a number of these, such as the potential for delay and administrative overload, the raising of expectations that it may not be possible to meet, the risks of unrepresentative views dominating the process, and the danger of providing a focus for the mobilisation of resistance. In addition, while there is considerable evidence of a real trend towards the embedding of approaches to and greater inclusiveness in the policy process, there remains the key question of the extent to which these approaches are effective in changing practices, including the ways and extent to which individuals and groups can become involved, and in altering policies and their outcomes.

'Inclusion' from the 1980s

Clearly, governments have for many years sought to achieve some form of 'inclusion' in the policy-making process, although historically much of what took place was typically limited to the publication of consultation documents, including Green Papers, and a dialogue with established key stakeholders such as the Confederation of British Industry (CBI) and Trades Union Congress (TUC) and a relatively limited range of pressure or interest groups. Clearly such approaches have significant limitations: they were restricted to those groups that had access to the consultation documents or to policy makers, and that had the resources to respond, to maintain dialogue or to lobby. During the 1970s and 1980s one of the responses to these forms of input and the otherwise limited opportunities to influence policy makers was the growth of lobbying, particularly of politicians and senior civil servants, a development that received a further spur from the growth of organisations seeking to represent the users of services and the providers of services, as well as from the emergence of professional lobbyists. However, the bulk of such input has historically been limited to pressure groups and commercial bodies or their representatives, and it is possible to identify a wide range of issues and concerns with such approaches (for example, Grant, 2000; Coxall, 2001).

More recently there has been a greater emphasis on 'user' or 'citizen' 'inclusion' in policy making. Under the Conservative governments of 1979-97 it is possible to identify two distinct approaches to this. One, and arguably the dominant, manifestation was embodied in a 'consumerist' approach (Newman, 2001), a key aspect of which was the view of individuals as consumers of services in a marketplace, able to exercise choice over a range of services, evidenced in attempts by the government to create 'parental choice of schools' and to encourage people to purchase council housing. In some areas of policy, therefore, a means of making decisions about the shape and, to some extent, the distribution of resources, was seen as being through empowering individuals to choose the services that they required, often involving market-like mechanisms. Other developments, such as the creation and publication of 'league tables', for services such as education and health, were intended at least in part to encourage competition and to provide information for consumers as a stimulus for improvements (Bochel and Bochel,

2004). A second aspect of this emphasis on the consumer was reflected in the widespread use of consumer satisfaction surveys across the public sector. Alongside this, albeit perhaps with a different imperative, there was a concern to encourage individual participation in society. In particular, Douglas Hurd, as Home Secretary, encouraged and articulated the notions of participative citizenship and active citizens as a way of improving both public services and 'the quality of life of the citizen' (for example, Stuart, 1998, p 163). Under Labour after 1997 there continued to be a general encouragement of volunteering and active citizenship, including the designation of 2005 as 'the year of the volunteer'. However, while there may be some links to inclusive policy making, this chapter will only consider such emphases where they are of direct relevance to its key foci.

Outside government, the 1980s also saw the separate development of a concern for the empowerment of individuals, particularly in relation to social policy, where a range of groups emerged seeking to encourage a shift in power to the users of services, a development that received significant support from some professionals involved in the delivery of such services.

For many people the dominant element in Labour's approach to inclusiveness in policy making since 1997 is arguably reflected in their modernisation agenda for public services, and attempts at 'democratic renewal'. In contrast with the market consumer approach favoured by the Conservatives, this can be seen to have some links with a 'democratic' perspective, associated to some extent with the growth of consumerism and with the emergence of user groups and self-advocacy organisations concerned to have a say in services and to gain more control over their own lives. This does not always fit easily, however, with traditional notions of representative democracy, where policies have been made by elected representatives whose primary accountability to the public has been through the ballot box. Under New Labour there has been a broad-based strategy, which has cut across a whole range of policy areas, and that might be linked to attempts to develop a 'Third Way'. Giddens (1998) says that 'The fostering of an active civil society is a basic part of the politics of the third way' (p 78), and that 'Government can and must play a major part in renewing civic culture' (1998, p 79). General statements from Labour about involvement appear to reflect this:'... democratic self-determination holds that we are only truly free when we participate in the self-government of our communities' (Blunkett, 2003, p 2); and '... that the freedom of citizens can only be truly be [sic] realised if they are enabled to participate constructively in the decisions which shape their lives' (Blunkett, 2003, p 3). The People's Panel, set up in 1998, was in part a recognition by government of 'the need to listen to, and learn from, people's views in order to be better able to provide services that people want' (http://archive.cabinetoffice.gov.uk/servicefirst/2000/panel/summary.htm) at the beginning of the policy process, rather than just taking note of their views after policies have been introduced. Although grounded in a more 'democratic' approach, this can also be seen as a development of the consumerist approach started under the Conservative governments in the 1980s, reflecting an interest in customer feedback that continues within central government and the wider public sector.

This emphasis is also reflected in the titles of various government publications; such as *Modern local government: In touch with the people* (DETR, 1998b), *Firm foundations:The government's framework for community capacity building* (Home Office, 2004a), and *Facilitating community involvement: Practical guidance for practitioners and policy makers* (Home Office, 2004b), as well as in the language used in government documentation, such as 'listening to and engaging with citizens and communities' (Home Office, 2004a, p 17), and the increasing stress on 'personalised services' so that 'The best councils already enable people to shape and choose those services they use on a personal basis.... We want this to be the normal pattern of working everywhere' (DCLG, 2006, p 26, para 2.5).

These general statements and the terminology used by government can be linked to a rather different rationale for this focus, an attempt to address the reasons for past policy failures, such as those that are perceived to have contributed to the 'erosion of social capital', created 'economic ghettoisation' of neighbourhoods and led to 'the failure of core services in deprived areas' (SEU, 2000, p 8), underpinned by attempts to develop a more rational approach to the policy process itself and thus to 'better' potential outcomes. These ideas were reflected by the Prime Minister in the foreword to *National strategy for neighbourhood renewal*, when he said 'Good policy depends on tapping into the widest base of ideas, knowledge and experience. Good implementation depends on having the broadest possible support behind what needs to be done so that it can be carried through over a full ten-to-20 years', and went on to suggest that 'unless the community is fully engaged in shaping and delivering regeneration, even the best plans on paper will fail to deliver in practice' (SEU, 2000, p 5).

The local government White Paper, *Strong and prosperous communities* (DCLG, 2006), continued the emphasis on inclusiveness, proposing a number of ways in which local people could be more involved, including 'securing participation' (p 31), 'listening to and acting upon local concerns' (p 34) and 'empowering local people to manage neighbourhoods and own community facilities' (p 38), as well as potentially requiring local authorities to ensure the participation of local citizens in their activities. It also set out the idea of 'double devolution', with power moving from Whitehall to local authorities and from them to citizens and local communities, although it provided no clear outline of how this might work in practice.

Post-devolution, it should be recognised that there is no longer a uniform UK-wide approach to inclusiveness. In Wales, for example, the consumer model has not found favour and the Welsh Assembly Government has developed a citizens model of public sector reform. The citizens model is part of a Making the Connections strategy (Welsh Assembly Government, 2004) for improving public service delivery, and encompasses both service users and the wider public who have an interest in the pattern of services and their efficiency. It has the potential to recognise a more complex and longer-term relationship with public services than that assumed by the customer model. It recognises that the public have both rights and responsibilities – rights to receive services but also responsibilities to be concerned about the services available to everyone else. It may, therefore, have potential to engage the public with the competing priorities for public investment within the context of limited budgets. However, the citizens model does place major responsibilities on service providers to engage effectively with service users and the wider public, and also poses a range of methodological challenges. The Welsh Assembly Government is therefore currently reviewing models for seeking the views of citizens at national and local levels (Welsh Assembly Government, 2004, 2005).

Inclusive policy making: participation, consultation and impact assessment

While the discussion above has examined some of the general thinking and reasoning behind the preferences for and development of more inclusive approaches to policy making, consideration now moves on to what this has meant in terms of methods. There is now a considerable amount of material available from government providing advice and guidance on different approaches to 'inclusive' policy making. In fact there is arguably so much literature and guidance available that policy makers are in danger of 'information overload'. However, taken together, the literature illustrates that while there may be real commitment to greater inclusion across all levels of government, there remains a lack of clarity around not only the use of different types of 'inclusion', but also around their precise aims and objectives, and as a result key questions, such as whether the emphasis on inclusive policy making has made any difference to policy outcomes, may sometimes be overlooked. As noted earlier in this chapter *Professional policy making for the twenty-first century* (Cabinet Office Strategic Policy Making Team, 1999) itself lacks specificity, implying that wider use of participation (in its terms 'involvement', 'consultation' and 'impact assessment') were key in aiding an inclusive policy-making process, but not providing any clear guidance on how these should be interpreted or operationalised. This chapter now considers developments in relation to participation and consultation, and in impact assessment.

One of the most familiar issues in relation to participation has been the different extent to which people may or may not be empowered, with Arnstein's (1969) well-known ladder of citizen participation illustrating some of the different levels at which people can participate. These range from non-participation methods, such as manipulation and therapy, through to methods that involve various degrees of tokenism such as placation and consultation, and finally degrees of genuine citizen power and control. From the perspective of the rungs on Arnstein's ladder, 'consultation' is not necessarily about empowering people, or being inclusive; indeed it may be more a tokenistic process to make people feel they are involved, but without giving them any decision-making power. It also may not include any feedback to those who have taken part. On the other hand, even if not associated with any shift in power, consultations do have the potential to be used to genuinely inform and influence decisions.

Guest (2003) builds on Arnstein's ladder and makes a distinction between '"how" to involve people' and '"what" people should be involved in' (p 5) (that is, which stages of the policy process). The first dimension very much relates to Arnstein's work, which recognises different levels of involvement, whether it be consultation, informing or decision making and so on. The second dimension emphasises what people can be involved in. Both are dependent on each other, since 'having a range of methods for involving people without clearly knowing what they are being involved in would be meaningless, as would knowing what people are to be involved in without any idea of how they will be involved' (Guest, 2003, p 6).

Participation and consultation

Taken as a whole, it is difficult to argue with the view that there are more widespread and more varied attempts at participation and consultation in policy making than was traditionally the case, and that this runs across all levels of government. Central government, the devolved administrations and local government now all employ a plethora of mechanisms to enable citizens and other stakeholders to respond to consultations and to provide other inputs into the policy process. For example, *Viewfinder: A policy maker's guide to public involvement* (Cabinet Office, 2002a) set out a range of 'types of involvement' that policy makers might use to enable public involvement with the aim of ensuring better policy making (see Table 6.1), while a report for the Scottish Executive identified 22 different consultation techniques used by public sector organisations (Scottish Executive Central Research Unit, 2000).

Clearly, the range of methods and techniques used for stakeholder consultation and participation is wide-ranging, extending well beyond the more limited range of techniques, such as consultation papers, questionnaires and public meetings that tended to be used in the past. While these more traditional methods are still used today, they have been supplemented by a whole range of other methods, frequently intended to be more inclusive and informative for both a wider constituency of stakeholders and for policy makers. However, while the opportunities for input into the policy process are now considerable, there remain major issues about their accessibility and acceptability to 'hard-to-reach' groups, such as some groups of women from the Asian community, refugees and economic or illegal migrants, the exclusion of whom from policy making can mean that their interests may be unheard, misunderstood or ignored (see Case study 6.1). Even within 'mainstream' society there is a danger that increasing opportunities for participation or consultation can simply reinforce existing social divisions, with middle-class, white interests potentially dominating debates.

Table 6.1: Types of involvement

Types/methods	Description
Written consultation exercises	The public is invited to comment on policies and proposals set out in a document
Questionnaires	The public are asked a set of questions; their responses are collected and analysed
Open/public meetings	An open invitation is extended to any member of the public to find out about a particular issue
Focus groups	They bring together 8-10 people, led by a trained facilitator, to discuss a particular issue
Reconvening groups	Similar to focus groups, except that participants are invited to reconvene on more than one occasion, having had time to read information, debate the issues with others outside the group, and reflect and refine their views
Citizens' panels	Made up of a statistically representative sample of the population, their views are sought regularly using a range of methods
Citizens' juries	A group of 12-16 citizens, recruited to be a 'best fit' of a population or a particular section of the population, are brought together to discuss a policy issue.
Workshops	Interactive session or sessions which allow policy makers to engage in a dialogue with a group of citizens or stakeholders on a specific issue
Deliberative polls	Used to measure the opinions of citizens before and after they have had the opportunity to become informed and discuss a particular issue
Consensus conferences	A panel of 15-20 people, recruited through random selection techniques, develop an understanding of a specific topic through briefing materials and in dialogue with experts, reports setting out their views
Issue forums	Ongoing bodies with regular meetings, but focusing on a particular issue
Working groups	Involve different groups in developing policy, for example government officials, ministers, experts, representatives of civil society groups, citizens
Visioning exercises	Participants take part in a structured meeting, where they develop a vision for the future and commit to action towards the vision
Planning for real	Often initiated by local communities on planning matters, a three-dimensional model of a particular neighbourhood is created. At a public event displaying this model, the public is invited to attach cards to identify problems, issues of concern and possible solutions
Electronic methods	
Email distribution lists	Used to circulate consultation documents to interested parties. Citizens can register for these lists via a website. Their comments can be forwarded to government
Electronic letterboxes	Email addresses on websites or documents give citizens opportunities to feedback to government
Internet-based fora	These can be limited to certain individuals (for example, a core group of stakeholders) or open to anyone. These can be designed to allow citizens to: respond to government proposals online; read and view the comments of all participants; and engage with other citizens in a dialogue on the proposals
Online live chat events	Participants exchange views, within a fixed period of time (usually 2 hours), with MPs, ministers etc
Interactive games and scenario planning	These can be used to engage citizens in developing policy options or proposals

Source: Adapted from Cabinet Office (2002a, pp 44-50)

Case study 6.1: Welsh Assembly Government: reaching 'hard-to-reach' groups

Making the Connections, the Welsh Assembly Government's public reform programme, includes a strong commitment to establish and uphold core customer service standards for public services in Wales. The development of five core principles in 2006 was supported by a programme of research to explore people's requirements of public services. The research programme, which included a literature review, household survey, citizens' forums, focus groups and in-depth interviews, placed considerable emphasis on including groups who could face particular barriers in engaging with public services, such as people with learning, literacy and numeracy difficulties, people with physical and sensory disabilities and impairments, lesbian/gay/bisexual/transgender people and those using languages other than English.

The core principles developed as a result of this feedback address issues of access, personal experience, responsiveness, language options and redress.

Source: Welsh Assembly Government (2006a).

Returning to a point outlined briefly previously in relation to the government's modernisation agenda, inclusive policy making is not solely concerned with the inclusion of the public and other stakeholders; it also refers to the greater involvement of frontline staff who are likely to be responsible for delivering and evaluating policies and programmes (see Case study 6.2). This is a significant dimension to 'inclusive' modern policy making: 'The NAO report *Modern Policy-Making* highlighted the importance of involving those that implement policy in its design, noting that: "Departments should make arrangements to engage implementers early so that the practicability of policies can be assessed.... Involving implementers closely as policies are designed can help identify and manage risks of their effectiveness, secure ownership and commitment from staff, and identify practical solutions ..."' (Cabinet Office, 2002b, p 1). This report also highlights the need for both policy makers and frontline staff to work together in this process. '... front line staff do not necessarily understand the "givens" or the purpose of new policy. The effective combination of the operational expertise of the front line with the contextual overview of policy makers offers a powerful synergy of knowledge and understanding that will inform all areas of policy development' (Cabinet Office, 2002b, p 2).

Taken together, the inclusion of different stakeholders (the public, frontline staff, policy makers) and the use of different methods might be described as a holistic approach to the policy-making process. Their combined knowledge and expertise has the potential to produce improvements in policy design, development, implementation and delivery, and to make a positive contribution to the modern policy-making process. However, it is not always clear the extent to which there is always the use of appropriate mechanisms and how questions such as those related to unequal access should be tackled.

> **Case study 6.2: Welsh Assembly Government: action research involving programme delivery staff**
>
> The Welsh Assembly Government's evaluation of its 10-year Communities First programme, aimed at improving the outcomes for individuals and communities in the poorest neighbourhoods in Wales, included a strong action research element. Three 'cluster groups' or forums were established of Communities First partnerships working in broadly similar contexts. The cluster groups were 'rural and small town', 'valleys' and 'urban'. As the programme, and its evaluation, progressed the action research element and the role of the cluster groups became an increasingly important mechanism for engaging the programme partnerships. The cluster groups also acted as a 'processing hub' through which other data (collected through case studies, survey work etc) could be interpreted and applied.
>
> A series of action research events with Communities First coordinators included a range of innovative engagement techniques. Researchers used a 'speedo exercise' that involved Communities First coordinators answering questions using a speedometer tool marked from 0mph to 100mph. Participants were asked to place their mark (speed) on the speedometer in relation to each question (such as how much impact they were having on mainstream services and how well they were working with the local authority). Participants were also asked to spend some time on their own writing one or two brief stories of what was working well and what was working less well in terms of Communities First. Over 200 stories were organised into eight key themes.
>
> Feedback from the cluster groups, including the action research events, was crucial to the development of a framework for local evaluation, including intermediate outcome measures.
>
> *Source:* Cambridge Policy Consultants et al, 2006.

Another area in which there is frequently a lack of clarity is what the purpose of stakeholder involvement is. Part of this may be associated with the confusion over the terminology around 'inclusiveness' and 'involving people'. For example *Viewfinder: A policy maker's guide to public involvement* (Cabinet Office, 2002a) defines 'consultation' as 'A two-way relationship in which government asks for and receives citizens' feedback on policy proposals' (p 41), and 'participation' as 'A relationship between government and citizens based on partnership. Citizens actively participate in defining the process and in developing a particular government policy' (p 42). On paper, these two distinct definitions suggest different degrees of involvement in the policy- and decision-making process. However, in practice, the concepts of 'participation' and 'consultation' are not necessarily easy to separate out and are sometimes used interchangeably. A consideration of *Professional policy making for the twenty-first century* (Cabinet Office Strategic Policy Making Team, 1999) reveals that it refers largely to 'consultations', but that these are depicted as taking different forms, such as involvement on steering groups, working parties and in seminars, which may involve more than just providing feedback. One example of good practice in 'inclusive' policy making cited in the document was the positive response to the competitiveness White Paper, which was felt to be as a result of the 'direct and close consultation with a wide range of business representatives' (Cabinet Office Strategic Policy Making Team, 1999, para 8.2), as 'some 200 business leaders contributed to six competitiveness working parties and eight Treasury/DTI productivity seminars. A number of specific proposals in the White Paper had their origins in the recommendations from the working parties' (Cabinet Office Strategic Policy Making Team, 1999, para 8.2). A further example cited was the Northern Ireland Development Strategy Review, the purpose of which was to come up with recommendations for the then new Northern Ireland Assembly on how 'a more vibrant, competitive and inclusive economy might be developed' (Cabinet Office Strategic Policy Making Team, 1999, Figure 16). Over 300 stakeholders from the public and private sectors were involved, including people from local government, trade unions, departmental officials, industry, business and academic communities, and this was contrasted to previous economic development strategies that were led by officials with advice from people in the community.

However, regardless of the success or otherwise of these initiatives, they do serve to illustrate that even within key government documents, on this competency there is a lack of clarity over the terminology and its meaning. For present purposes, therefore, 'consultation' is perhaps best viewed as one subset of 'participation'. Nevertheless, one of the major difficulties for those who seek to understand, analyse and indeed enable different forms of inclusion and participation in policy making is this very blurring of boundaries and concepts. If it is not clear what these terms mean, then the purposes of participation may become confused at the outset.

While, as noted above, involvement in policy making may bring a range of potential benefits, further major issues relating to the purpose of involvement are what exactly policy makers are expecting of the people they wish to involve, and how the results of this will inform policy. These in turn raise a whole series of further questions, which it is frequently not clear that policy makers have thought through sufficiently. What will the role of participants be? For example, are their views primarily being sought in response to a plan or document that is largely or fully formed, or is it really empowerment at an early agenda-setting stage of the policy process? Who do policy makers wish to involve and why these groups or individuals (as opposed to others, who may therefore be likely to be excluded); and what feedback will they provide? Each of these questions will have implications for the nature and perhaps for the success or failure of the inclusive initiative, as well as potentially for the policy itself.

It is not only policy makers who require clear guidance about the purposes of participation and consultation; this is also of great importance for participants. To maximise the value of their input, as well as in relation to other social benefits (the development of social capital, and so on) they need to be clear: why they are being asked to participate; who they are expected to represent (for example, are they participating to represent themselves, the views of a particular group or organisation, or a local community?); what their participation will involve (attending meetings, becoming a member of a user forum, having their views listened to, being involved in taking decisions, and so on); and what they can expect in return, for example, written feedback or a meeting to explain which policy options were selected and why. Thus the capacities in which people participate may be an important consideration in inclusive modern policy making (see Bochel, 2006). A truly inclusive process requires that policy makers and those who commission participatory projects and initiatives be clear about what they are setting out to achieve, including establishing the purposes and parameters of involvement, and only then should they select their method(s).

Impact on outcomes

Stakeholder involvement in the policy process has arguably been increasing in complexity for the past two decades in terms of the range and number of groups and citizens from whom input is sought, the variety of tools and mechanisms used, and the different stages of the process at which involvement is sought. However, a key question is whether it is any more successful than past attempts. It is clearly difficult to provide a definitive answer to this. At the level of individual projects, some will be successful and others less so, but in terms of the overriding aim of making modern policy making more 'inclusive', then there are a range of issues worthy of further discussion.

The trend towards encouraging involvement is generally seen to be a good thing, but is this necessarily the case? The discussion above has highlighted some of the many potential pitfalls that can occur, and underlines the importance of how and why such processes are undertaken. Given this, it is important that the availability of existing research and evidence is fully explored to find out what is already known before embarking on another 'inclusive' initiative.

As noted in the preceding section, participants' experience of involvement and the way in which they feel about their involvement has implications for the extent to which policy making is truly inclusive. This can be illustrated by *The Social Exclusion Unit's Policy Action Team approach to policy development*: 'Those interviewed expressed clear appreciation for the PAT [Policy Action Team] approach as a new and inclusive approach to policy making' (SEU/CMPS, 2002, p 12). The areas highlighted as part of this included, inter alia: the diverse membership from within and outside government; process and mode of operation – 'Open and inclusive discussion … which had moved beyond consultation or acting as a "sounding board", to active, equal involvement in policy development' (p 13); government commitment; briefing and preparation of key players; the inclusiveness of the Policy Action Team process; and the importance of building a team. Inclusivity was seen to be one of the fundamental tenets of the Policy Action Team approach. However, it is still unclear whether those consulted actually had any influence on the policy question. This raises an interesting issue about whether it is the fact that people are consulted that matters, or whether they actually influence outcomes. Do people feel included just because they have been consulted? *The Social Exclusion Unit's Policy Action Team approach to policy development* (SEU/CMPS, 2002) clearly created a positive experience for those involved, and so perhaps being consulted was enough for this group. However, there are equally many experiences of involvement that are less satisfactory and lead to those participating feeling frustrated and confused by the experience of involvement (see Bochel, 2006). It is possible that in some cases people may have their expectations unduly raised and/or feel that simply being consulted is not enough and may expect to see their involvement resulting in outcomes (see Cabinet Office, 2002a).

Impact assessment

While different forms of consultation and participation with the public and other stakeholders are clearly seen as a fundamental part of approaches to inclusive policy making, another area of potential significance, although one that is perhaps less known and not immediately thought of as part of the 'inclusiveness' agenda, is the use of impact assessment. Documents such as *Modernising government* (Cabinet Office, 1999) and *Professional policy making for the twenty-first century* (Cabinet Office Strategic Policy Making Team, 1999) make it clear that the government sees impact assessment as one of the tools that can help in delivering their modernising agenda. For example the former talks about '… producing and delivering an integrated system of impact assessment and appraisal tools in support of sustainable development, covering impacts on business, the environment, health and the needs of particular groups in society' (Cabinet Office, 1999, p 20). In addition, as with many other aspects of 'modern policy making', the general approach taken by the government suggests that the use of impact assessment is grounded in attempts to approach the policy-making process in a more rational way, and to improve the quality of policy making and through it the quality of policy outcomes.

The best known forms of impact assessment include health impact assessment (HIA), environmental impact assessment (EIA), social impact assessment (SIA) and regulatory impact assessment (RIA). Guidance makes clear that there is not a 'one size fits all' approach to impact assessment, but most incorporate a checklist, with RIA, for example, aiming to get policy makers to work their way through a structured list of requirements and encouraging them to think through all the possible implications, impacts and outcomes on different groups (see, for example, Davies, 2004b).

Impact assessment is intended to be inclusive of a wide range of individuals and groups, including recognising that individuals and groups will have different needs and that different policies will impact on them differently, and thus it is important that this is taken into account in policy making. Policies developed using impact assessment as a tool may incorporate gender, ethnic, disability, rural and urban dimensions, among others, helping to create a better understanding of what the impacts on particular groups or on people living in certain areas might be. In addition, impact assessments should seek to incorporate the views of wider stakeholders, including those inside and outside government.

As noted earlier in the chapter, a lack of clarity about the purpose and objectives of participation and consultation is a frequent weakness of participatory initiatives. In contrast, impact assessment should be clear about its objectives, although one of its weaknesses may be that there are too many impact assessment tools, making it difficult for analysts to know which they should use in different situations. *Professional policy making for the twenty-first century* (Cabinet Office Strategic Policy Making Team, 1999) also suggested that there is patchy awareness of the role and importance of impact assessment as a tool for policy makers.

One of the most widely known uses of impact assessment is in relation to the removal of unnecessary regulation:

> ... where departments are preparing policies which impose regulatory burdens, high quality Regulatory Impact Assessments must be submitted to Ministers and the Cabinet Office must be consulted before decisions are taken. This process should ensure that any new regulations do not impose unnecessary burdens and can be managed so as to minimise cumulative effects and business uncertainty. (Cabinet Office, 1999, p 21)

However, their use has increasingly spread to other areas of public policy, so that there is now considerable experience of their use in the health arena (see, for example, the HIA Gateway – www.hiagateway.org.uk), where HIA is seen by some as a way to potentially bring about reductions in health inequalities. However, in line with some of the weaknesses of impact assessments mentioned above, Parry and Scully (2003, p 243) contend that 'most, if not all, published health impact assessments have not considered the effects of public policies on health inequalities in a robust or reliable manner'.

Other areas where it has frequently been suggested that the use of impact assessment might be beneficial are in promoting disability equality and gender equality. The Disability Rights Commission has argued that:

> For new policy development, or situations where the policy is undergoing an evaluation or review, it will be more effective to build disability equality impact assessment into the development of the policy. This is more likely to lead to robust and inclusive policy development, whereas simply undertaking a formal disability equality impact assessment at the end of the policy-making process will simply

lead to piecemeal changes and the danger of disability equality being bolted on as an afterthought. (DRC, 2006, p 19)

Similarly, the Women and Equality Unit (2002) produced guidance on gender impact assessment as part of the move towards inclusive policy making (see Figure 6.1). The guidance noted that even policies that at face value appear to be gender neutral do have a gender perspective. For example, research on transport reveals differences in patterns of use and access to transport among women and men. Women often use public transport more and fewer have access to private transport. Thus policies on vehicle usage and public transport will have differential impacts on men and women and undertaking some form of impact assessment when devising policies, such as to improve the cost and availability of public transport, would highlight that women are more likely to be the 'losers' if such policies were assumed to be 'gender neutral'.

However, as with the implementation of the 'participation' and 'consultation' aspects of inclusive policy making, the use of impact assessments is not unproblematic. In the same way as other participative techniques, the practice of impact assessment can be challenging. While there may be scope to have impact assessments ranging from 'rapid' to 'comprehensive', in the latter case in particular, the very process of undertaking an impact assessment can be considerable, not only being time consuming, but also likely to be costly in terms of resources. Given that the process is likely to place additional burdens on policy makers there is a risk that the requirements may only be fulfilled 'in a superficial way and without

Figure 6.1: An aide-memoire for equality impact assessment

1. Define issues and goals
- What is the policy trying to achieve?
- Understand different problems and concerns
- Enable equal contribution

2. Collect data
- Gather gender, race and disability disaggregated statistics
- Consult experts, women and men, black and minority ethnic and disability groups
- Interpret from different perspectives

3. Develop options
- Determine impact/implications for different groups
- Offer real choice and opportunities
- Remove stereotyped perceptions

4. Communicate
- Integrate with equality commitments
- Design different strategies
- Use inclusive language

5. Monitor
- Use the community
- Develop indicators
- Examine differential impact

6. Evaluate
- Achieve equality of opportunity and equal outcomes
- Learn lessons
- Spread best practice

Source: Women and Equality Unit (2002, Appendix B2)

the detailed consideration, appraisal and evaluation that is necessary' (Davies, 2004b, p 13). An evaluation of RIAs by the National Audit Office (2004), which highlighted variation in the way in which these were undertaken, underlined this very point. Impact assessment also shares similar problems, in seeking to ensure that the voices of some stakeholders do not drown out those of less powerful or excluded groups, and the challenge of ascertaining the views of hard-to-reach groups remains significant. And, while it can be argued that, for example, HIAs are underpinned by a set of underlying principles – democracy, equity, sustainable development, scientific and robust practice, and a holistic approach to health (www.hiagateway.org.uk/page.aspx?o=Underpinningprinciples) – a contrary argument can be advanced that approaches such as these, while in some respects technocratic, remain value based. Finally, there is a point that is relevant to much of the development of 'modern policy making', which is the relationship between decisions based on rational processes and evidence, including impact assessments, and political decisions. Clarence (2002), in relation to evidence-based policy, argues that 'By seeking to utilise rational policy making, what is effectively being argued for is depoliticisation of the policy process' (p 4). However, ultimately policy making remains political and in impact assessments, as with other areas, much depends on which voices are chosen to be listened to, and the relative weight given to them, both against each other and against other, different, factors.

Conclusions

It is apparent from the discussion in this chapter that 'inclusive' policy making remains a contentious and elusive aim. In recent decades there have been significant attempts to achieve wider participation of users and other stakeholders in policy making, whether through consumerist approaches, as emphasised in many aspects of Conservative policy making during the 1980s and early 1990s, or in wider consultation and other forms of involvement under Labour since 1997. Developments over the past two decades, and perhaps in particular since 1997, have demonstrated that the government has placed inclusiveness at the heart of the public service reform agenda, and expects government and other public service agencies to be both energetic and innovative in their approaches. However, it remains extremely difficult to be certain what difference these are making, particularly across broad areas of policy. In part this results from a lack of clarity about the purpose and objective of inclusive initiatives at the outset, for policy makers and for those other stakeholders who become involved in these participatory schemes. However, in relation to the 'modernisation' of policy making it is possible to highlight a number of features and issues associated with these developments:

• There are a variety of different, but frequently overlapping, imperatives associated with inclusiveness, from those rooted in principles such as 'active citizenship' and democratic renewal to more pragmatically based drivers such as the desire to legitimise policy decisions and avoid policy failures.

- It is difficult to judge the impact of inclusive initiatives, individually or collectively, largely because their aims and objectives are rarely explicitly set out, nor is their effectiveness systematically evaluated.

- There are questions over the extent to which many of these initiatives have been 'inclusive' in the wider sense of the term, and over the extent to which they have sought to shift the balance of power away from professionals and policy makers towards citizens and the users of services.

- Rather, it is perhaps possible to depict much of what has happened, particularly since 1997, as attempts to improve the quality of policies, and to some extent to take account of the input of a wider range of stakeholders and the groups who are likely to be affected by policies.

- While impact assessment may be a valuable tool, the wider use of which might help inform policy making in a range of areas, it has a number of limitations, including in relation to the appropriate level of resources to be invested in such exercises; at present the potential value of such methods also appears not to be widely recognised across government departments.

- Inclusive policy making requires the significant input of time and resources, and there may be a tension with the need to make decisions in a timely fashion, as well as the costs and benefits associated with attempts to be more inclusive.

- Inclusiveness brings with it responsibilities. For example, how do we know that the views we are hearing are representative? Have vulnerable, difficult-to-reach groups been included? How do we deal with conflicting interests? And how do we manage expectations? These are important ethical issues that much of the literature and guidance on inclusiveness only touches on.

- Policy making ultimately remains political, and while attempts to develop and use a wider range of participative approaches should lead to better policy making and better policy outcomes, it is important to recognise that political values, priorities and pressures are also fundamental to the decision-making process.

Further reading

Bochel, C. and Bochel, H. (2004) *The UK social policy process*, Basingstoke: Palgrave Macmillan – a review and analysis of the policy process, Chapter 7 considers 'participation'.

SEU (Social Exclusion Unit)/CMPS (Centre for Management and Policy Studies) (2002) *The Social Exclusion Unit's Policy Action Team approach to policy development: The views of participants*, London: SEU/CMPS – a report that examines the experiences and perceptions of some of the individuals who participated in the Policy Action Team process.

Welsh Assembly Government (2005) *Delivering the connections: From vision to action*, Cardiff: Welsh Assembly Government – provides a perspective from one of the devolved administrations that arguably reflects a somewhat particular approach to 'inclusiveness'.

Useful websites

www.policyhub.gov.uk/policy_tools/ – the Policy Hub website's Policy Tools section provides access to a variety of resources including a number relating to public involvement; elsewhere the site also gives access to documents such as *Viewfinder* and *Involving the front line in policy making*.

www.hiagateway.org.uk – the HIA Gateway contains a large selection of information about HIAs.

SEVEN

Joined-up policy making

Richard Parry with Marion Kerr

Over the past two decades there have been a variety of approaches by governments to 'joining up' their activities, and the period since 1997 has arguably seen added impetus for this, even before the scale of the government's commitment to the 'modernisation' of policy making became fully apparent. This chapter:

- examines a variety of influences and approaches on the development of joined-up policy making;
- discusses initiatives involving attempts to change cultures and structures since 1997; and
- considers the extent to which new approaches to joined-up policy making have been successful.

Joined-up government is one of the great mantras of our time, but its continued use suggests that there remain problems of definition and application that need to be addressed. A significant problem is that which arises from the intrinsically fissile nature of government activity under the pressure of political power and public business. Business organisations may typically be 'joined up' by a strong sense of culture and socialisation related to a product-led mission. Even the most multinational of corporations is likely to have strong joined-up influences equipped to integrate staff of different disciplines and nationalities. Government is different. The cultural affinities may be strong (as in the traditional UK civil service collegiality, driven by a career-long fast-stream elite, albeit now under erosion from more varied recruitment patterns). Financial protocols (in the UK driven by HM Treasury) may impose uniformities of behaviour and approach, but on the policy side the power of the bureaucracy is deployed in favour of particular agencies, professions, territories, ministers and causes.

The reciprocal nature of government as a channel between the governors and the governed means that control from above is matched by pressure from below. Even in an apparently directive system like the US federal government, in which the will and charisma of the President are meant to be a decisive force, the dominant impression to observers has often been of a loose, and particularist bureaucracy.

The idea of 'joined-up government' extends well beyond the policy-making arena; however, the focus of this chapter is on new approaches to *policy making*, so it approaches the concept from that perspective rather than more generally. The chapter considers the extent to which cross-cutting planning and objective setting have been achieved, the success or failure of joint working, collaboration and partnership arrangements, and the extent to which these have become a normal or embedded part of the policy process. This implies an evaluative approach based on the premise that after a decade of New Labour joining up, and many more years of aspirations in that direction from UK government more generally, it should be possible to identify the degree of success of the policies, the extent to which they have been normalised within the policy process, examples of good and less good practice and lessons for future action.

Professional policy making for the twenty-first century, the report prepared by the Cabinet Office Strategic Policy Making Team in 1999, was cautious and wide-ranging in its approach to joined-up policy making. The driver was the government's focus on cross-cutting outcomes: 'policymaking built around shared goals, not organisational structures and functions' (para 9.1). Setting out an important distinction, it argued that 'joining up is not just about shared approaches to cross-cutting issues. Horizontal joining up between organizations needs to be supplemented by better co-ordination between policy makers in the same departments and by better "vertical" joining up with service deliverers and those who implement policy. It is not an end in itself but should be undertaken where it adds value' (para 9.1). The document's confession that 'policy makers … are still feeling their way when it comes to how best to achieve it' (para 9.2) points to the difficulty of making progress beyond good intentions, including when primary loyalties are not problem related.

The complexity of joining up reflects the complexity of modern government. The academic industry around the word 'governance' expresses a search for a more ambitious conceptualisation of the role of government as an organiser and steerer of economic and social life. Modern governance requires a deeper reach into the reality of social experience in an era when direct government control has been discredited.

Joined-up working is about interactions between the agencies of government, and we need a model of these interactions and the ways that they happen. An influential approach from the 1990s is to distinguish between *markets, hierarchies* and *networks* (Thompson et al, 1991). All three have promoted bodies of descriptive and prescriptive literature. The important lesson from this literature is that we should not try to choose between them, or favour one over another, but should understand the relations between them and the way that they are combined in real-world political situations.

The classic political approach is that of *hierarchy*. This derives from constitutional theory and the legal disposition of authority in public organisations and those who work for them. The UK lacks a formal codification of administrative law, but it has a practical equivalent in the form of ordinary Acts of Parliament and of codes and regulations. For instance, the ultra vires rule prevents local authorities from acting outside explicitly granted powers, and there is a history of cautious advice by local officials on this point and legal cases. Devolution within the UK has been legislated by ordinary statute that can be amended by the Westminster Parliament by further ordinary statute. Outside Northern Ireland, the organisation and denomination of government departments is at the discretion of the Prime Minister or First Minister. The legal position of civil servants, although based on royal prerogative expressed through Orders in Council rather than by statute, does not, in the words of the Armstrong memorandum of 1985 (Treasury and Civil Service Committee, 1986, pp 7-9), give them a constitutional position distinct from that of the government of the day.

In principle, 'joining up' could be hierarchically initiated and enforced: the government would instruct government agencies to work together. But the combination of horizontal and vertical imagery is rightly uncomfortable. Indeed, the scope of local jurisdictions to exercise general powers in the interest of the people of an area has tended to increase over time. This leads us to the idea of *networks*, where organisations and actors of varying statuses from inside and outside government choose to relate. Their motives for doing so can include shared interest in an issue, a sense of good practice in relation to an issue, advisory or research-based recommendations, or potential access to resources. There are two particularly important facilitators of network formation: insider access to policy formation and funding under various kinds of conditionality. A major line of academic literature is that working relationships end up being structured by resource dependencies, both between central and local levels and governmental and non-governmental organisations.

Rhodes (1997) distinguished between *issue networks* and *policy communities*, the former being loose coalitions of interested parties, the latter active policy makers delivering the compliance of key actors (typically in fields like agriculture and health, where producer interests have been dominant). Network theory has been less good at analysing complex service delivery networks, which pose problems of network management akin to game management. In the UK, Friend et al's idea of 'reticulist' skills was a pioneering approach from the planning tradition (Friend et al, 1974).

The relation of networks to *markets* is a neglected area. The resources of public policy are becoming increasingly measurable and tradeable. Policies to contract out public functions require an accurate measurement of cost in order that the in-house operation can submit a competitive bid (such as cleaning and catering). Once the market-testing approach was extended in the 1990s from well-defined support services to core functions, the way was open for innovations like management contracts for schools or independent treatment providers in the health service. It can be argued that the simplest way to join up an operation is to force relationships into a market of supply and demand. The National Health Service (NHS) in England has moved in this direction as the previously internal market with incomplete charging has been replaced by active and competitive purchasing relationships with the NHS and independent providers.

There are two major issues that emerge here: what is to be joined up, and how are they to be joined up? A model of what is meant to be joined up will include at least three variables:

- the *functions* of government, the various policy areas that structure a bureaucracy but are constrained by professional and organisational traditions and never fully match the experience of service delivery or the needs of clients;
- the *levels* of government, the territorial structuring that lies at the heart of constitutions, everywhere encompassing central and local government and usually federal, devolved and regional structures;
- the *political accountabilities* of government, the various mandates and loyalties that operate within and across jurisdictions. A rhetoric of agreed goals, common purpose and national roll-out of piloted programmes has to coexist with different functional priorities and political pressure for urgent attention to specific problems. Political parties may seek to impose a consistent line on their activists in different jurisdictions, a variable often neglected in prescriptive models of policy making. *Professional policy making for the twenty-first century* spoke of a wide desire for 'a greater sense of "corporacy" for the civil service, turning it into an organisation with a much stronger sense of common endeavour to achieve shared goals' (Cabinet Office Strategic Policy Making Team, 1999, para 9.5). The 'corporacy' concept opens up the important question of whether joined-up policy making is, or should be, anything different from officials performing their traditional constitutional role of serving the government's pursuit of its objectives.

The question of how the joining up is to be done has inspired an extensive literature, both analytical and prescriptive. De Bruijn and ten Heuvelhof (1997) speak of three kinds of instruments: regulatory, financial and communicative. Some of these instruments are aimed at the actors, stimulating their creation or structuring their behaviour; others are designed to manage the relations between actors.

The power of all these kinds of instruments in modern policy making is readily evident. Regulation in the form of reporting procedures, inspection, audit, requirements for institutional creation and so on is the typical response to the wish of government to maintain its reach into the economic and social system without the creation of big institutions or direct public expenditure or public employment.

Financial instruments are not just concerned with the spending of money but various kinds of imaginative pump-priming or cost-shifting mechanisms including joint ventures and public–private partnerships. The UK system has a structural imbalance between the allocation of policy responsibility and the allocation of financial instruments, and so requires grant transfers from central government to delivery agencies. A three-stage process has been evident. Traditionally financial transfers were function-specific (local authority services or items of NHS spending). The problems of managing these interactions led to a vogue for consolidated grant transfers to more powerful institutions with better financial capacity in local government and the health service (such as unitary authorities and hospital trusts). But the subsequent lack of political trust by the centre in these institutions led to the reinstatement of financial controls in the form of technical stratagems like pilot projects, action zones and challenge funding, that aimed to combine low cost with effective stimulus to 'correct' action.

Communicative instruments include: the rhetorical or conceptual framework in which policy is set; the prescription of 'buzzwords' that enter into public discourse; the citing of good and normative behaviour as a tool of benchmarking and policy learning; and the specification of reporting formats. These can be powerful tools but they can also be a substitute for action rather than an articulation of it.

Another useful conceptualisation comes from the National Audit Office in their work on the 'public sector delivery chain' (2006a). They distinguish internal links (direct management); contractual or regulatory links (in which one party uses legal or financial instruments to control the actions of another); links of common purpose (where there are 'parallel missions' that the parties choose to express by joint working); and links to the wider community (without formal authority and reliant primarily on persuasion). The heterogeneity of these various kinds of links and the difficulty of combining them are clear.

Reciprocity is another key driver of joined-up behaviour. Parker (2007, p 115) sets out a model of 'networked governance': networks require connected actors, shared power, information transfer and reflexivity, while governance requires density of linkages between nodes, a breadth of incorporation of institutions and, again, trust, mutuality and common identity. These qualities are needed in the economic and environmental schemes that Parker describes, but have a wider application. Again, the identification of desirable qualities is easier than the specification of how they are to be secured.

Many writers, including Bogdanor (2005), Pollitt (2003) and Mulgan (2005c), have addressed these issues directly or indirectly in recent years. Mulgan, as a former key policy adviser at No 10, has set out his definition of joined-up government as 'cajoling' organisations to point in 'the same broad direction, and at the very least not to undermine each other's work', and aligning 'incentives, cultures and structures of authority to fit critical tasks' (Mulgan, 2005c, p 1). He identifies the key impediment as the autonomy, in the sense of relatively undisputed jurisdiction, that organisations seek. Other think-tank productions, including Demos' work on the 'collaborative state', explore the moral as well as the financial motivations of working together (Parker and Gallagher, 2007). Theories of policy design and of policy implementation have influenced them as well as the textbook-type approach of *Professional policy making for the twenty-first century*, but they typically stop short of more explicitly political interpretations of the reasons for resistance to joined-up approaches in the UK.

Policy trend

In the UK, the question of how to join up has attracted a mixture of long-term themes and more recent emphases, including:

- *Forming mega- or conglomerate departments*, especially in the 1960s and 1970s (Environment, Health and Social Security) and recently (Work and Pensions). There are also examples of imaginative pairings (foreign policy and trade in Australia; industry and post-16 education ('education and lifelong learning') in Scotland). Debates about the 'fitness for purpose' of government structures have been raised, particularly in connection with the Home Office and its ability to organise the internal relationships between its components (as discussed in its 2006 Capability Reviews Capability Reviews Team, 2006e), with political debate about whether the answer is tighter integration or division into two or more departments (resolved in favour of a transfer of functions to a new Ministry of Justice in May 2007).
- *Changing the distribution of functions between central and local levels:* in the UK, there is a presumption that cash transfers should be centralised and related to the tax system, whereas personally delivered services should be localised under elected local government, with the important exception of health; but there is a lack of confidence in local service decisions leading to national targeting and political direction.
- *Special-purpose regional bodies* rather than uniform regional government (the latter now rejected following North East England's 78% 'No' vote in a referendum in November 2004).
- *Fragmented and contractorised local service delivery*, with growing use of public–private partnerships and independent service providers.
- *Opportunistic and manipulative funding mechanisms*, including action zones, challenge funding and comprehensive star ratings as a route to 'earned autonomy'.

The historical trend before the Blair government was to promote more trade-offs between policies. In the 1950s the Treasury suggested that there might be a Social Services Ministry that would stop health, housing, pensions and education from picking off the Treasury in pursuit of individual political goals (Deakin and Parry, 2000). From 1961 the Public Expenditure Survey system was supposed to be organised around programmes not agencies, and to include policy analysis. In local government, the many specific grants were consolidated into the Rate Support Grant in 1966, allowing authorities greater discretion in their policy choices. Local government reorganisation, planned from 1966 and implemented in 1974, created larger authorities bridging urban–rural divides and charged with addressing the needs of their areas as a whole. In 1968 Richard Crossman became Secretary of State for Social Services, a title different from that of his new mega-department (Health and Social Security), but the mechanics of fully merging the previous ministries were never fully resolved (they were redivided in 1988) and the wider coordinating role got lost.

In 1975 the *Joint framework for social policies* (CPRS, 1975) set out both an aspiration and an institutional mechanism. Impossible for Labour ministers to resist in the abstract, it fell victim to Whitehall silo-protection at a time when the brakes were being applied to public spending as a whole. Despite efforts to revive it later in the 1970s, it was fatally damaged by its association with the Central Policy Review Staff at No 10 (Challis et al, 1988). However, many of the framework analyses and prescriptions seem accurate even from today's perspectives. The issue is therefore not so much diagnosis but the best path to dealing with it. Here we can see that the main variable is the character of the central government machine. In the 1970s the power of institutions was greater than the power of programmes, and so spending power came to be devolved to departments. As the departments were defined by the ownership of government resources (money, employment, legal authority), joined-up initiatives became contests for control and self-protection.

In the 1980s the Thatcher government introduced new mechanisms into public policy that were ultimately very important for joined-up government. By forcing contestability into the pattern of service delivery through privatisation, contracting out and market testing, they infiltrated the market into hierarchies and networks. The mechanisms included explicit joint working between health and social services on community care. However, the Conservatives became so mired in conflict on local government finance and the challenge to welfare state professionals that the potential of their instruments was not fully realised.

Joining up since 1997

It was only under New Labour that a self-regulating form of joined-up government, based on incentives to act in a cross-institutional way, took shape. Labour first went through a phase of soft rhetoric on partnership, as it dismantled internal markets and allowed Best Value to be set up as a benign alternative to competitive tendering. But the concept of action zones allowed targeted funding and promoted behavioural patterns of bidding and conformity to central norms. 'Challenge funding' laid down an incentive to comply that managers were in no position to resist. From 1998 Public Service Agreements (PSAs) laid down performance targets that mandated particular forms of compliance. These developed into the concept of 'earned autonomy' in which good ratings produced more money and more freedom from scrutiny. (Glendinning et al, 2002, provide a good account of the philosophy and policies of these years.)

From the perspective of the end of the Blair era in 2007 a longer view of joined-up policy can be taken. Much of the action before 2001 was under the influence of *Modernising government*, the name of the 1999 White Paper that expressed aspirations for civil service reform, more responsive services (using e-government means), continued faith in devolution and regionalism, and better resourcing for service delivery in the 1998 Comprehensive Spending Review. The power of this rhetoric was propelled by the political success of the Blair government. It was novel but it was also untested in long-term practice.

Janet Newman's *Modernising governance* (2001) provided an important analysis of this approach. Newman identifies three bodies of theory:

- *governing the nation:* globalisation, supranational bodies, internal devolution ('decentring') – new political and economic forces that make it hard to 'govern the nation' in the old way;
- *coordinating economic activity:* markets, hierarchies and networks – fragmented and dispersed patterns of service delivery and regulation, not just markets;
- *steering the social:* responding to complexity, diversity and dynamic change – governments cannot control complex behaviour in society, households and the labour market.

This then generates 10 hypothesised 'governance shifts' (Newman, 2001):

1. from hierarchy and competition to networks and partnerships
2. blurring of boundaries and responsibilities for tackling issues
3. recognition and incorporation of policy networks
4. from command and control to 'governing at a distance'
5. more reflexive and responsive policy tools
6. government offers leadership, steering, integration
7. 'negotiated self-governance' in localities
8. participation in decision making
9. innovations in democratic practice
10. government's concerns broaden from the institutional to the involvement of civil society in governance.

This cumulative 'narrative of change' is clearly closely related to the joining-up agenda: the direction of movement is from a tight top-down structure towards a looser and more participatory style. But, as Newman recognised, the achievement of these shifts requires a redistribution of power that may be resisted. Power relations remain strong even if dispersed around professionals, bureaucracies, political institutions and agencies of service delivery. Even if the narrative is a powerful one, Newman was prescient in her conclusion that New Labour's approach was selective and did not properly reckon with the political dynamics of change: 'the process of realigning and dispersing state power interacted with, rather than displaced, a process of centralisation and the exercise of more coercive and direct forms of control' (Newman, 2001, p 163).

Professional policy making for the twenty-first century was in many ways a sketchy document. One elaboration of it was *Better policy making*, a glossy account of various departmental initiatives that identified general difficulties of maintaining departmental 'buy-in' and of the time-consuming nature of joined-up activity, especially where there were diverse consultation processes (Bullock et al, 2001). A stronger analytical line came from two reports issued in 2000 by the Performance and Innovation Unit (2000a, 2000b). *Wiring it up* took the conventional line of a strong centre driving the cross-cutting mechanisms (and it was to be the Cabinet Office rather than the Treasury, reflecting a pervasive tension within the Blair government). The tone was realistic: 'more needs to be done if cross-cutting policy initiatives are to hold their own against purely departmental objectives. There is no simple or standard answer' (2000b, p 5). Much of the report's focus was on removing unintended barriers and perverse incentives.

Adding it up approached the issue from the perspective of evidence-based policy, and the way that government might go beyond microeconomic modelling. In 18 case studies it analysed the cross-cutting issues in terms of trade-offs (departments asking for incompatible things), gaps (where whole groups are excluded, like the non-economically active young who are not registered for benefits) and coordination (as when departments prefer to guard their own data sources and models of behaviour rather than cooperate on interdepartmental ones) (Performance and Innovation Unit, 2000a). The report sounded an early note of caution that cross-cutting issues might be insufficiently planned or provided for in normal governmental processes. Its endorsement of *Wiring it up*'s 'presumption that central intervention in the everyday work of departments is justified only when joining-up is difficult and the issues are important' (p 34) proved a poor predictor of New Labour behaviour.

The two reports offered a toolkit for designing policies, but they were never properly incorporated into Whitehall structures and were overtaken by the dual focus on strategy and delivery within Blair's central operation – reflected in the establishment of two separate units – the Performance and Innovation Unit becoming the Prime Minister's Strategy Unit, and a new unit, the Prime Minister's Delivery Unit, focusing on the delivery of government priorities.

Ling's (2002) survey of joined-up practices, based on his work for the National Audit Office, assessed the early phase of Labour policies by grouping practices associated with joined-up government into four clusters or dimensions:

- the internal life of each organisation (such as culture and values, information management and training);
- interorganisational life (such as shared leadership, pooled budgets, merged structures and joint teams);
- the delivery of services (such as joint consultation with clients, developing a shared client focus, and providing a 'one-stop shop' for service users);
- accountabilities 'upwards' and target setting from above (such as PSAs and other shared outcome targets, performance measures and shared regulation).

With such a broad definition it is not surprising that for Ling 'outcomes are fluid and contested' (2002, p 624) and that 'the role of the centre in how to facilitate the local implementation of joined-up government has never been satisfactorily established' (p 640). He takes five pages to summarise recommendations about joined-up government only up to 2000. Writing in 2001, Ling saw joined-up government as a defining principle of the Blairite modernisation project and suggested that a test of its success would be its ability to resolve old control problems and prevent new ones emerging. The associated National Audit Office report (2001c) is a valuable statement of progress up to that point, focusing on risks and system design.

In the second half of the New Labour decade it is possible to identify new themes emerging. These include 'capability', the 'fitness for purpose' of departments, and the focus on 'strategy' expressed in the unit of that name in No 10 and in the directors of strategy in government departments. While civil service reform has remained a major preoccupation, e-government, although still a priority, has been affected by some change of direction, and devolution to the English regions has suffered a major loss of impetus. Overall, the preoccupation of the centre during this period can be seen as a concern with delivery mechanisms that produce perceived improvements in service quality. Particularly in the NHS, selective central intervention when things go wrong has replaced the building of self-sustaining joined-up mechanisms.

The practical issues that are now being faced link theory and practice in important ways. Both the underlying theory and the particular institutional design need to be right. The issues include:

- the machinery of government, with changes bringing together parts of departments previously separated – most recently the formation of the Department of Communities and Local Government – but dividing the responsibilities of the Home Office with the creation of the Ministry of Justice;
- other joining up at the centre, including a host of cross-cutting programmes and targets – initiatives around community cohesion, the third sector and 'respect' are all recent examples, but these are many and various. Some include real system reform, of which there is further discussion below;
- developing the joined-up agenda at the regional level through the expansion of the work of Government Offices that now do business on behalf of 10 departments;
- joining up at the local level, including through Local Strategic Partnerships in each local authority area, building on one of the first major joined-up programmes, neighbourhood renewal;
- the characterisation of departments as strategic centres devolving delivery to regional and local authorities and agencies, but also looking at how to get the feedback loops between policy development and frontline authorities and agencies right;
- 'double devolution' to neighbourhood level as a political requirement of the strengthening of elected local government.

One culmination of all of these initiatives was the policy reviews of 2006/07, which, in some respects, can be seen as characteristic statements of the frustrations and possibilities of 'late Blairism'. The policy review dealing with public services (Cabinet Office, 2007) marked an explicit statement of the move away from joined-up processes engineered by government to a personalised service driven by user choice. The emphasis in the document is on plurality of supply, the contestability of existing delivery patterns, and market incentives to suppliers on the model of the energy or telecommunications industries. The section on multiagency working mentions public service hubs, dealing with significant life events like childbirth and bereavement, and the National Offender Management Scheme. The model seems to be that of a self-regulating market for 'normal' services coupled with top-down managed networks available for moments of personal or political risk.

What defines the joined-up agenda?

One clue to the agenda comes from the role of the Treasury. Its concept of 'total managed expenditure' includes local government and the devolved administrations, allowing it to survey the whole of public expenditure, and its perceptions of what is deficiently joined up are of great interest. These perceptions can be tracked in the Treasury's choice of cross-cutting issues in its Comprehensive Spending Reviews from 1998 (see Table 7.1). These represent areas of government business where either the Treasury was not happy with the existing links within government, or the policy challenges were so novel that they wanted to initiate a review under their leadership.

Table 7.1: Cross-cutting Spending Reviews

1998	Local government finance, the criminal justice system, illegal drugs and provision for young children ('Sure Start') – total 4.
2000	Government intervention in deprived areas; Sure Start and services for the under-5s; young people at risk; welfare-to-work and 'ONE' (the single gateway for working-age benefit and employment services, later called Jobcentre Plus); criminal justice; crime reduction; illegal drugs; the 'active community' (volunteering etc); care and support for older people; rural and countryside programmes; local government finance; science research; the knowledge economy; conflict prevention; nuclear safety in the former Soviet Union – total 15.
2002	Science and research; services to small businesses; the public sector labour market; children at risk; tackling health inequalities; role of the voluntary sector in public services; improving public space – total 7.
2004	Criminal justice system; action against illegal drugs – total 2.
2007	Children and young people; counter-terrorism and security; mental health and employment outcomes; sub-national economic development and regeneration; supporting housing growth; future role of the third sector in social and economic regeneration – total 6.

Source: Spending Review reports

Over time, the areas covered by the reviews have narrowed into ones with major cost implications and alternatives that cannot be considered in the normal bargaining processes between the Treasury and spending departments. The high tide for this approach arguably came in 2000, the year of *Wiring it up* (PIU, 2000b), which cited the studies intensively.

Generally budgets for the cross-cutting areas have been held by departments, but there are some 'pooled budgets' controlled by committees of ministers. What the Spending Review documents do not explain is the role of the Treasury in choosing the topics for these reviews and chairing them (for example, in 1998 Gill Noble [later project director on *Wiring it up*] on criminal justice and Norman Glass on Sure Start). The choice of areas seems to reflect a reciprocity and partial overlap between policy areas that are inherently difficult to organise for government action, and those that have traditionally posed boundary problems within UK government.

Joint targets between the Treasury and departments have been difficult: the National Audit Office (2005) reviewing four in the international arena (conflict prevention, debt relief, millennium development goals, trade barriers) found that targets were understood and coherently structured, but had lacked impact on working arrangements and the pattern of activities undertaken – again a familiar line of evaluation.

In the Comprehensive Spending Review of 2006/07 the approach was different, as the cross-cutting reviews merged with the Treasury approach of using expert reviews (see also Chapter Eight, this volume). In the 2007 Budget speech the Chancellor announced that interdepartmental reviews of youth services and disabled children, mental health and employment, and the future of regions and localities were all nearing completion. The main impetus for this was arguably managerial. Sir David Varney's review of the user perspectives on services (2006) became the guide to the Service Transformation Development Plan designed to promote better procurement, property management and government websites. The Budget report of 2007 reported that a feasibility study into a 'single point of contact change of circumstance service' was under way (HM Treasury, 2007, p 148).

It is apparent that by this stage a rather different approach to joining up was evident, one that suggested that 'citizen and business insight must become central to the design and delivery of public services' (HM Treasury, 2007, p 149). The model here is of the accessible and seamless service, experienced as a whole and indifferent to the political construction of the managerial processes that lie behind it. This has profound implications for Cabinet government and multi-level government, for if the experience of service use is to be corporatised and homogenised many traditional notions of accountability and transparency may have to be abandoned, or at a minimum redefined.

Debate continues about whether the primary role of the Treasury is necessary or desirable. Observing that in practice the Treasury does get involved in the detail of welfare policy, despite all its pretensions to work alongside departments, Deakin and Parry (2000) argued that the best approach was for the Treasury to reinforce its own expertise and make its decisions better informed. To some extent this was done in Gordon Brown's Treasury, especially through the Work Incentives and Poverty Analysis team. But the more typical approach was to use outside experts to cut through complex policy matters and drive towards conclusions that were often implemented by the Chancellor, as with Martin Taylor on the tax–benefit system, Derek Wanless on health, and Kate Barker on housing. Policy on income maintenance was made by a fusion of the Treasury and the Department for Work and Pensions, notably in the Freud report of March 2007 (Freud, 2007) that was interested in joined-up approaches.

Is the answer to leave it to the Treasury? Former Cabinet Secretary, Andrew Turnbull, famously commented on the effect of vesting so much power in the Treasury on the efficient working of government (Giles and Timmins, 2007). While there have been widely different interpretations of such views, undoubtedly joining up through Treasury expenditure manipulation is among the most potent of all mechanisms, although exposing the joined-up agenda to the vulnerabilities of Treasury–departmental relations may also bring its own risks.

Institutional innovations in England

Both the preceding structures of government and the creation of devolved administrations in Northern Ireland, Scotland and Wales have led to what may be increasingly distinctive approaches to parts of the modernisation agenda, including joining up. These mean that to some extent the experience in England has been different from the other parts of the UK.

Government Offices (for the Regions)

Many UK government departments have had a regional field organisation, with offices in the standard English regions and where appropriate Scotland and Northern Ireland. However, the boundaries of these networks were often not standardised and there was a particular problem about South East England – should there be one large region, London as a distinct region taken out of it, or three or more regions with London distinct and other regions extending from it? The treatment of Cumbria (relating to Newcastle or to Manchester?) and of South West England (based on Bristol or on Plymouth?) detained administrators and commentators for decades as the geographical basis of joining-up services seemed to be the dominant policy goal. Meanwhile the delivery of services became much more fragmented and diversified, with central government increasingly preoccupied with securing a direct reach into local service delivery that might attract them political blame.

Integrated Government Offices grew from the regional offices of the Department of the Environment when it encompassed housing, planning and transport from 1970-1976. The offices served as a vehicle for territorial policy interests but were firmly part of the central government machine, often serving to give officials experience of a 'provincial' location within their career development. Other departmental networks had developed separately, notably for the Department of Trade and Industry.

In 1994 a significant step was taken with the establishment of Government Offices for the Regions (GOs) in each English region to bring together previously separate government programmes. They originally comprised staff from the then Department of the Environment, Department of Transport, Department of Trade and Industry and Department for Education and Employment. GOs were then responsible for housing and transport investment programmes, European structural funds and regional selective assistance, contracting with Training and Enterprise Councils and Business Links.

Following the publication of *Reaching out* in 2000 (PIU, 2000c), GOs were made the key representatives of government in the regions and were involved more directly in policy making. In 2001 they took on support for the Connexions service and for Neighbourhood Renewal programmes. The Department for Environment, Food and Rural Affairs joined the GO network, and the Home Office built co-located crime and drugs teams. By 2002 the Home Office teams had integrated with the GO network as had Department for Culture, Media and Sport representatives, and Sure Start/Children's Fund teams co-located. In 2003 additional responsibility for street crime and community cohesion initiatives as well as regional resilience and decent homes passed to the network and public health teams were also co-located. From April 2006 the Department for Education and Skills also fully integrated its GO-based activity.

As a result of these developments, the GO network now delivers on behalf of 10 government departments and in an increasingly integrated way. Their original role, which was largely to be an administrator of grant programmes, has been transformed into one that is much more clearly the government's presence in the regions. GOs are intended to support and challenge local partners and to provide key input from regions and localities into policy development. They support Whitehall in delivering specific PSAs, including on improvements to housing and deprived areas; crime and drugs reduction; third sector engagement; sustainable development; children and learning; land use planning; and culture. They are also involved with negotiating and monitoring delivery of Local Area Agreements (LAAs), supporting the local government improvement strategy, and developing a more tailored dialogue with individual localities about priorities and performance; and they are supporting and challenging regional partners to strengthen regional strategies. Accordingly, the organisational structure of GOs has been changing, becoming more flexible and joined up, and with staff being valued for their influencing and negotiating skills. Teams have become more focused around localities rather than departmental boundaries, helping GOs to see the interconnectedness of policy problems and thus to effect or promote joined-up solutions.

From treatment to prevention

Perhaps the classic expression of joined-up problems is through the concept of 'social exclusion'. The Unit of that name was established in 1997 and produced over 40 reports on eye-catching issues, such as rough sleeping, and on potentially marginalised age groups like children, young adults and older people. A further theme of the physical context of lives emerged with the spin-off Neighbourhood Renewal Unit. Sometimes the themes multiplied, such as one report on multiple exclusion and quality of life among older people in disadvantaged neighbourhoods.

By 2006 planning had become more intensive, with a minister (Hilary Armstrong) and a Cross-government Social Exclusion Plan. The Unit was renamed the Social Exclusion Task Force. The stated aim is to build on reforms that aim to shift efforts from 'treatment' to 'prevention' by developing tools to identify those most at risk; by systematically identifying what works; by promoting multiagency working and strengthening the role of LAAs; by piloting budget-holding lead practitioners; and by rigorous management of wider performance. The point of all this activity is to set up an alternative analytical focus by working across government to ensure the generation of PSAs address the needs of the most excluded. Case study 7.1 describes an approach to services for children which is joined up in terms of both policy and delivery and reflects wide stakeholder engagement. It also places emphasis on prevention and early intervention, encouraged by closer inter-agency working.

Case study 7.1: Every Child Matters: joined-up services for children

The original impetus for Every Child Matters was Lord Laming's report into the death of Victoria Climbié that recommended that child protection should not be separated from policies to improve children's lives as a whole. In the development of the Green Paper and of the subsequent Every Child Matters: Change for Children programme, there has been strong involvement from ministers across government. The programme is led by the Department for Education and Skills – to whom children's social care transferred from the Department of Health. The Department of Health remains as a joint sponsor, together with the Cabinet Office, HM Treasury, Department for Work and Pensions, Department of Communities and Local Government, Department for Culture, Media and Sport, and the Home Office.

Every Child Matters establishes a national framework for programmes of local change, building services around children, young people and families. The focus is on maximising potential as well as minimising risk and on moving towards a system that is characterised by prevention and early intervention. Children's well-being is defined by reference to five outcomes – be healthy,

---

stay safe, enjoy and achieve, make a positive contribution and achieve economic well-being. This outcomes framework was developed in collaboration with statutory, voluntary and private sector stakeholders, and with input from children and young people themselves.

The 2004 Children Act provided the legislative foundation for whole-system reform. This encompasses integrated frontline delivery, with multiagency teams providing joined-up services; integrated processes, including a Common Assessment Framework to improve referrals between agencies; an integrated strategy including joint strategic needs assessment and planning, joint commissioning of services and joint budgeting; and integrated governance, via Local Safeguarding Children Boards. Local authorities have a duty to promote cooperation between agencies and have a new power to pool resources in support of joint actions. A new local authority post of director of children's services covering education and children's social services was introduced, as was an equivalent lead member role. A single Children and Young People's Plan replaced individual plans for various services and functions and an integrated inspection framework was established, focused on how children's services as a whole operate across each local authority area.

Area-based initiatives: the 2006 local government White Paper

By 2006 the emphasis of the Blair government had moved to bottom-up approaches to resolving the delivery problems of public services. Its White Paper on local government had as an opening line: 'this White Paper is on the side of individuals and families who want to make a difference, both to their own lives and to the communities in which they live' (Department of Communities and Local Government, 2006, p 7). Community initiative from below was to replace institutional engineering from above, but this still left the question of who was to do the coordination and joining. The answer was local government as a 'strategic leader and place-shaper' (p 10) putting together standardised LAAs.

But, arguably, it is a local government whose governance is very much that specified by the centre, as is evident in the annexes on how cross-cutting is to be achieved in seven areas – community safety; health and well-being; vulnerable people; children, young people and families; economic development; housing and planning; and climate change. When the White Paper says that 'delivery of local priorities will be the responsibility of partners in key local partnerships ... once agreed with Government, local partners will be required to have regard to these priorities for improvement' (Department of Communities and Local Government, 2006, p 11), there is a sense that the balance between the centre enforcing and letting go remains elusive.

Joining up under devolution

The devolved administrations in Scotland, Wales and Northern Ireland face a particular challenge of 'joining up'. Because they were an additional level of government, they risked perpetuating a congested political system, in which issues were divided up both horizontally and vertically and the leadership potential of the system diluted. In Wales, there was a strong political theme of bringing quangos (quasi-autonomous non-governmental organisations) under control and of reviewing local government. In Northern Ireland, the profusion of special-purpose delivery agencies, the inclusion of several local services in civil service departments, and the small size and limited powers of the 26 local authorities had long been noted. In Scotland, the large number of local authorities (32) was identified as a problem.

In a contrasting theme, the Scottish and Welsh administrations were already joined-up 'brands' because of the previous history of the Scottish and Welsh Offices, and were often cited as exemplars of policy coordination. This cohesion has been maintained without break-ups into ministerial silos, and the pursuit of joined-up economic and social objectives has generally been more convincing than in England, although there remain issues such as different organisational cultures and boundaries (see Case study 7.2).

Case study 7.2: Community planning in Scotland: comprehensive service provision at the local government level

The Community Planning Working Group was set up in July 1997, to study existing best practice in local authorities' relationships with other public, private and voluntary sector bodies. It recommended the establishment of three to five 'pathfinder' areas and projects in Edinburgh, Highland, Perth and Kinross, South Lanarkshire and Stirling. Evaluation indicated that there were tensions (top-down or bottom-up; local authority leadership or partnership between equals; strategic aspirations and operational reality; an improved process or measurable outcomes). A Community Planning Task Force established in 2000 split into four sub-groups to focus on: clearer shared visions; effective partnering; involving communities and other interests; and charting success, added value and learning lessons. The Task Force further examined progress in community planning across Scotland, reporting in June 2001. Finally, a Community Planning Implementation Group was established in 2003 and reported in June 2004.

The 2003 Local Government in Scotland Act gave a statutory basis for community planning and linked it to Best Value policy, mandating a leading role to local authorities; formalising the link between community planning and Best Value; creating a clear community leadership role for local authorities; and

---

placing a duty to participate on health boards, Scottish Enterprise, Highlands and Islands Enterprise, joint police boards and chief constables, joint fire boards and the Strathclyde Passenger Transport Authority. A Community Planning Network has from 2005 brought together representatives of all 32 community planning areas.

The process offers the possibility of rationalising existing partnerships and sustaining networks that offer a framework for joint planning. The process has been partly owned by CoSLA (Convention of Scottish Local Authorities) throughout and respects the boundaries and authority of existing bodies.

The Audit Scotland investigation of 2006 found that 'community planning can add value to joint working by providing a local strategic framework and building a culture of co-operation and trust' (Audit Scotland, 2006, p 2); but the report commented on the complexity and inconsistency of structures, the number of other national policy initiatives that had to be considered and the primacy of corporate plans and performance targets of all the partners.

Northern Ireland and Wales have run their own investigations into congested government under Lord (Herman) Ouseley and Sir Jeremy Beecham respectively. Ouseley's work, later taken over by direct rule ministers, led to fairly conventional rationalising proposals, including fewer, more powerful local authorities and single education and health authorities (Northern Ireland Review of Public Administration, 2006). The Beecham report is a more interesting conceptual statement drawing on academic models and, interestingly, not holding any public consultations (Welsh Assembly Government, 2006b). It identifies cross-cutting themes that can influence the performance of services, including organisational structures that promote a defensive compliance culture, capacity constraints within the business process (including leadership), and a multiplicity of performance targets and funding streams all championed by different parts of central government.

Beecham sets up a 'citizen' model of services based on voice in contrast to the English consumer model based on the possibility of exit (see also Chapter Six, this volume). It expresses the vision of 'small country governance' in which local ambition is supported by an involved and accessible centre. The Welsh orthodoxy is that the nation is indeed small, and that alternative suppliers are not sustainable in typical Welsh communities. In fact this logic could be applied elsewhere in the UK and expresses the devolved model of joining up through a professionally driven consensus. It is very different from, and potentially challenging to, the norms set by the Blair government.

Sometimes joint working has been necessary to make sense of the division of responsibilities. *Closing the opportunities gap* is the Scottish Executive strategy, agreed by the Department for Work and Pensions, relating to the devolved responsibilities for active labour market policy and skills training to the retained areas of social security, tax credits, welfare-to-work and poverty reduction. It has worked because of the wish of the two Labour-led administrations to present themselves as partners in economic development. Executive ministers and officials have deferred to the policy lead of the Treasury and Gordon Brown and the uniform Britain–wide administration of Jobcentre Plus.

Scotland's approach has been an implicitly centralist one, based on Executive regret that the 1996 reorganisation produced as many as 32 authorities of varying size and capacity. Work has been done on the sharing of council services and some functions (such as inspection of care facilities) transferred to national-level quangos. The NHS structure of 14 area boards represents a more logical territorial division but it too is part of a centralised delivery apparatus, without any hospital trusts since 2004.

A wider perspective: 'whole of government' approaches

Adding it up (PIU, 2000a) introduced the term 'whole of government' into UK discussion. This has been taken furthest in Australia, an exemplar for the UK even though it is a federal system. The Australian Public Service's Whole of Government project, launched in 2004, is attempting through pilot projects and cultural change to improve coordination and 'seamlessness' and to improve the government's engagement with individuals and communities, including the handling of emergencies. The idea of 'connecting government' has, like 'joined-up government' in Britain, a sense that the rhetoric of horizontality is a cloak for the reality of verticality. The 'government' here is the (federal) Australian government but there is little sense of a non-unitary political system. States are characterised as 'external stakeholders' who are to be consulted but who are not to stand in the way of centrally led delivery (Australian Public Service Commission, 2004). This report notes intergovernmental mechanisms such as the Council of Australian Governments and the functional Council of Ministers (Australian Public Service Commission, 2004), but the line is strongly centralist: the centre must have 'clout on the ground' and 'on occasion the government will simply decide that a matter is not (or no longer) open for debate' (Australian Public Service Commission, 2004, p 97).

There is also an agenda of further centralisation within the Australian government through a Cabinet Implementation Unit. This approach sets a strategic focus at the centre but moderates its political force with rhetoric about joined-up, user-serving action and decentralised delivery. The reality is that at the federal level in Australia – and even more so in Canada – a great deal of the action is to do with the political management of relations with intermediate governments who more often than not are controlled by other political parties. In a situation where the main tax instruments are controlled by the centre, even a federal constitution is no guarantee against an attempt at joining up through a top-down reach into local delivery processes.

Conclusions

The central question is whether we are making real progress towards more genuinely joined-up processes and relationships, or whether the constantly recycled exhortations and innovations reflect underlying political problems in addressing the fissile nature of government. Our conclusion is that effective joining up is evident in parts and is getting better. The early days were characterised by initiative overload and there has continued to be a lot of process-related activity, much of it very time-consuming. But there is now evidence of a more sustained kind of joining up that is likely to be increasingly recognised in performance management systems focused on key (and joined-up) outcomes – both for central and local government.

Seen from inside government, joining up is not just a mantra for the sake of it – a simple fad or fashion. It is a genuine attempt to respond to a genuine set of problems. Governments have attempted this in the past but this may well be the most sustained attempt, driven by a government in office for an extended period and impatient with some of the impediments to achieving results on service delivery. The evidence so far suggests that:

- Solutions to historically intractable problems, or the so-called 'wicked issues', can only be achieved by agencies working in consort rather than in silos. Vertical organisation can skew government efforts away from prevention – since the benefits of preventive action could come to another department – and it may make the government less sensitive to particular client groups whose needs cut across departmental boundaries.
- Joining up needs to be driven from the top. This means being championed by ministers – with clear accountabilities throughout the system – supported by PSAs that are themselves joined up – and with the capacity to enable local solutions tailored to meet the needs of the local population – signalled, for example, in the approach to performance management outlined in the local government White Paper (Department of Communities and Local Government, 2006). Users must be able to have their say in the system if the solutions are to be sustainable – thus the emphasis on user voice in the White Paper and the increasing emphasis on the 'personalisation' of the offer to individuals, which perhaps ironically requires a strategically joined-up system to deliver.
- Effective feedback loops are essential – between central and local government and between local government and the communities and individuals they serve – in order to ensure that policy remains grounded in reality and capable of flexing when tested, and that implementation is effective and sustained.
- Performance management systems need to be tailored around outcomes and the partnerships necessary to achieve those outcomes. PSAs have started to be more joined up, a trend that might be expected to see an increase in the Comprehensive Spending Review 2007, and an assessment on the effectiveness of partnership arrangements is already reflected in comprehensive performance

assessments for local authorities; again a trend we expect to see enhanced in the revised performance management system for local authorities currently being formulated.

- Joining up is about a focus on place as well as a focus on outcomes. The transformation in the GO role in England – whose organisational structures and ways of working are now being focused around localities rather than departmental boundaries – is a telling development here, as is the focus on the place-shaping role of local authorities in the *Strong and prosperous communities* White Paper (Department of Communities and Local Government, 2006).
- One model would take the form of a whole-system change in which: central government sets the agenda in collaboration and consultation with local government and other key stakeholders; GOs help to drive the system change through the support and challenge of local delivery partners; local authorities take responsibility for local delivery tailored to local circumstances, providing a leadership role to Local Strategic Partnerships; and users and citizens make their contribution and help identify what works.
- In the terms set out in *Professional policy making for the twenty-first century*, clear progress has been made in improving the compatibility of systems (as broadly defined, including information technology [IT], culture, structures and lack of time). On the criterion of greater 'corporacy' (within the civil service or more widely) the position is less clear, and the Labour government's faith in personalised initiatives is likely to be a challenge to all established institutions.
- Joining up risks transitional problems, and the reality may never be entirely straightforward. Even in an apparent success story, such as the merger of employment and benefit offices into Jobcentre Plus, Karagiannaki (2007) found that 'the main lesson to be learned by Jobcentre Plus is that extra care is required when designing such multi-tasking organizations in order to balance the delivery of differing elements of service', and noted the 'negative transitional effects' of the programme (p 193).

No one should be surprised by this. At the root of joining-up problems is a psychological preference for the particular to the general. The political system does not admit its actors into a single entity: it is approached through a particular organisation, profession, territory, ideology or policy approach that becomes a vehicle for loyalty and focus. Federal systems typically have more structured horizontal and vertical mechanisms that have developed over time into cooperative procedures. The UK, although potentially a more flexible system, tends to combine unrealistic rhetoric with deep-seated centralist attitudes. These are difficult and challenging ideas, and the impact on outcomes will not be evident in many cases for some time to come. However, over 10 years a direction has been set and there is evidence that new systems and approaches are being embedded within government.

Further reading

Department for Communites and Local Government (2006) – the local government White Paper and the latest atempt to set out a citizen-centred approach to joining up fragmented services at the local level.

Mulgan, G. (2005c) www.youngfoundation.org.uk/node/223 – a concise statement of the issues from a former key policy adviser to the Blair government.

National Audit Office (2001c) – the most important review of the possibilities and limitations of joined-up government in the early years of New Labour.

National Audit Office (2006a) – this report goes beyond the government-centred focus to take on board the experience of policies and the latest business-related thinking on integrated service delivery.

Welsh Assembly Government (2006b) – this review was led by Sir Jeremy Beecham for the devolved Welsh administration and is also a useful general analysis of the issue.

Useful websites

www.cabinetoffice.gov.uk/social_exclusion_task_force – reports on the UK government's work on joined-up social policy and provides links to other government websites.

www.nao.gov.uk – the National Audit Office's reports, some of them mentioned in this chapter, are both supportive of good practice and sceptical about government rhetoric.

www.hm-treasury.gov.uk/spending_review – this site gives access to the reports of the cross-cutting reviews done in these exercises since 1998, a clue to both the substance of joined-up issues and to the Treasury's changing agenda of the issues needing attention.

EIGHT

Policy review

Martin Powell and Warwick Maynard

Of the nine competencies identified in *Professional policy making for the twenty-first century* (Cabinet Office Strategic Policy Making Team, 1999), 'review' is in many respects the most problematic to define, and thus to analyse. This chapter therefore:

- begins with a consideration of the ways in which the term is used in key government documentation;
- examines the conceptual and theoretical material on review within the policy process;
- outlines some dimensions of review, and suggests a typology of review;
- explores New Labour's reviews with reference to the typology; and
- discusses the changing nature of review under New Labour.

The aim of this chapter is to examine the competency of 'review', but reviewing 'review' is problematic for a number of reasons. First, it is a difficult term to define. According to *Chambers dictionary*, it can mean:

> A viewing again; a looking back; retrospect; a reconsideration; a survey; a revision; a critical examination; a critique; a periodical with critiques of books, etc; a display and inspection of troops and ships; the judicial revision of a higher court.

Second, the term remains elusive in *Professional policy making for the twenty-first century* (Cabinet Office Strategic Policy Making Team, 1999) in that definitions change and the term disappears from parts of the document. The core competency of review – 'keeps established policy under review to ensure that it continues to deal with the problems it was designed to tackle, taking account of associated effects elsewhere' (para 2.11) – is included. However, a slightly different definition appears in Annexe A: constantly reviews existing policy to ensure it is really dealing with problems it was designed to solve without having unintended detrimental effects elsewhere. More importantly, the idea disappears from later parts of the text. There are chapters on the other competencies (chapters 4-10) but no chapter on review (or evaluation). Annexe A gives the definition and evidence for review, where 'the ideas for "evidence" have been suggested by policy makers from a range of departments'. Placed under the theme of continuous improvement, review is defined as constantly reviewing existing/established policy. Under evidence is given: 'worked closely with international divisions, agencies etc, use made of OECD, EU mechanisms etc. Looked at how other countries dealt with the issue. Worked closely with colleagues in Welsh, Scottish and Northern Ireland Offices. Carried out international benchmarking; recognised regional variation within England. Communications/presentation strategy prepared and implemented'. However, review disappears in Annexe B (summary of suggested levers for change to policy making), which lists eight 'features' (that is, competencies) among which 'evaluates' and 'reviews' are not present, although 'cross-cutting actions' is added.

Third, there is the problem of overlap with other competencies; although none of the competencies are entirely self-contained, many appear to have links with 'review'. These include: using evidence ('uses best available evidence from a wide variety of sources and involves key stakeholders at an early stage'); inclusive ('takes account of the impact on the needs of all those directly or indirectly affected [that is, everybody?] by the policy'); evaluates ('builds systematic evaluation of early outcomes into the policy process'); and learns lessons ('learns from experience of what works and what does not') (Cabinet Office Strategic Policy Making Team, 1999, para 2.11). Chapter One of this book suggests that an exploration of the term 'review' might consider different approaches to reviewing key areas of policy and delivery, how evidence and opinion are sought, how stakeholders are involved, and how this feeds backs into policy and legislative change. However, while providing some direction, such an approach maintains an overlap with 'outward looking' (evidence from elsewhere), 'using evidence' (how can policy be reviewed without evidence?), 'inclusive' (stakeholders), 'evaluates', and 'learns lessons' (experience of what works and what does not).

Finally, as we shall see, the government uses the term 'review' in a variety of ways. A quick internet search revealed many 'reviews' in different forms (see Table 8.1). For example, the work of the Prime Minister's Strategy Unit (PMSU) does not quite go from A to Z, but lists over 50 documents from 'active ageing' to 'workforce development' (www.cabinetoffice.gov.uk/strategy/work_areas/past.asp).

Never in the field of government has so much been reviewed by so many! In other words, an audit state or an evaluative state is also a 'reviewing state'.

Table 8.1: Reviews under New Labour

Department + Health + Review: about 1,200,000
Cabinet Office + Review: about 1,100,000
Department + Pensions + Review: about 1,090,000
HM Treasury + Review: about 901,000

A: Results of search (pages from UK: 28 March 2007)
- HM Treasury and the Cabinet Office launched the third sector review on 15 May 2006.
- The Cabinet Office appointed Professor Baker (University of Salford) to examine 'equalities' (October 2006).
- The Department of Health is to carry out a review of the new system to select doctors for specialist training (7 March 2007).
- The Department of Health publishes a review of seasonal influenza programme arrangements (8 March 2007).
- The Centre for Economic and Social Inclusion are doing a review on behalf of the Cabinet Office, taking the form of an online questionnaire, to identify how services for excluded families can be improved (12 March 2007).
- Stern review on *The economics of climate change*, published 30 October 2006.
- Davidson review of the implementation of European Union legislation, final report (28 November 2006).
- Thornton review of pensions institutions, consultation paper (7 March 2007).
- Lyons inquiry into local government, final report (launched 21 March 2007).

B: Reviews recently appointed or reported
- Health Committee: produced over 25 reports since the 2001 Election.
- Committees of both Houses of Parliament: produced about 70 reports in March 2007.

C: Work of the House of Commons Select Committees
There have been concerns at the reduction of parliamentary scrutiny, as seen in the increasing use of 'external' inquiries (Public Administration Select Committee, 2005) and the government attempting to replace independently minded chairs of committees. A series of reports from the Liaison and Modernisation Committees, the Conservatives Commission to Strengthen Parliament (the Norton Commission) and the Hansard Society Commission on Parliamentary Scrutiny from 1999 onwards have led to a number of changes in the operation of Select Committees (House of Commons Library, nd). The Modernisation Committee recommended a core set of tasks for Select Committees. The Health Committee (2007) examined 10 tasks under four broad objectives:

Objective A: to examine and comment on the policy of the department
Task 1: to examine policy proposals from the UK government and the European Commission in Green Papers, White Papers, draft guidance etc.
Task 2: to identify and examine areas of emerging policy, or where existing policy is deficient, and make proposals.
Task 3: to conduct scrutiny of any published draft bill within the Committee's responsibilities.
Task 4: to examine specific outputs from the department expressed in documents or other decisions.

Objective B: to examine the expenditure of the department
Task 5: to examine the expenditure plans and out-turn of the department, its agencies and principal BDPBs.

(continued)

Table 8.1: (continued)

Objective C: to examine the administration of the department
Task 6: to examine the department's Public Service Agreements, the associated targets, and the statistical measurements employed, and report if appropriate.
Task 7: to monitor work of the department's Executive Agencies, non-departmental public bodies, regulators and other associated bodies.
Task 8: to scrutinise major appointments made by the department.
Task 9: to examine the implementation of legislation and other major policy initiatives.
Objective D: to assist the House in debate and decision
Task 10: to produce reports that are suitable for debate in the House or debating committees.

Sources: Public Administration Select Committee (2005); Health Committee (2007); House of Commons Library (nd)

Review and the policy process

Most textbooks on the policy process contrast the 'rational' with the 'incremental' approach to policy making. The rational model is usually traced to Simon (1945/57) (see Bochel and Bochel, 2004), while 'incrementalism' or 'muddling through' is associated with Lindblom (1959). In this chapter, we concentrate on the rational model that generally sees policy making as a series of sequential and linear 'stages' or as part of a 'policy cycle' with a series of 'feedbacks' or 'loops'. The 'stages' model is sometimes referred to as 'the textbook model', 'the stages heuristic', and so on. Different models have slightly different terminology about stages (see Parsons, 1995), but most stagist models have some form of 'review'. For example, Parsons (1995) outlines seven 'stages' models. Six of them include some form of 'review' such as 'termination' and 'appraisal'; 'correction and supplementation'; 'policy evaluation' and 'feedback'; 'evaluation' and 'termination'; and 'evaluation and review' and 'policy maintenance, succession and termination'. The Cabinet Office Strategic Policy Making Team (1999) contrasts its *Professional policy making for the twenty-first century* with (presumably) the amateur and traditional policy making of the twentieth century. The document claims that, traditionally, the policy-making process has been regarded as a sequence of closely related and interdependent activities that, together, form a cycle geared towards the progressive improvement of outcomes (para 2.6). It goes on to state that, 'we found in our discussions with policy-makers that policy making rarely proceeds as neatly as this model suggests' (para 2.7). Eight years on, most policy makers would probably recognise that aiming to form policy using a rational cycle or stages model is often overtaken either by responding to demands for speedy action or to 'events' in the words of the late Prime Minister, Harold Macmillan, either of which will leave implementation as king. This is hardly surprising, as the rational stages model is widely seen as an 'ideal type' or heuristic device. Moreover, the rational model is important as it fits well with the ideas of evidence, evaluation and review (Sanderson, 2000; Bochel and Bochel, 2004; Hudson and Lowe, 2004). Most studies of policy making differentiate between formative and summative evaluation (discussed in detail in Chapter Nine, this volume). Palumbo (1987) relates the 'policy cycle' to the 'information cycle'. Formative evaluation takes place at the implementation stage, while summative evaluation occurs at the impact stage, examining the degree to which the policy has impacted on the problems to which it was addressed. Similarly, Spicker (2006) writes that formative evaluation is undertaken at intermediate stages in the policy cycle, while summative evaluation is the evaluation of a whole policy, focusing on the impact of policy. The distinction between them is basically a technical one, concerned with the stage when evaluation takes place.

According to Hudson and Lowe (2004), the classic or rational view of evaluation research is retrospective; has a narrow focus; and is concerned with causal issues. Summative judgements and quantitative approaches dominate, with experimental research regarded as the 'gold standard'. On the other hand, Bochel and Bochel (2004) claim that 'much of the assessment of policy success or failure in social policy has been impressionistic and anecdotal' (p 179). Hudson and Lowe continue that, in response to the limitations of the rational model, a more bottom–up approach of formative evaluation has emerged, which is based on a more qualitative evidence base, is characterised by the active participation of stakeholders, and with feedback appearing as (rather than after) the policy is being rolled out. From this perspective 'review' might be seen as formative evaluation, but in the view of *Professional policy making for the twenty-first century*, a focus on 'established policy' appears to fit more with summative evaluation. However, as the policy cycle leads back from evaluation into policy formulation and development, in a sense all evaluation is formative, as Spicker (2006) points out. As we shall see below, 'review' appears to occur at all stages of the policy process.

A review of reviews

As we saw earlier, the term 'review' covers a huge variety of studies, which might vary in terms of purpose (to identify problems, generate solutions, improve accountability, and so on), triggers (such as scrutiny of government policy, and contribution to wider policy debate), leadership and membership (for example, civil servants, academics, judges, users and 'stakeholders'), and method (including internal review, public inquiry and parliamentary scrutiny). In order to explore the diversity of reviews, this section examines three basic dimensions (see Table 8.2).

The first dimension is the 'who' question, concerned with membership, which has links to 'stakeholders' and issues of 'inclusiveness' (see Chapter Six, this volume). The second dimension concerns the 'when' question or the stage of the policy process, and links with issues of formative versus summative evaluation and research for policy and research of policy. The final dimension revolves around the 'how' question or different ways of reviewing the evidence. Before examining the dimensions, it is worth detailing some examples of reviews. As we will see later, reviews can combine the who, what and how dimensions in different ways.

Table 8.2: Dimensions of review

Who?	When?	How?
Government internal review	Review for policy/formative evaluation/problem review	Judicial or legal review
Government external review	Review of policy/summative evaluation/policy review	'Traditional' literature review
External review		Rapid review
		Scoping review
		Systematic review
		Meta-analysis

Who?

There are three types of 'who' reviews. The first is set up by government and is composed largely of civil servants. The second is set up by government but is headed by or composed of 'external' or 'independent' members. The third is set up by an external body. One type of traditional government 'external' review is the Royal Commission. This is a body of the 'great and the good' who examine an issue in detail, although cynics point out that it is sometimes a useful device for 'kicking a problem into the long grass'. The late Prime Minister, Harold Wilson, is reported to have favoured Royal Commissions as they 'take minutes and last years'. For example, Secretary of State Barbara Castle recorded that the British Medical Association asked her to postpone the phasing out of pay beds in the National Health Service (NHS) while the Royal Commission looked at it (hopefully, from their point of view, until there was a Conservative government) (Castle, 1980). The Royal Commission on the NHS was announced in Prime Minister Wilson's statement of 20 October 1975. The Royal Commission of 16 members was appointed by Royal Warrant on 19 May 1976. Its remit was 'to consider in the interests both of the patients and of those who work in the NHS the best use and management of the financial and manpower resources of the NHS' (Royal Commission on the NHS, 1979, p 1). It had 35 meetings, including five conferences lasting two or more days, received 2,460 written evidence submissions and held 58 oral evidence sessions. In addition, members met and spoke informally to about 2,800 individuals. Its report of nearly 500 pages with 117 recommendations (Royal Commission on the NHS, 1979) was presented to Parliament in July 1979.

Another type of independent review is the public inquiry (Sulitzeanu-Kenan, 2006). Bochel and Bochel (2004) note the recent tendency for government to use judges to head inquiries (for example, Scarman on the Brixton riots [1981]+Taylor on Hillsborough [1993]; Scott on weapons to Iraq [1994]; and Nolan on standards in public life [1995]).

The Griffiths Review of NHS management provides a contrasting 'external' review. In January 1983 the Managing Director of Sainsbury's, Roy Griffiths, was asked to look at manpower in the NHS. He refused, arguing that 'if the manpower is out of control, you have got management problems' (Timmins, 2001, pp 406-7). Griffiths, with three other businessmen, took no formal evidence, and produced a 'letter' rather than a report. Timmins (2001) considers that it proved 'the most unconventional NHS report of all time' (pp 406-7). It was 'written backwards' with seven pages of recommendations followed by 13 pages of diagnosis, while the evidence, so beloved of most formal inquiries, was simply omitted. It warned that speed was 'essential': the NHS could not afford 'any lengthy self-imposed Hamlet-like soliloquy as a precursor or alternative to the required action' (p 407). The 24 pages demanded not a paragraph of legislation, yet its recommendations proved the single most important change to the NHS since 1948.

On the other hand, a health review set up by Mrs Thatcher at the end of January 1988 can be seen as an 'internal' review, which has been termed 'one of the strangest and most secretive reviews ever of a major British institution' (Timmins, 2001, p 458). This is said to have had an unusual birth, in an interview on the TV programme 'Panorama', which stunned ministers and civil servants. It consisted of a ministerial group, chaired by the Prime Minister herself, with a plentiful supply of competing ideas from right-wing think-tanks, but with limited 'producer' input (such as two seminars with doctors and administrators respectively who were regarded as NHS 'trusties'), which led to a White Paper entitled *Working for patients* (DH, 1989) (see Thatcher, 1993; Timmins, 2001).

A rather different type of review is provided by House of Commons committees that include departmental Select Committees as well as the Public Administration Select Committee and the Public Accounts Committee (Dorey, 2005). Membership of these committees is limited to 'backbenchers' generally in proportion to the strength of the parties in the House of Commons. Under the 1983 National Audit Act, the National Audit Office examines the 'three Es' – economy, efficiency and effectiveness, or spending less, spending well and spending wisely – of public spending. Its 'value for money work' covers a wide range of issues. Relations with Parliament, and in particular with the Public Accounts Committee, are central to its work, with the Committee undertaking further investigation of about 50 National Audit Office reports each year. The Committee will then issue its own report, and the government must reply to its recommendations within two months. The National Audit Office claims – rather optimistically – that 'in this way, a cycle of accountability operates' (www.nao. org.uk/about/role.htm; for example, NAO, 2006c).

The first dimension, membership, can thus be seen on a rough 'insider–outsider' spectrum. We might expect internal reviews to produce relatively predictable conclusions that are largely in line with government thinking – that there is a clear correlation between membership and independence – but such an expectation would be erroneous in some cases. Some internal reviews – particularly where there are no plans to publish their findings and/or where the subject is unlikely to attract media interest – may in fact produce extremely unpredictable conclusions that result in policies being abandoned or step-changes in particular courses of action. The two examples in Case studies 8.1 and 8.2 are just such examples. It is possible to choose 'sound' people ('one of us') for external reviews, although there are some famous instances where inquiries came to the 'wrong' conclusions. Sir William Beveridge was 'kicked upstairs' to chair a committee regarded as a 'tidying up operation' with its terms of reference made 'as harmless as they can be made', dealing with administrative issues rather than issues of policy. However, this led to the famous Beveridge report, signed by Beveridge alone, with departmental representatives regarded as merely 'advisers and assessors', and not being associated in any way with the views and recommendations of policy (Timmins, 2001).

When?

The second dimension concerns the 'when' question, or the stage of the policy process. This also relates to the 'why' question, or the issue of rationale. As we saw above, evaluation is generally differentiated into 'formative' and 'summative'. *Professional policy making for the twenty-first century* talks of keeping 'established policy' under review, implying summative evaluation. However, as we have seen, 'review' can include issues at all stages of the policy process from policy formulation to policy termination. We can differentiate reviews very broadly into review *for* policy and review *of* policy, or problem and policy reviews, although reviews for policy will necessarily include some examination of existing policy.

The first category focuses on a problem that needs to be solved. This may be linked with agenda setting (Kingdon, 1984). 'Think-tanks' are sometimes seen as 'ideas brokers' or 'policy entrepreneurs' (Dorey, 2005). While right-leaning think-tanks such as the Institute of Economic Affairs, the Adam Smith Institute and the Centre for Policy Studies claimed to have influenced the Conservative government in areas such as health policy (see, for example, Timmins, 2001), centre and left-leaning think-tanks such as Demos, the Institute for Public Policy Research (IPPR) and the Fabian Society claim to produce ideas for New Labour. The Borrie Commission on Social Justice was set up by Labour leader John Smith (CSJ, 1994). These bodies tend to be concerned more with policy formulation or policy proposals – some more realistic than others – rather than with reviewing established policy, but the IPPR set up a commission on public–private partnerships (PPPs) (IPPR, 2001) that gave PPPs a guarded welcome, and the Fabian Society set up a commission on taxation (Fabian Society Commission on Taxation and Citizenship, 2004). However, the links between these think-tanks and political posts (such as John Redwood and David Willetts for the Conservatives; David Miliband, Geoff Mulgan and Matthew Taylor for New Labour; see Dorey, 2005), mean that it is often difficult to draw a clear line between stages.

The second category of review of policy, or policy review, is concerned with scrutinising established policy in a particular area. Two recent reviews conducted by the Home Office illustrate this difference between a review *for* policy and a review *of* policy (Case studies 8.1 and 8.2).

Case study 8.1: A review of partnership working between the Home Office and business 2006: a review *for* policy formulation

The Home Office decided that it needed to engage business more fully in supporting its strategic objectives. It needed a clearer view of what it had to offer business; what the business sector could or should deliver to further Home Office aims; and overall how to ensure that these opportunities for both Home Office and business were more successfully met.

The department recognised that its engagement with business was uncoordinated, with different policy areas pursuing partnerships and selling the value of working with the Home Office in different ways across a range of agendas. There was also a belief that individual companies and business sectors failed to associate their working partnerships with the Home Office as an entity. Some parts of the Home Office had built excellent working relations with the business sector, but others struggled to get any leverage. It was also apparent that the business sector's view of the Home Office was often framed either in terms of imposing costs on the sector through regulation (for example, corporate manslaughter; barriers to recruiting employees from outside the European Economic Area); or through a policy priorities framework that places, as they see it, business at the bottom of the list when it comes, for example, to dealing with crime.

A review aimed to identify how the department engaged with business; to analyse the success of this and identify future engagement opportunities; to develop a core departmental narrative for approaching and engaging business in the delivery of Home Office objectives; to identify innovative ways of better partnership working with business for areas already engaged; and of developing new partnerships in areas not yet engaged.

The review considered what the department could do to help business; whether there were particular Home Office policies that imposed restrictions on business; whether certain policy developments that would greatly aid the business sector – for example, enhanced crime prevention in town centres – would be likely to assist the retail industry; whether corporate social responsibility could act as a non-financial incentive to business, given it could bring an increased focus and benefits both to the Home Office, government in general and individual businesses themselves; and whether there were areas where business could help the Home Office achieve its objectives. Implementation of the recommendations is leading to a change in the way the Home Office engages with the business community across a range of policy areas.

Case study 8.2: A review of child evidence 2005: a review *of* a current policy

In 1998 the Home Office published *Speaking up for justice*, the report of the interdepartmental working group on the treatment of vulnerable or intimidated witnesses in the criminal justice system. The report made 78 recommendations that formed the basis for the 1999 Youth Justice and Criminal Evidence Act. This set out, for the first time, a comprehensive set of special measures to assist children, vulnerable adults and intimidated witnesses. In July 2002 special measures began a phased roll-out across both Crown Courts and magistrates' courts.

In 2003 consideration was given to how best to implement the special measure, 'video-recorded cross-examination or re-examination' (Section 28 of the Act) in the earlier Pigot report on video evidence (1989). It would provide for the examination and cross-examination of the child witness in informal surroundings with the proceedings being video-recorded and shown at the trial. Professor Diane Birch, a respected academic, was commissioned to produce *Meeting the challenges of Pigot: Pre-trial cross-examination under s.28 of the Youth Justice and Criminal Evidence Act 1999* (Birch and Powell, 2004). It reviewed the reasons for the Pigot report conclusions and academic and professional opinion at the time; considered relevant changes since 1989; and what practitioners and academics today regard as the major difficulties with implementing this measure. It concluded that there was little optimism that piloting Section 28 would provide tangible benefits for vulnerable witnesses and recommended that the government should explore alternatives.

On 21 July 2004 the government announced that it would not be implementing Section 28 (*Hansard*, col 40WS) and that the related provisions in Section 21 would be reviewed. It committed the government to embarking on a wider review of how child evidence is taken and presented in criminal courts. On 1 December 2004 the review of child evidence was launched to review Section 28 (video-recorded cross-examination and re-examination) in light of the recommendations in Professor Birch's report; and to review the performance of the special measures as they are applied to child witnesses and other aspects of child evidence.

First thoughts were presented to the Criminal Justice Council, an advisory body, then views of academics and practitioners were sought, including the judiciary, the magistracy, the bar, solicitors, the Crown Prosecution Service, the police, the court service, witness care units, voluntary services and social services childcare workers. Recommendations were submitted to ministers in July 2005 and implementation of the recommendations has led to direct changes in the policies and practices around children giving evidence in court.

How?

The third and final dimension relates to the type of evidence used. The term 'review' as used in this chapter excludes primary, academic research and international policy transfer (see Chapter Three, this volume), but this still leaves a great diversity of evidence and 'style'. On the issue of style, one type of review is the legal or judicial style, where a great deal of stress is placed on interrogating witnesses. This tends to occur in judicial reviews and Parliamentary Committees (see, for example, Sampson, 2005). A different style relies largely on synthesis or 'desk research' that can include 'traditional literature reviews', 'scoping reviews', 'rapid reviews', 'systematic reviews' and 'meta-analyses'.

Rightly or wrongly, 'personal experience' does appear to influence policy. It is reported that Members of Parliament's postbags and surgeries can influence policy. For example, Rawnsley (2001) writes that former Minister of Welfare Reform, Frank Field's, 'ungenerous' view of single mothers was formed by his experience in his constituency: 'There are no single mums in Birkenhead', he liked to claim. 'They all have a boyfriend somewhere' (p 111). Similarly, it is claimed that two events contributed towards Blair's Sunday morning television announcement in January 2000 that NHS spending in Britain would rise to the EU average in five years. First, an article in the *New Statesman* reported the experience in hospital of the mother of New Labour peer Lord Winston, leading him to claim that the health service was much the worst in Europe. Second, Blair received a letter from the daughter of 73-year-old Mavis Skeet whose throat cancer had become inoperable after operations were cancelled four times in five weeks because of bed shortages. As a Cabinet minister put it, 'The budget was written by Mavis Skeet and Robert Winston' (quoted in Rawnsley, 2001, p 337).

Similarly, New Labour has been accused of being obsessed by 'spin' and 'focus groups', concerned about what the *Daily Mail* might say (see Gould, 1998; Rawnsley, 2001). In a memo to Alistair Campbell, Philip Gould reported that 'TB is not believed to be real. He lacks conviction, he is all spin and presentation, he says things to please people, not because he believes them'. Rawnsley (2001, p 380) comments that 'the focus grouper was telling the spinmeister that too many voters saw them as the ventriloquists and Blair as the dummy' (see also Cohen, 2003), although Cohen – in a 'heads I win; tails you lose' argument – goes on to say that 'No focus group instructed New Labour to part-privatise the NHS or fight Iraq. Blair was prepared to be unpopular when he wanted to be' (2003 p 38).

Reviewing New Labour

Since 1997 New Labour has placed a great deal of stress on different types of 'review'. Table 8.3 classifies some of New Labour's reviews using the framework introduced earlier, while Case studies 8.1 and 8.2 give brief case studies of two reviews for and of policy.

Like the Conservative government of 1979, New Labour has set up few Royal Commissions. As Timmins (2001) writes, the existence of the Royal Commission on Long-term Care was not 'a happy one' (p 587). The problem of long-term care for elderly people, where some had to sell their homes to finance the care that they considered they should get 'free' due to a lifetime of paying taxes, emerged as a major issue for the Conservative government, and led to a series of reports by the Health Select Committee (see Baggott, 2004). In opposition in 1996, Blair had condemned a country where elderly people had to give up their homes to acquire the care they needed (Timmins, 2001). In government, Blair set up a Royal Commission on Long-term Care under Stewart Sutherland. However, its report in 1999 (Royal Commission on Long-term Care, 1999) produced a majority and minority report. Both agreed that the government should pay for nursing care and that residents, or their families, should pay the cost of food and accommodation on a means-tested basis. However, the majority considered that the government should pay for 'personal care' such as dressing and washing, while the minority argued that it was a personal responsibility. Alarmed by the cost, New Labour sided with the minority, while the Scottish Parliament (although not initially the Scottish Executive) sided with the majority (Baggott, 2004; Stewart, 2004).

Although New Labour has set up few Royal Commissions, it has relied heavily on what the Treasury terms 'independent review' (see www.hm-treasury.gov.uk/Independent_Reviews/independent_reviews_index.cfm and www.hm-treasury.gov.uk/Independent_Reviews/independent_reviews_archive.cfm). Although the

Table 8.3: Reviews under New Labour from 1997

Who?	When?	How?
Government internal Strategy Reviews; Capability Reviews	Review for policy: Lyons, Barker, Wanless, Henshaw, Turner	Judicial or legal: Royal Commission on Long-term Care (Sutherland); Nolan, Hutton, Butler, Turner, Wanless; Select Committees
Government external Royal Commission on Long-term Care (Sutherland); independent reviews, eg Lyons, Barker, Wanless, Henshaw, Turner, Select Committees	Review of policy: Select Committees; Butler; IPPR Review of PPPs; King's Fund Review of Social Care (Wanless)	'Traditional' literature review: Ford and England (2000)
External IPPR review of partnerships; King's Fund review of social care (Wanless)		Rapid review: Butler et al (2004)
		Scoping review *Service Delivery and Organisation*
		Systematic review Hasluck (2000)
		Meta-analysis

review team draws on departmental staff, it is headed by – and in the name of – an 'outsider', for example, the Lyons inquiry into local government, the Wanless review on health (Wanless, 2002), and the Barker review of housing supply, of which Toynbee and Walker (2005) wrote, 'it will rank as one of the principal state papers of the Blair era' (p 134). Like Royal Commissions, these are also generally protracted inquiries that usually produce a series of recommendations to which the government makes a formal response.

A different type of 'external' review is one set up by an external body, for example, the IPPR Commission on PPPs (IPPR, 2001), the Fabian Society Commission on Taxation (Fabian Society Commission on Taxation and Citizenship, 2004) and the King's Fund report on social care (Wanless, 2006).

Turning to internal reviews, the PMSU (2002a) produced *Health strategy review. Analytical report*. The June 2002 report focused on 'situation analysis' and was part of a wider piece of work that also included implications of context for supply-side design; organisational effectiveness; audit and recommendations for change; organisation philosophy and future vision; and summary of recommendations. The situation analysis describes the context against which supply-side effectiveness and organisation must be assessed, and analyses the trends shaping that context, and the challenges the UK's health system faces. It was composed of five sections on: (1) health outcomes – trends and drivers; (2) demand – past and future; (3) Britain's key problem – capacity; (4) potential efficiency improvement; (5) and capacity, growth and efficiency improvement – an integrated challenge. The overall message is that while Britain's health outcomes will continue to improve, healthcare demands will continue to increase, with only limited potential to mitigate that increase by focusing instead on public health initiatives. Continued increases in demand will need to be satisfied, in line with Wanless's forecasts. Given this context, Britain's key problem is a shortage of medical system capacity. Overcoming that capacity shortage requires both efficiency improvement and capacity increases. Finally, the key priority for the NHS is to implement an integrated capacity gap-closing plan that is likely to take five to eight years at least.

In early 2006, the Cabinet Office initiated a rolling programme of Capability Reviews on government departments along the lines of those that have been conducted for a number of years by departments on their non-departmental public bodies. These examine each department's capability to meet their future challenges. The review teams have been drawn from the private sector, the wider public sector and board-level members of other government departments. The Prime Minister declared that 'Capability Reviews mark a watershed in the history of British public administration. For the first time, government departments have been publicly assessed on how well placed they are to meet the demands of the future' (Capability Reviews Team, 2006a, p 1). Although some 'common themes' are set out, the document appears to be a strange mix of expenditure savings and reduction of posts on the one hand, and changes at director level to strengthen leadership on the other. The document is written in obscure jargon, going against one of its main themes of public and stakeholder engagement. The language is guarded, for example, 'The Home Office's problems are well known and documented' (Capability Reviews Team, 2006a, p 25), in contrast to Home Secretary Dr John Reid's pithy comment describing his department as 'not fit for purpose'. Moreover, it is difficult to see beyond the mix of generalities, banalities and specifics exactly how the reviews will result in departments being run any better. Finally, events may quickly overtake the reviews. For example, the Home Office Capability Review, published in July 2006 (Capability Reviews Team, 2006e), set out a 'reform action plan' (p 5) arguing that 'Governance needs to be strengthened to enable the Home Office to operate as a single entity with a specific culture' (p 15). However, early in 2007 the Home Secretary John Reid announced a rather different 'emergent' and opposite strategy of breaking the Home Office into two separate departments.

Other reviews draw extensively on the views of external stakeholders (see Chapter Six, this volume). For example, the National Institute for Clinical Excellence (NICE) is reviewing coronary artery stents. It lists 'stakeholders' who are divided into 'consultees' (such as manufacturers/sponsors; patient/carer groups; professional groups; and 'others') and 'commentators' (with no right of appeal). The provisional schedule involved consultation on draft scope by stakeholders (January 2005), an information meeting for consultees (March 2005), a closing date for invited submissions (July 2005) and three appraisal committee meetings (in February, March and July 2006), with an expected date of review by October 2006 (www.nice.org.uk/page.aspx?o=239915). Similarly, the Department of Health is undertaking a project to review NHS implementation of the guidance on safeguarding children in whom illness is induced or fabricated. As part of the review the Department of Health is keen to hear the views of all staff working with children to find out what can be learnt from their experience and views of the guidance and any issues it raises (www.library.nhs.uk/childhealth/ViewResource.aspx?resID=155598). Both these examples, in that they include the views of producers and consumers, initiate debates involving the place of 'peer review' and 'personal experience' in the hierarchy of evidence, and of getting beyond the views of the 'usual suspects' (see, for example, Harrison, 1998; Davies et al, 2000a; Taylor, 2005).

As Table 8.1 shows, many different styles of review exist. Chapter 2 of *The magenta book* (PMSU, 2003; www.gsr.gov.uk/professional_guidance/magenta_book/index.asp) examines 'what do we already know'. It states that 'an essential first step in planning a policy evaluation is to determine what is already known about the topic in question'. It notes that two common methods of synthesising research evidence are narrative reviews and vote-counting reviews. Major limitations of the 'traditional literature review' or narrative review are that they almost always involve selection and/or publication bias, and do not involve a systematic, rigorous, transparent and exhaustive search of all the literature. Vote-counting reviews attempt to accumulate the results of a collection of relevant studies by counting the direction and significance of results. However, they have problems of treating studies of unequal quality equally, and of ignoring contextual factors. For these reasons, *The magenta book* tends to favour systematic reviews and meta–analysis. Systematic reviews (see Chapter Five, this volume) are seen to be more rigorous, with explicit and transparent inclusion and comparability criteria. Meta-analysis is a type of systematic review that aggregates the findings of individual studies. However, given the need for quick information, rapid review or rapid evidence assessment is a tool for getting on top of the available evidence on a policy issue, as comprehensively as possible, within the constraints of a given timetable, typically within three months. Rapid evidence assessment tools are less comprehensive than systematic reviews, and ideally should be further developed into a full-blown systematic review. In this case, the rapid evidence assessment is better referred to as an interim evidence assessment (www.gsr.gov.uk/new_research/archive/rae. asp; PMSU, 2003, chapter 2, pp 17-19; see also Butler et al, 2005).

This bland description disguises the protracted and bitter 'paradigm wars' fought over gathering evidence (see Davies et al, 2000a; PMSU, 2003, chapter 2; Becker and Bryman, 2004; Wallace et al, 2004, 2006). This is not the place to open a new front, but it should be noted that review evidence for government comes in a variety of types such as the traditional literature review (Ford and England, 2000), rapid review (Butler et al, 2005), systematic review (Hasluck, 2000), and meta-analysis. Wallace et al (2006) note that people understand the terms to mean different things, and that the field lacks an agreed vocabulary to facilitate discussion of the development of the methods. Boaz and Pawson (2005) compare 'five journeys' on 'the perilous road from evidence to policy' that are termed 'meta-analysis'; 'phenomenological review'; 'evidence nugget'; 'literature review'; and 'synthesis'. They note a propensity for delivering unequivocal policy verdicts on the basis of ambiguous evidence (for which the media have recently coined the term 'dodgy dossiers'). Even more disconcertingly, the five reviews head off on different judgemental tangents, one set of recommendations appearing to gainsay the next.

Current state of review

This section considers three main issues at a fairly speculative level. First, to what extent has the volume and type of review changed as part of New Labour's 'modern' policy making? Second, are there differences in the effectiveness of the different types of review? Third, are there differences in the impact of the different types of review?

Dorey (2005) points out that the use of task forces, working groups and ad hoc advisory groups, while not new, has massively expanded under the Blair government. During its first 18 months, 295 task forces and ad hoc advisory groups were created (Barker et al, 1999). They were concerned either 'to investigate and recommend new policies and practices or, in some cases, practical means of implementing policies on which Labour had already settled' (Barker et al, 1999). In addition to the cynical response that setting up bodies indicates 'doing something' (see Harold Wilson's phrase about Royal Commissions, above), Dorey (2005) suggests three rather more charitable interpretations, each of which is reflected in *Professional policy making for the twenty-first century*: achieving a more inclusive approach to politics (chapter 6); enhancing expertise by involving experts in 'evidence-based policy making' (chapter 5); and tackling 'wicked issues' through 'joined-up government' (chapter 7).

With regard to New Labour's social policy, Timmins (2001) states that 'A whole host of welfare state reviews had been set up from Martin Taylor's report on the Modernisation of Britain's Tax and Benefits System, to work on the New Deal, a pensions review, the comprehensive spending reviews, a planned green paper from [Frank] Field on welfare reform, the work of the Social Exclusion Unit, a promised Royal Commission on long-term care, and much else. It was far from clear who was talking to whom, and who, if anyone, was in control' (p 568).

As Table 8.4 suggests, the volume and diversity of reviews under New Labour is very impressive. It is difficult to give clear views on the type of review, except to say that recent Conservative and Labour governments have tended not to resort to Royal Commissions, and that there is increasing interest by government in the relatively new types of rapid review, systematic review and meta-analysis.

Turning to the second issue of effectiveness, it is clear that different reviews have different mixes of advantages and disadvantages. Judicial reviews are normally very comprehensive, but this has the knock-on disadvantage that by the time

Table 8.4: Effectiveness of review

Who?	How?
Government internal + focused – high impact?	Judicial or legal + can be comprehensive – outcomes often vary with chair's relationship with the 'sponsor'
Government external + focused + independent? – variable impact	'Traditional' literature review – biased? – not comprehensive?
External + independence? – limited influence?	Rapid review + rapid – not comprehensive
	Scoping review + fairly rapid – not comprehensive
	Systematic review + comprehensive – method disputed
	Meta-analysis + comprehensive – method disputed

they report their sponsoring Secretary of State may have moved on (or even be out of government). A powerful example of the strength of continuity was the judge Sir William McPherson's inquiry into the death of Stephen Lawrence, set up by Home Secretary Jack Straw, who was still in that position when the inquiry reported, which may explain why so many of its recommendations were accepted by the government. The when question is not considered in Table 8.4, as both review for and review of policy are suitable for different purposes (see, for example, Case studies 8.1 and 8.2).

Sulitzeanu-Kenan (2006) argues that public inquiries tend to be judged on outcomes (giving the 'right' answer) rather than on process, pointing to the 'perceptual U-turn' following the report of the Hutton inquiry into the death of Dr David Kelly, transforming Hutton from a 'fearless forensic investigator' into 'an establishment lackey' (see also Cohen, 2003). Moreover, Sampson (2005) claims that the very fact that the Prime Minister needed to turn to a senior judge to reassure the public and unearth the truth indicated the loss of trust in both government and Parliament, whose Select Committees had failed to uncover the key facts (Cohen, 2003). There have been some significant changes in the operation of departmental Select Committees under New Labour, and Dorey (2005) considers that departmental Select Committees may have played a part in encouraging a recent trend both to more 'rational' policy making, and in evidence-based policy making. We noted above the 'contested and antagonistic' views on different styles of reviewing evidence (Wallace et al, 2006, p 300; see also the journal *Evidence and Policy*).

The final issue of impact is perhaps the most problematic. It is difficult to trace the causal chains or the 'smoking gun'. For example, is the health policy of New Labour more attributable to the internal health strategic review or the Wanless reports? Are health inequalities targets attributable to the Acheson Committee, given that the 1998 Green Paper on public health dismissed them, but they were included in the 1999 White Paper? Moreover, impact may be seen only in the long term, and it is unlikely that the legislative changes prompted by the Pensions Commission (2006) will be the last word on the subject.

Paxman (2003) considers that departmental Select Committees 'have produced a number of coruscating reports, in which the incompetence, inadequacies and indolence of government have been laid bare' (p 186), but Dorey (2005) comments that the impact of Parliamentary Committees is not clear. As they tend to examine the implementation and impact of policy after its enactment, they cannot prevent 'policy disasters', but by examining the causes and origins, may reduce the likelihood of them in future. They are increasingly engaged in 'pre-legislative scrutiny' where they conduct inquiries into draft Bills or White Papers. He continues that Select Committees normally contribute only to relatively modest or technical policy changes. However, in 2002 Stephen Byers resigned as Secretary of State for Transport following serious criticism of the government's transport policies and strategy by the Transport Select Committee; and the issue of foreign national prisoners simply being released at the end of their custodial sentences rather than being considered for deportation – as recommended for many of them when they were sentenced – was originally raised by the Public Accounts Committee and ultimately led to the resignation of Home Secretary Charles Clarke. The Health Committee (2007) considers that it makes an impact in a variety of ways: affecting policy, changing policy during an inquiry, acting as a forum where major health issues are aired, and acting as a way of publishing important information. It claims that its report into smoking in public places 'seems to have played a part in the House's decision to amend the Health Bill and introduce a comprehensive smoking ban' (p 18).

A case study of the review of the child support system is considered in Case study 8.3. In our terms, this is a government external review, a review *of* policy and probably a mix of 'judicial' (witnesses) and narrative review.

Case study 8.3: Review of the child support system

In February 2006 the Secretary of State for Work and Pensions asked Sir David Henshaw to undertake a fundamental review of the child support system. In his report Henshaw (2006) stated that the current child support system was failing to deliver, for children, parents and the taxpayer, and that this failure was the result of policy and operational issues. He argued that the role of the state should be very different, focusing on a smaller number of more difficult cases, that the Child Support Agency was not capable of the radical shift in business model, culture and efficiency required to deliver this new role and that a new organisation should be set up.

The government's response was set out in a statement by the Secretary of State for Work and Pensions in July 2006. It agreed that the delivery of child support required a fresh start, but stated that this document marked the first stage in the government's response, setting out a series of questions around the broad principles of the proposed system, and inviting views. The government was to publish a White Paper with detailed proposals in autumn 2006 (issued in December 2006), with the aim of seeing aspects of the new system in place from 2008.

It is pertinent to consider three sets of issues on the Henshaw report: firstly, one of Henshaw's recommendations was to introduce strong new sanctions, including the withdrawal of passports, to ensure that parents comply with their financial obligations to their children. The government's response stated that it would bring forward legislation to allow this, but 'we think we must go further' (DWP, 2006, p 10). The government had its own views and stronger sanctions were clearly a policy option; this raises questions about the added value of an independent review.

Secondly, the view that the Child Support Agency was failing was hardly a new one, and the agency had been criticised almost from its foundation. Previous reforms had largely failed, with the National Audit Office (2006c)

---

claiming that the reforms of 2003 had failed to bring about significant improvements. The government admitted that the recent Operational Improvement Plan did not go to the heart of the current problems. The child support system had been the focus of substantial 'review' (with some of the reports cited in the text). If previous 'review' had failed to deliver the goods, why should this one succeed?

Thirdly, neither the Henshaw report nor the government's response appears to take seriously the problems of the conflicting requirements of different stakeholders. The child support system has multiple objectives for different stakeholders and the best ways of delivering for some stakeholders may be in conflict with the requirements of others. At root, taxpayers, the caring parent (usually mothers) and different classes of absent parents (usually fathers) have different aims. The Child Support Agency was accused of going for 'easy wins' by 'hounding decent fathers' who were prepared to contribute towards their children and largely ignoring the 'difficult cases' of fathers who wished to evade all financial responsibility. There is also the problem of the 'can't pay' against 'won't pay' cases. Although Henshaw clearly understands these issues, and says that 'the state should only get involved when parents cannot come to agreement themselves, or when one party tries to evade their responsibilities' (Henshaw, 2005, p 5), there is no explicit focus on the tensions.

Conclusions

It is difficult to specify what would be the 'proper' place of 'review' in the policy process, or to evaluate what its effects may have been. As we have seen, there are a large variety of types of review, and some of them blend into other competencies. The lowest common denominator of many of the competencies is 'evidence'. As the Cabinet Office (1999) puts it, the raw ingredient of evidence is information. Good quality policy making depends on high quality information, derived from a variety of sources – expert knowledge; existing domestic and international evidence; existing statistics; stakeholder consultation; evaluation of previous policies; new evidence; or secondary sources. There is a tendency to think of evidence as something that is only generated by major pieces of research. In any policy area there is a great deal of critical evidence held as often untapped operational data and in the minds of both frontline staff in departments, agencies and local authorities and those to whom the policy is directed.

Similarly, as Davies et al (2000a) point out, the definition of 'evidence' varies, including at its widest 'almost any conscious assembly of facts' (p 3), which excludes anecdotes, but includes 'output from more formal and systematic enquiries, generated by government departments, research institutes, universities, charitable foundations, consultancy organisations, and a variety of agencies and intermediaries such as the Audit Commission, or Office for Standards in Education [Ofsted]' (p 3).

However, as Chapter Five, this volume, shows, 'evidence' can be problematic. The Prime Minister considered evidence to be 'extensive, detailed and authoritative', while it consisted of two articles and a PhD thesis from the internet, subsequently termed the 'dodgy dossier' (Sampson, 2005, pp 157-8).

Professional policy making for the twenty-first century recognises some problems in reviewing evidence. First, while there is plenty of evidence available in areas such as education, social services and criminal justice, the coverage is patchy and there is little agreement among the research community about the appropriateness of particular methodologies or how research evidence should be used to inform policy and practice. Second, there is a need to improve the accessibility of research evidence (Cabinet Office, 1999). The document notes that moves are already under way to address the 'user friendliness' of the evidence base, giving examples of the national Electronic Library for Health, the Economic and Social Research Council (ESRC) Centre for Evidence-based Policy, the Cochrane Collaboration in health and the Campbell Collaboration in education (see also Davies et al, 2000a; Sanderson, 2002; Becker and Bryman, 2004; Wallace et al, 2004). It stresses the importance of creating a 'knowledge pool', but passes over the problem of stocking the pool and the methods of fishing from it.

There will be much material for future historians to review in the way that current historians examine government Blue Books. These have grown significantly not simply in volume but also in variety. Reviews come in all shapes and sizes, and formats (although some reviews have mysteriously disappeared; see Powell, 2002).

Almost a decade on from *Professional policy making for the twenty-first century*, what conclusions can we draw about the role and status of 'reviews' in relation to policy making?

- A basic problem concerns the validity and reliability of review. It is not as simple as reviewing the evidence to discover 'the answer' as this depends on what questions are posed, who carries out the review, and which methods they use. Put simply, would different answers – and so recommendations – have been produced if, say, Smith had been asked to write the review on housing rather than Barker, or if Jones had been invited to conduct the Kelly inquiry rather than Hutton?
- It is possible that politicians may not like the answer that is found. Governments have a wide variety of tactics for ignoring uncomfortable research findings (best illustrated, albeit light-heartedly, in the TV series 'Yes, Minister'). Two possible outcomes are being ignored and being rendered irrelevant – powers of research: 0; Realpolitik: 2 (Becker and Bryman, 2004). Cynics believe that evidence may be used selectively in order to reach the preferred answer and any conflicting evidence discarded. In other words, evidence-based policy may be used more for support than for illumination. For example, David Blunkett

argued in 2000 that 'social science should be at the heart of policy making' but was ready to reject any unpalatable social science evidence:'... no-one with the slightest commonsense could take seriously suggestions by Durham University researchers that homework is bad for you' (quoted in Davies et al, 2000a, pp 13, 23). This suggests that the status and findings of reviews may depend on the willingness of politicians to accept them.

• All of this adds up to the 'big question' of the counterfactual – how would government have been different without review? There are claims that 'old' reviews led to changes. Historians may point to the impact of the Royal Commission on the Poor Laws of 1832 that led to the 1834 Poor Law Amendment Act. However, the Royal Commission on the Poor Laws of 1905-09, with its majority and minority reports, led to little change in the short term, but the minority report is said to have mapped out the form of the classic welfare state of the 1940s. Moreover, there must be many instances where review produced little effect in the short or long term, and even where the review led to change (such as the abolition of the Child Support Agency), it may not have needed a review to come to that conclusion. It is likely that (to adapt the words of the late Prime Minister, Harold Macmillan), it continues to be 'events' rather than reviews that shape policy (for example, Rawnsley, 2001; Cohen, 2003).

Further reading

Different styles of review are covered in this chapter. Contrast, for example:

IPPR (Institute for Public Policy Research) (2001) *Building better partnerships*, London: IPPR.

Royal Commission on Long-term Care (1999) *With respect to old age: Long-term care: Rights and responsibilities* (Sutherland Report), London: The Stationery Office.

PMSU (Prime Minister's Strategy Unit) (2002a) *Health strategy review. Analytical report*, London: PMSU.

An academic view of policy making is given in:

Dorey, P. (2005) *Policy making in Britain*, London: Sage Publications,

while entertaining accounts can be found in texts by politicians, advisers and commentators, with a good example being:

Rawnsley, A. (2001) *Servants of the people*, Harmondsworth: Penguin.

Useful websites

The most useful website is a search engine to find the required reviews (see Table 8.1)!

www.gsr.gov.uk/professional_guidance/magenta_book/index.asp (chapter 2) of *The magenta book* gives useful 'official' guidance on reviews.

www.policyhub.gov.uk/better_policy_making/review.asp gives access to relevant documents and a 'Policy Library'.

www.parliament.uk can be used to find full text versions of reports by Select Committees.

Websites of government departments (for example, www.hmtreasury.gov.uk) can be used to find reviews commissioned by departments.

NINE

Policy evaluation

Robert Walker and Sue Duncan

This chapter examines the complex interplay between evaluation and policy and the growing prominence of public sector policy evaluation. It discusses:

- how policy evaluation has developed and become more complex;
- how evaluation works in a political environment and the challenges this poses for evaluators;
- current thinking in policy evaluation; and
- how the government uses evaluation results to inform the policy process.

It seems inevitable that policy makers would ask whether a policy has worked, is working or would work if implemented. A recognition of the value of policy appraisal and evaluation is not new (HM Treasury, 1988) yet, until comparatively recently, such questions were not routinely asked by policy makers in Britain and it is only within the past decade that procedures have been formalised and promulgated to help answer them. Within central government, processes for ensuring that the cost implications of policies are evaluated pre-implementation – policy appraisal – are well established, guided by the Treasury *Green Book* (HM Treasury, 1997, 2003), but concern with the behavioural and attitudinal drivers of policy – how consumers will respond and how policies are affected by those responsible for delivery – is less well established. There is now a recognition that implementation can be an important factor in achieving policy intent (Cabinet Office, 2002b). The growth in use of 'policy experiments' (Cabinet Office, 2003), where policies are tested before national roll-out, reflects, among other things, an acknowledgement that attention to the drivers of policy success at the design phase can pay dividends in helping to ensure that policy intent is achieved. In recent years, the emphasis on performance measurement overseen by HM Treasury and the Prime Minister's Delivery Unit has acted as a key driver in encouraging policy evaluation.

A moment's thought reveals that policy evaluation is not a necessary concomitant of a democratic system, especially an adversarial one such as exists in Britain. Politics is a battle for minds that is won by ideas and driven by ideology and the ballot box. Hence policies have not only to 'work', but also to be seen to work; public opinion is a key ingredient in the policy process. If politicians are ideologically committed to a policy, they may be less amenable to the 'wait and see' logic inherent in prospective evaluation. This is particularly so when policies have been publicly endorsed by inclusion in a successful political manifesto. Moreover, the ideological presumption that drives democracy is that one party's ideas and policies are better than another's. In this context, evaluation outcomes can be politically difficult to handle and evidence that a policy does not work in terms of meeting its policy objectives can be unwelcome. This really reflects that, in a political environment, the notion of policy success is more complex than 'what works' in objective terms; what works in terms of supporting political ideology may be equally important. This dilemma is inherent in the relationship between policy and evaluation and to ignore it is to oversimplify the process. Expressed simply, politicians have a mandate to govern and ultimately to decide policy direction. This dilemma has been clearly articulated by politicians yet is underemphasised in the notion of 'evidence-based' policy making. Where policies are not driven by ideology, they are sensitive to wider influences, not least public opinion and media reaction.

The generally accepted view is that the increase in policy evaluation by successive British governments was a consequence of the advance of the school of new public management that took hold in the early 1990s, the notion that the ideas and techniques of business could be applied to good effect in the public sector (Pollitt, 1996; Stewart, 1996). The reality is a little more complex in that changes had already occurred that made government more open to adopting new approaches. Consensus about the benevolent role of government had broken down by the late 1970s and concerns about the level of public expenditure and its impact on international competitiveness had been rife since at least the 1976 Sterling Crisis and the intervention of the International Monetary Fund. Likewise, the change from volume to cash planning of public expenditure in 1982-83 shifted attention away from policy demand towards a focus on the cost of policies and their cost-effectiveness.

There were also early examples of policy evaluation that yielded unanticipated benefits. The Thatcher government, for example, instigated the first formal evaluation of a national social security scheme, Supplementary Benefit, introduced in 1980 (Berthoud, 1984). This happened to report into an unexpected review of social security triggered by the press exposing the administrative failings of another new scheme, Housing Benefit. The results were used to justify and inform a radical redesign of the complete benefit system (DHSS, 1985; Walker, 2000).

The emphasis given to policy evaluation witnessed a step-change with the 1997 election of a New Labour government with a public commitment to evidence-based policy making (Davies et al, 2000a), although, recognising wider influences, commentators have reframed the concept as 'evidence-informed' or 'evidence-inspired' policy making (Duncan, 2005; Levitt and Solesbury, 2005; Duncan and Harrop, 2006). Existing procedures advocated by the Treasury for the appraisal of policy were systematised in the publication in 1997 of the so-called *Green Book* (HM Treasury, 1997). This, in its latest reincarnation, presents a sequential model of policy making under the acronym, ROAMEF (Rationale, Objectives, Appraisal, Monitoring, Evaluation and Feedback). This differentiates between appraisal (the 'assessment of whether a proposal is worthwhile'), evaluation ('similar in technique to appraisal, although it obviously uses historic [actual or estimated] rather than forecast data, and takes place after the event'), and monitoring (HM Treasury, 2003, pp 3-5). However, this rather narrow interpretation of evaluation already looks anachronistic alongside New Labour's desire to pilot policies ahead of full implementation and the rubric developed elsewhere within the Whitehall 'village' following the 1999 White Paper, *Modernising government* (Cabinet Office, 1999). *Professional policy making for the twenty-first century* (Cabinet Office Strategic Policy Making Team, 1999) and *Better policy making* (Bullock et al, 2001) both place evaluation at the heart of policy making rather than at the end, the former arguing that:

> ... new policies must have evaluation of their effectiveness built into them from the start; established policies must be reviewed regularly to ensure that they are still delivering the desired outcome; and the lessons learned from evaluation must be available and accessible to other policy makers. (Cabinet Office Strategic Policy Making Team, 1999, para 10.1)

It is this more ambitious conceptualisation of evaluation and its role that provides the stimulus for this chapter. What does it mean in theory and practice? Is it rhetoric rather than reality and, if the former, is it reasonable to expect that reality can be forged from the rhetoric?

Rationale and goals for evaluation

The dynamic foundation for the current emphasis on evaluation, and evidence-informed policy more generally, is provided by former Prime Minister Tony Blair's assertion that what counts in third way politics is what works (Powell, 1999). Signalled in this approach is the precedence given to rational policy making, effectiveness and practicality over ideology. Even though policy making under successive Blair governments has always continued to be influenced by politics and presentation, and often by expediency (Ludlam, 2000), the scaffolding for evidence-based policy making has been assembled, if not the full architecture. Hence, *Professional policy making for the twenty-first century* (Cabinet Office Strategic Policy Making Team, 1999, para 7.1) emphasises that 'the raw ingredient of evidence is information', but that this, and the policy process as a whole, needs to be understood in context. Thus, policy makers are encouraged to set out the desired policy outcomes and to consider the most effective outputs for achieving such outcomes. But they are also urged to ask what evidence is available, relevant and useful, what evaluation systems and performance targets are needed, and even whether there are different solutions that should be tested.

The 1999 document asserts that evaluation should be systematic, analytical, study actual effects and judge success; as a salutary aside, it reminds readers that this was often not the case (Cabinet Office Strategic Policy Making Team, 1999). It also sets out the purpose or 'key objectives' of evaluation. Evaluation should aim to 'improve decision making, help resource allocation, enhance accountability' and 'bring organisational learning' (para 10.1). It also envisages that evidence includes, among other things, expert knowledge, stakeholder views and knowledge gained from previous policy experience as well as formal policy evaluation.

This formulation is important in that it characterises policy evaluation as a process rather than as an event. While evaluation aims to establish whether a policy works, it has a broader, more sustained purpose that can be beneficial even if the results of the evaluation itself are inconclusive. It requires policy makers to be specific about the objectives of policy, to express them in ways amenable to measurement and, ideally, to assign objectives different priorities (since the practical methodology of evaluation makes it virtually impossible to assess multiple outcomes with equal precision; Orr, 1998; Walker, 2001). Evaluation demands that policy makers articulate a theory of change by which it is anticipated that the policy will affect individual and/or institutional behaviour so as to produce the desired outcome. Similarly it requires policy makers to give thought to the possible unintended consequences of policy so that appropriate evidence may be sought to identify them.

As well as enhancing policy making, evaluation can contribute to effective resource allocation. First, it may allow policy makers to choose between competing alternatives that are shown to be differentially effective. In making such choices, policy makers will be wise to not just focus on average impacts. In addition, they should consider the relative size of the groups that exhibit the most positive effects, compared to those for whom the effect is less marked, in order to assess how best the policy intervention should be targeted.

Second, the best policy evaluations include a cost–benefit analysis that indicates whether benefits exceed costs, judged from different perspectives: typically government's, society's and those of the service user. Determining the true cost of an intervention is exceedingly difficult, especially if it is delivered by non-public agencies; it is necessary to separate set-up from running costs and to partial out additional costs associated with special one-off implementation, piloting and monitoring. In the case of 'policy experiments' it is also essential to consider the costs and savings associated in scaling up from a demonstration scale pilot to full (often national) implementation, all of which requires the foresight to place cost monitoring systems in place right from the start of evaluation. Moreover, a policy may appear to perform very differently according to perspective: the New Deal for Disabled People brings marked savings to government, notably through benefit savings, but leaves the average participant only marginally if at all better off (Greenberg and Davis, 2007). Nevertheless, it is always wise to temper enthusiasm about a policy's impact with knowledge as to its cost.

Third, evaluation results may be used to influence strategic resource allocation decisions quite distant from particular interventions. HM Treasury is increasingly insisting that government departments support their claims for sustained or increased expenditure with evidence of the effectiveness of their programmes. Strong evaluation evidence may therefore give one department a competitive edge over another, resulting in substantial shifts in programme funding between departments. The analytical work conducted to inform the 2007 Comprehensive Spending Review illustrates this point; it includes an examination of key long-term trends and challenges and a review of evidence on cross-cutting policy issues where innovative policy responses and coordination across departmental boundaries will be required; it also makes explicit the evidence that supports spending priorities (HM Treasury, 2006).

Evaluation also makes real the prospect of both internal and public accountability since, without the clear statement of objectives and evidence to measure outcomes against target objectives, it is impossible to assess whether policy is effective, whether achievements match political rhetoric, and whether resources have been used wisely. In 1998 the government conducted a Comprehensive Spending Review that examined the resources allocated to each area of spending and, for the first time, decided on and published the service improvements and reforms required in return for resources allocated to the department's spending programmes (HM Treasury, 1998). These requirements are set out in Public Service Agreements (PSAs) for every central government department. PSAs are three-year agreements negotiated between departments and HM Treasury during the Spending Review process. Each PSA sets out a department's high-level aim, priority objectives and key outcome-based performance targets. PSAs are supported by Technical Notes that set out how performance against PSA targets will be measured; the Notes set down baselines and set out clearly how success will be assessed and describe the data sources that will be used. Service Delivery Agreements (SDAs) for each government department were published for the first time in autumn 2000 (HM Treasury, 2000). SDAs set out how a department would deliver its PSA targets but were abolished in 2003 as part of a more integrated approach to targets and other controls (HM Treasury and Cabinet Office, 2004). Policy evaluation is seen as playing a clear role in the PSA process, and departments are expected to assess the evidence base underpinning departmental delivery of PSA objectives and to fill 'evidence gaps' using research, evaluation and analysis.

So, the guidance emphasises the scope for institutional learning arising from systematic policy evaluation. This potential is not bounded by the evaluation of specific interventions but embraces the possibility of systemic learning both at the level of implementation and policy making. The detailed understanding of how policy is delivered and is affected by the response of staff, management and end users derived from comprehensive evaluation of particular interventions can often be fruitfully applied, with suitable discounting, to other programmes in different settings. Likewise, the formal articulation of goals and mechanisms demanded by formal evaluation offers a rigorous model for policy making in general.

Types of evaluation

While *Professional policy making for the twenty-first century* adopted a broader definition of evaluation than *The Green Book*, it derived most of its examples of best practice from evaluations of individual policies and programmes. *The magenta book* (PMSU, 2003), comprising 'guidance notes for policy evaluators and analysts, and people who use and commission policy evaluation' (p 2), was part-published (electronically, and with the intention of adding further chapters) in 2003 to complement *The Green Book*. It is necessarily more specific than either *Professional policy making* or *The Green Book*, differentiating different kinds of evaluation, while also being wide-ranging in terms of expanding the number of evaluative questions addressed. What is important is that evaluation tools suit the task in hand, rather than being dictated by other concerns. One means of categorising the various forms of evaluation is by differentiating the nature and timing of the evaluative question being asked (Table 9.1). At risk of oversimplification there are two basic questions that evaluation seeks to answer. One is descriptive: 'Does the policy work?'. The other, 'Why?', is analytic, and could also be formulated as 'How does the policy work?', or, if it does not, 'How come the policy does not work?'. Evaluations that address the first question are variously termed 'summative', 'programme' or 'impact' evaluations and are typically quantitative (Orr, 1998; Greenberg and Schroder, 2004). Those that focus on the second question are frequently called 'formative' evaluations and are often qualitative (Pawson and Tilley, 1997; Yanow, 1999; Patton, 2002). There is, however, a plethora of different terms used to describe formative evaluation that reflect subtly, and sometimes radically, different ontological positions.

Table 9.1 serves to illustrate the complex relationship between policy and evaluation and underlines the role of evaluation at different stages in the policy process, from policy development, through implementation, to review. It also emphasises the need for clarity about the question being asked. The simple assertion 'what counts is what works' belies the complexity of the process. In recent years, many of the largest policy evaluations reflect this complexity and have sought to combine elements of summative and formative evaluation (Gibson and Duncan, 2002). This move represents an acknowledgement that the success or otherwise of a policy depends as much on the processes of implementation and delivery as on the design of the policy itself. Knowing how these contribute to a policy's success is essential if the outcome is to be replicated when the policy moves to full implementation (Ritchie and Lewis, 2003).

Programme evaluation

Addressing the question 'will a policy work?' usually involves conducting a policy experiment or programme evaluation, the terminology in common use until recently (Greenberg and Schroder, 2004). Conceptually policy experiments are the most straightforward form of evaluation. Certain people are subjected to a

Table 9.1: Questions of evaluation

Time perspective	Evaluation question	Illustrative evaluation method(s)	Counterpart formative evaluation question	Illustrative formative evaluation approaches
Extensive past	What worked?	Meta-analysis Systematic review	How did it work?	Systematic review
Past	Did the policy work?	Retrospective evaluation	How did it work/not work?	Retrospective interviews Participative judgement (Connoisseurship studies) Retrospective case study
Present	Is this policy working?	Monitoring • Interrupted time series • Natural experiments	How is it working/not working?	Process studies Implementation evaluation Ethnography
Present to future	Is there a problem?	Basic research Policy analysis	What is the problem?	Basic research Rapid reconnaissance
Close future	Can we make this policy work?	Prototypes Micro-simulation	How can we make this policy work?	Theory of change Participative research Action research
Future	Will this policy work?	Programme evaluation (impact or summative evaluation) • Random assignment • Matched designs • Cohort designs • Statistical controls	How will it work/not work?	Theory of change Laboratory evaluation
Expansive future	What policy would work?	Prospective evaluation • Micro-simulation • Laboratory experimentation • Gaming	How would it work?	Laboratory evaluation Delphi consultation Gaming

Source: Adapted from Walker (2004)

policy intervention (the programme group) while others are not (the control group), and the outcome is observed for both groups. The control group defines the counterfactual, the situation that would have obtained had the policy to be evaluated not been introduced. Any difference in outcomes established between the two groups provides a measure of the impact of the policy. Without a counterfactual, it is possible only to determine what happens to people subjected to the intervention being evaluated, not to gauge the extent to which what happens is a direct consequence of the policy intervention itself.

Evaluators regularly debate the various methods of defining action and control samples and it is widely accepted that technically the best method is to randomly allocate people to 'action' or 'control' groups, because it gives the clearest picture of policy impact. It guarantees that any initial differences between the two groups are random and that differences in the outcomes for the two groups can confidently be attributed to the effects of the policy since all other changes will randomly influence both groups. Randomisation thereby separates out the impact of a policy with minimum bias and maximum precision. However, this method is rarely used in government policy evaluation with a notable exception being the Employment, Retention and Advancement Demonstration that sought, using random allocation of 16,000 benefit recipients, to assess the impact of various measures to encourage people to gain and keep employment (Morris et al, 2004; Hall et al, 2005). The more usual method in the UK is the use of matched 'action' and 'control' areas, despite the technical problems of matching and the difficulty of accurately measuring policy impact. A key reason for this is concern by politicians and others about the morality and/or political acceptability of selectively allowing access to resources perceived as valuable (Bottomley and Walker, 1996; Stafford et al, 2002). Of course, matched area designs could be criticised for the same reason but have tended to be regarded as less unacceptable. Yet again, this illustrates the importance of understanding the political context within which policy evaluation occurs. But 'acceptability' of random allocation is only one problem with policy experiments. Other issues are discussed more fully elsewhere (Cabinet Office, 2003), but one obvious drawback is the time it takes to measure a true policy outcome, balanced against the political imperative to deliver quickly. A further consideration is the risk involved in setting up a high-profile policy experiment that by definition may not 'work'. For this reason, policy experiments have tended to concentrate on 'low-risk' policies in the sense that the idea has been tried elsewhere, as with the welfare-to-work programme, which draws heavily on US evaluation and Swedish experience (Cebulla et al, 2005), and/or the experiment is testing a modification of policy, rather than a radical departure.

For these reasons experiments hailed as policy pilots are more commonly tests of implementation methods, or are designed to 'fine-tune' policy. The key question is 'How can we make this policy work?'. Less emphasis is placed on measuring outcome and more on understanding the process of implementation. This 'prototype' approach has the advantage of speed in comparison with a true policy experiment, but, despite this, in Britain full policy implementation has often preceded the results of the prototype evaluation becoming available (Walker, 2001). It is interesting to further note the wide variety of terms adopted, including 'policy pilot', 'pathfinder', 'trailblazer' and 'pioneer' (Cabinet Office, 2003). Some of the more emotive terms suggest a concern with making an impact, as much as measuring the success of an experiment.

Case study 9.1: Education Maintenance Allowance (EMA): the complexity of the evaluation–policy relationship

The policy was based on research that indicated that 16-year-olds from low-income families were less likely to remain in education. The evaluation was a longitudinal cohort study with matched comparisons using propensity score matching.

The Department for Education and Skills (DfES) set up the EMA pilot to examine whether financial incentives could improve further education participation, retention, achievement and motivation of 16- to 19-year-olds and to explore the optimum level of allowance, who it should be paid to and to inform how it should be administered and delivered. The EMA pilot began in 1999 in 15 local education authorities and was later extended to 41 areas. It tested eight variants of the scheme. The pilots demonstrated improvements in participation and retention and indicated that payments to students rather than parents and higher bonuses were most successful. Transport variants were not successful but have been used to shape other DfES initiatives. It also showed that additional support and flexibility could benefit vulnerable young people and demonstrated the value of multi-agency working. Later results showed that support and guidance following the end of compulsory education were important to sustain the benefits of retention in post-16 education.

The integration of negative and positive findings into policy roll-out, which took place in 2004, make clear that for evaluation findings to be useful, research expertise needs to be combined with the experience and knowledge of policy makers and practitioners; evaluation rarely points in an unequivocal policy direction.

Monitoring and retrospective evaluation

Before 1997, most policy evaluation conducted in Britain was either undertaken retrospectively, asking 'Has the policy worked?', or took the form of monitoring and focused on whether the policy was working. In some cases, success was commonly measured against a pre-implementation baseline. A counterfactual was rarely defined since full implementation generally made this impractical, with, for example, removing the right to access a programme being likely to raise ethical and political concerns.

The methodologies employed in retrospective evaluations tend to be eclectic and adverse circumstances can stimulate creative designs (Huby and Dix, 1992; Thornton and Corden, 2002). Pluralistic approaches are often used in which the experiences and opinions of key actors in the policy implementation are collated and triangulated to reach an overall judgement on policy effectiveness. Personal interview surveys may be used to solicit the views of policy recipients, qualitative interviews conducted with administrators and other interest groups and observational techniques used at the point of service delivery. These accounts can provide irrefutable evidence about the efficiency or lack of efficiency of implementation and provide a sound basis for reform.

Monitoring and retrospective evaluation probably still account for most evaluative research undertaken in Britain, especially that by local government. This is partly because both form part of the normal process of policy audit, which seeks to establish who has received the service and at what cost, often by reference to administrative information. Retrospective evaluation may also be triggered by suspicion, often aroused by monitoring, that the policy is not working well. These modes of evaluation do not require the same level of institutional commitment to evidence-based policy making as programme evaluation. They are not, for example, located on the critical path from policy idea to policy introduction that demands policy makers rein back their enthusiasm for implementation to await the outcome of a lengthy evaluation.

The historic emphasis on monitoring and retrospective evaluation probably has its roots, at least in part, in the traditional organisation of the policy and analysis functions. Until relatively recently, policy making and analysis were seen as largely separate functions; 'policy makers' designed policy and social scientists, fulfilling different analytical functions, advised. This was reflected in their organisational separateness; policy makers were in 'policy divisions', while analysts tended to be brigaded together in 'analytical services divisions': this was symbolised in the language that referred to a 'customer–contractor' relationship, often referred to as 'the Rothschild Principle' (Rothschild Report, 1971). A string of reports, most notably *Adding it up* (Performance and Innovation Unit, 2000a), encouraged closer working between the two functions and, notably, a 'challenge' function for analysts. Current arrangements where analysts are more usually integrated, or at least co-located, with the policy function has facilitated the development of evaluation as an ongoing process rather than one that contributed at discrete stages. This role change is reflected in the wider Professional Skills for Government initiative that aims to ensure that civil servants are equipped with the skills to make use of the diverse range of resources at their disposal; 'analysis and use of evidence' is now regarded as a core competency for the whole senior civil service (Civil Service Management Board, 2005). Similarly Professional Skills for Government, among other things, takes the approach that all civil servants should be valued for their professional expertise, whatever it is.

Prospective and meta-evaluation

Prospective evaluation that looks to the future and meta-analysis that draws insight from the past lie adjacent in the policy cycle, when the challenge is to consider how to respond to a defined problem – prospective evaluation – and the sensible first step is to determine what worked well in similar settings in the past (and perhaps elsewhere) – meta-evaluation. These approaches play to the assertion that modern policy making should be both 'forward looking' and 'learn(s) lessons' (Cabinet Office Strategic Policy Making Team, 1999).

Most policy scoping exercises review past research although not necessarily with the comprehensiveness and rigour that is increasingly demanded of systematic reviews of medical interventions. There have been recent attempts made to establish 'knowledge pools' of evidence on past policies, as portended in *Professional policy making for the twenty-first century* (Cabinet Office Strategic Policy Making Team, 1999), most notably the EPPI-Centre (Evidence for Policy and Practice Information and Coordinating Centre), based at the Institute of Education, University of London, and funded to produce a number of systematic reviews for the Department for Education and Skills. But this systematic approach is still gathering momentum. Within the Government Social Research service, too, there is increased emphasis on the techniques of 'systematic review' (PMSU, 2003) and professional training reflects this (see also Chapter Five, this volume). Again, the lengthy process of full-blown systematic reviews can sit uneasily with the policy timetables; this has been addressed in government by the development of rapid evidence assessment techniques (Davies, 2004c; Butler et al, 2005). But formal statistical meta-analysis of policy evaluations is still relatively rare. This matters since meta-evaluation does more than summarise the existing evidence about what works; it offers insight into how policies work. Whereas a single programme evaluation will determine the cost-effectiveness of a particular policy, and associated formative (process) analyses will point to aspects of its delivery that may contribute to its effectiveness, meta-analysis can provide a quantitative estimate of the added value of each feature of a policy and its administration, both in isolation and in combination. Unlike a single evaluation, meta-analysis can also establish whether a particular policy would work as well in a different location or, indeed, whether the apparent success of a policy implementation is due in large measure to the idiosyncratic nature of its policy environment (Ashworth et al, 2005). The occasional report that covers several evaluations illustrates the value of synthesis (for example, Hasluck and Green, 2007).

Most prospective evaluation undertaken by and for the UK government, asking 'What policy would work?', is currently based on static micro-simulation models and, more recently, dynamic micro-simulation although variants of meta-evaluation and experimentation could be used (Brewer et al, 2001; Walker, 2004). Micro-simulation attempts to predict the likely impact of a policy change on individual people or families, aggregating the individual effects to provide estimates of the total impact (Klevmarken, 1997). It is particularly important to government because the introduction of a new policy must be underpinned by reasonably robust estimations of how much the policy would cost, the extent of take-up, and so on. However, success of micro-simulation depends on the quality of data and modelling, something that is surprisingly often forgotten. Moreover, the modelling is in turn dependent on prior understanding of the system being modelled and the appropriateness and specificity of underlying theory. Of critical importance is the validity of the behavioural assumptions embedded in the modelling that is often difficult to establish.

Formative evaluation

For each summative evaluation question, there is a set of corresponding formative ones that seek explanations for, or understanding of, the outcomes of policy (Table 9.1). These questions lend themselves to qualitative research and so formative evaluation is characterised by heavy reliance on qualitative techniques such as in-depth interviews, focus groups, observation and case study.

The broad approach of most formative evaluation is pluralistic and investigative, assembling whatever relevant information it is possible to obtain, and comparing and contrasting insights gleaned from the perspectives of different policy actors and sources of data.

Acceptance of qualitative analysis as providing both valid and valuable insights for policy came relatively late to government, which had a long tradition of dependence on quantitative analysis, supported by government statisticians and economists. From the 1970s onwards, the steady growth of the social research profession in government brought with it new analytical tools which, for some time, tended to be regarded with suspicion. An evaluation of rent allowances in the 1970s using qualitative techniques (Ritchie and Matthews, 1982, 1985) was regarded as ground-breaking at a time when the commercial sector already depended on the insights that qualitative research could bring. Now, qualitative techniques are a regular part of the toolkit used in government evaluation and, more recently, have stimulated debate on the role they can legitimately play (Ritchie and Lewis, 2003). Perhaps, not surprisingly, the design of the flagship pilots commissioned since 1997 has been driven by the quantitative concern of measuring impact with formative evaluation being only partly integrated into the overall design and analysis. However, the rolling out of national policies has necessarily been heavily dependent on the results of formative evaluation and, where the results of summative evaluations have been equivocal, either because of immeasurable small policy impact or inadequate design or both, qualitative findings have legitimated the entire evaluative project. For example, the evaluation of the New Deal for Lone Parents pilots, which aimed to assist lone parents into work, showed a modest overall impact on labour market participation, while the qualitative elements of the evaluation demonstrated clearly the positive role that personal advisers could play (Lewis et al, 2000).

Managing policy evaluation

Many of the policy evaluations conducted since 1997 are among the largest social science enterprises ever undertaken in Britain, with multi-million pound budgets, large teams of researchers and large field staffs. In many respects, managing an evaluation is similar to managing any large project and requires many of the standard project management techniques to be deployed. However, perhaps more than anything, successfully undertaking a policy evaluation demands effective management of the relationships between four key sets of policy actors: politicians and policy makers; service users who constitute the target of policy; evaluators and the wider research community; and the media. These relationships are depicted in Figure 9.1 with respect to four components of the evaluative process: policy design, design of evaluation, implementation, and analysis and dissemination. Certain of the relationships exist by definition. Some are a requirement for effective management, others are desirable, and yet others are possible and may have either beneficial or deleterious consequences that have to be managed. Successful management entails fully exploiting definitional, necessary and desirable relationships while being appropriately responsive to possible relationships when they occur. The research manager needs to protect the integrity of the evaluation

Figure 9.1: A relational model of the management of policy evaluations

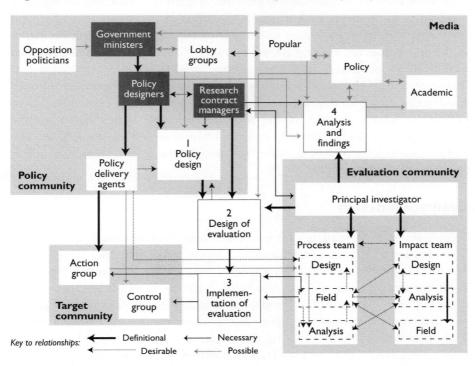

Source: Adapted from Walker and Wiseman (2006)

and keep the end user engaged, without making huge demands on their time, or allowing non-research factors to unduly influence design. The end game must always be that evaluation is a complex exercise in stakeholder management.

Policy design

There is not the space here to explore all the relationships portrayed in Figure 9.1 (see Walker and Wiseman, 2006). It is sufficient to draw attention to key points of tension. Policy design is often driven by the aspirations of politicians and shaped by crises or unanticipated events. Officials tasked with designing the details of policy and its implementation have to accommodate both the bidding of their political bosses and practical realities that are often well articulated by staff and organisations charged with implementation and delivery. This typically results in complex policies with multiple, often imprecisely defined objectives that are variously tailored to different subgroups. Similarly, implementation is often intricately varied. Such policies are very difficult to evaluate and constrain the use of experimental and quasi-experimental designs.

If the typical model is that of policy-driven evaluation, an alternative one is evaluation-led policy in which a policy experiment is designed to test a nascent policy concept or strategy. Evaluation-led policy increases the chances of obtaining precise estimates of impact by explicitly designing the policy and its implementation to be amenable to effective evaluation. Evaluators are typically involved from the beginning of policy development (or closely thereafter) and often have a quasi-management role to ensure that day-to-day implementation of the policy does not corrupt any aspect of the evaluative design. Policies tested in this way are necessarily simple, and subtle changes to fit local circumstance or unanticipated developments are rarely possible. From the perspective of policy makers, this may be a disadvantage, but the real aim of such experiments is to evaluate an idealised policy model or policy principle rather than a specific implementation. This approach is strongly represented in the US but the aforementioned Employment Retention and Advancement Demonstration is the closest British example.

Evaluation design

Politicians may have conflicting expectations about what they want from evaluation. They may hope to demonstrate that a policy works, rather than determine whether or not it does. They may be keener to learn how to fine-tune and implement a policy rather than wait to determine whether it has the desired effect. They may be eager to cherry-pick components of a policy or implementation without paying much attention to the context that allows the cherries to appear ripe for picking. They may wish to do all these things, despite some being mutually exclusive. Policy officials have the combined task of providing ministers with evidence and arguments to inform their decision making, while supporting them in achieving their political objectives. Managing these complex relationships and competing expectations is often the task of the government researcher.

Evaluation timetables are generally tight, with political pressure for quick results competing with concerns over robustness. This means evaluation design is often a compromise between the ideal and what can be achieved within a preordained policy timetable. Although frustrating, this is the reality of the evaluation–policy relationship.

Evaluative designs can be seriously disrupted by changes in the policy and policy environment. Sometimes changes in governments, ministers or even policy officials, can lead, for example, to the cancellation of policies or the modification of existing evaluations to test out new policy variants (Walker, 2001). This can mean that evaluators are faced with large challenges, as the questions the evaluation was designed to answer are modified or are no longer relevant to current policy. As a consequence, the evaluation sometimes comes to be seen as a 'handling problem', rather than a contribution to the policy process. Case study 9.2 illustrates the need for a flexible approach.

Case study 9.2: New Deal for Disabled People personal adviser pilots 1998–2001: a flexible approach to evaluation

The New Deal for Disabled People personal adviser pilots are a good example of the complex interplay between policy and evaluation and demonstrate how evaluators need to be flexible if they are to play a role in informing policy.

The policy objective was to increase workforce participation among disabled people by providing them with personal advisers. The policy was initially introduced as a 'quasi-experiment' in 12 areas, where performance was compared against a matched national sample of disabled people. The initial aim was to test how disabled people can be helped into work, but was later modified to place emphasis on getting as many disabled people as possible into work. The basic design of the national scheme was decided a year after the evaluation began, before the impact evaluation had delivered robust results.

The initial multi-method programme and process evaluation design was modified early on to meet cost constraints, reducing the robustness of evaluation results. Implementation problems – slow scheme take-up and a decision to include those who requested inclusion in the scheme, but were not part of the sample – necessitated further modifications to the evaluation design and further reduced the robustness of the evaluation results. This reflects how on the ground practical problems can necessitate refinements to technically ideal evaluation designs.

The evaluation results, initially envisaged as informing policy design, in practice, informed only the design of implementation, reflecting the pressure that can be exerted by political timetables. The impact evaluation was contaminated by a policy change and policy decisions were anyway taken

---

before results were available. The evaluation nevertheless yielded valuable data on barriers and incentives, to inform the broader policy objective.

Sources: Walker (2000a); Loumidis et al (2001); Sainsbury (2004).

Delivering evaluation

Evaluators have to balance the needs and concerns of staff responsible for delivery with demands for rigorous evaluation. This is not always as straightforward as it might appear. Staff delivering services may aspire to minimise inconvenience and maximise benefits for their clients and for themselves. They are also typically concerned by the prospect of their own work being appraised and, for the most part, have limited understanding of the niceties of evaluation research. Their concerns therefore have to be allayed, usually through tiers of explanation and negotiation with management, trade unions and individual members of staff. They need to appreciate the importance of the evaluation and of rigour; to be convinced that confidentiality will be respected; to believe that their voice will be heard; to know what is expected of them; and, finally, to be aware from whom to seek advice and who to advise if things go wrong. This is yet another layer in the complexity of the evaluation–policy relationship.

Impact of evaluations

Evaluators, and even government research managers, have limited control over the contribution of a particular evaluation as an agent of policy change. Much depends on timing, the receptiveness of policy makers and politicians of the time to the results and their willingness, and ability, to use them to some effect.

Timeliness is as important as the quality of the evaluation and the robustness of the results. Good evaluation is of limited value if policy decisions have already been taken although, in the right circumstances, results can be used to promote and/or defend a chosen course of action. The strength of the relationship between evaluators and government researchers and the latter's relationship with policy makers is important here. The more that each knows about the policy imperatives and the tone of the emergent findings, the more likely it is that the results will be interpreted sensitively and used productively within the policy process.

The evaluation of the New Deal for Disabled People personal adviser pilots (see Case study 9.2), for example, had relatively little impact. This was partly because policy interest shifted away from discovering how best to help people into employment towards getting as many as possible into work but also because contamination and low take-up destroyed the design based on a natural experiment. Also, within a year of commencing the two-year evaluation, the basic design of a national scheme to supersede the pilots had already been determined (Walker and Wiseman, 2006). In contrast, some evaluations have an impact even in the most inauspicious circumstances. The Major government initiated a policy pilot, Earnings Top-Up, which was abandoned by the incoming Blair Labour government but, after much lobbying by civil servants, the pilot continued and the results were subsequently used to shape policy on the Minimum Wage (Cabinet Office, 2003).

Evaluators are often challenged to justify their contribution to the policy process, but the influence of evaluation, or indeed any research, on policy is complex and often diffuse and long term. There is rarely a linear relationship between research insight and policy innovation or change. There is a growing literature that discusses these relationships, with a linear or 'instrumental' relationship being the simplest form and other forms, such as 'conceptual', where research insights influence policy indirectly via changes in knowledge, understanding and attitude, seen as equally important (Davies et al, 2000a; Nutley et al, 2007).

While the fate of individual evaluations is determined by exogenous factors largely beyond the control of evaluators, their cumulative effect is sufficient to shape institutions and policy-making practice. The move towards evidence-informed policy was facilitated by the growth in the volume and use of policy research within, and for, government over a period of 30 years, and by the belief that the private sector was making extensive use of prototyping and statistical analysis. After 1997, evaluation was given added momentum by the conviction, especially among economists and policy advisers within HM Treasury, that the effectiveness of policy making in the US was enhanced by extensive use of experimentation. To the extent that policy evaluation continues to be accessible, robust and relevant, it is likely to continue to be used and to reinforce an environment in which evidence is demanded. Moreover, to the extent that evaluation is seen to be unbiased and immune from political interference, it is likely to be relied on by governments (and opposition) regardless of political colour. In this regard, the growing commitment to publication and to peer review, facilitated in part by the growing influence and confidence of professionals within Whitehall, is an important institutional support to continued production and use of high quality evaluation, research and analysis.

Equally, any erosion of the highest professional standards, a process that can cumulate from deficiencies in individual studies and the occasional misuse of evaluative evidence, is likely to rapidly undermine conviction in the value of policy research and evaluation. Some have expressed concern that compromises made in the design of policy evaluations to accommodate perceived political necessities of timing and cost, may undermine the ability of evaluations to detect true policy impacts or to offer insight into the processes of implementation (Walker, 2004), while others have argued that useability is an inherent element of research quality (Duncan and Harrop, 2006).

Ethics of policy evaluation

The extent to which policy evaluation can contribute to policy is also tempered by ethical concerns, which can sometimes demand that the technically optimum evaluation design be modified. Policy evaluation falls under the same ethical rubric as policy research. However, it is indisputable that prospective forms of evaluation, programme evaluations and prototyping, that involve establishing policy interventions for the purpose of determining whether they work, raise ethical issues not encountered in other forms of research. Such evaluations explicitly place people in situations where they risk lack of benefit or lack of treatment, thereby adding risks connected to the consequences of the policy intervention to those associated to the research process itself. In appropriate circumstances, these additional risks may be justified with respect to the resultant policy knowledge that is to be used to enhance the common good.

The principles underpinning research can be reduced to three: beneficence, justice and respect for people (Blustein, 2005). The beneficence principle states that harm should not be done to research subjects, that potential harms should be minimised and possible benefits maximised. In applying this to policy evaluations, uncertainty as to the outcome of the intervention assumes great importance: there must be uncertainty as to whether people in the programme or control group will fare better, otherwise one group will be knowingly disadvantaged. In practice, policy trials have tended to offer additional 'benefits' such as cash payments and additional advice, so the risk of 'harm' to the trial group does not assume the same importance as it does in medical trials where the impact of the intervention is unknown. The beneficence principle is also generally interpreted to mean that an existing proven policy or treatment cannot be withdrawn to create a control group. Hence, the overall efficacy of a new programme cannot be directly established, only its performance relative to the existing one.

In the UK, the design of policy trials has drawn heavily on the model developed in the US, but policy trials developed in the UK differ from their US counterparts in a number of important ways and these differences have been the subject of debate (Blustein, 2005). The essential dilemma is defining the balance between the interests of research subjects and benefits to society – the principle of justice. Blustein (2005) has opined that the tendency in the US for policies aimed at welfare recipients to be more often piloted than those directed towards the middle class smacks of injustice. In the UK, trials have extended to policies covering the middle classes as well, being applied, for example, to court services and house purchase (Cabinet Office, 2003). A further response to justice issues is the requirement for government-sponsored research in the UK to meet 'a clearly defined, legitimate and unmet need to inform the conduct of government business' (GSRU, 2005, p 6) although occasionally the implementation of this principle has been questioned (Bee, 2007). Concerns of 'justice' relating to evaluation have also been addressed by the greater reliance in the UK on action and control areas, rather than individual random allocation, in some cases weighing fairness above precision of evaluation results. In truth, the justice issue still applies in these circumstances and should be confronted, although it is less 'visible'.

There are also differences between the UK and the US in connection with the third principle, that of respect. This is most evident in relation to the principle of 'informed consent' and the balance to be struck between research integrity and respondent rights. The US Common Rule, 'The Federal policy for the protection of human subjects' (Federal Register, 1991), explicitly excludes research designed to study or evaluate public benefit or service programmes from informed consent requirements. Thus, in the US evaluations of mandatory programmes that employ random assignment, participants typically have no choice over being assigned to action or control groups. In the UK, to date, consent has typically been solicited from potential participants prior to random assignment. Experience to date suggests that such practice need not undermine the integrity of experiments although doubts have been expressed about the extent to which participants have always been adequately informed (Stratford et al, 2005; Walker et al, 2006).

Conclusions

It is only 20 years since policy evaluation fully entered the lexicon of Whitehall policy makers and little more than a decade since policy pilots and their evaluation were thrust centre stage by enthusiasm within HM Treasury. Since then, tens, perhaps even hundreds, of policies have been subject to evaluation, varying markedly in scale and level of sophistication. Whitehall is not immune to fads and fashions and it remains to be seen whether the performance-based culture will continue as now. The simple notion that 'what matters is what works' has needed to be considerably refined to make it workable in policy making and has required a consideration of what is meant by 'works'. It seems likely that a commitment to piloting and evaluation will be strengthened by the demand for increased value for money. From the discussion in this chapter we can conclude that:

• The gains from evaluation have been far more wide-ranging than simply knowing what individual policies achieve. Indeed the process of setting up an evaluation is often as important as its outcome. It encourages policy makers clearly to specify policy objectives and to prioritise them. These in turn need to be translated into performance goals specified in terms that can be measured. There are benefits from articulating a theory of change setting out the process by which the intervention is likely to achieve its objectives, distinguishing between the resource inputs, service outputs and final outcomes. The process encourages ongoing communication between policy makers and analytical specialists and between analytical specialisms within government and has led some departments to adopt multi-disciplinary policy teams. There has also been an increased involvement of academics and other experts from outside government at early stages in the process of policy development. In effect, the vision outlined in *Modernising government* and *Professional policy making for the twenty-first century* has become more of a reality, with evaluation being a major component of the evidence-informed policy decisions.

- Conducting evaluations of policy pilots has also focused more attention on the process of implementing policy, on the mechanisms of delivery and on the significance of frontline staff, and especially supervisory level management, in attaining outcome goals. Policy makers have become more aware of the time needed to set up systems, for procedures to bed down and structures to adjust before there is any semblance of the stability necessary for meaningful measurement. The gulf between piloting and the national rolling out of policy has been highlighted, together with the difficulty of replication; the uniqueness of pilots tends to attract more competent staff and greater resources and to attain higher levels of success than is generally possible in mainstream implementation. Piloting has also emphasised the complexities of joint agency working, the intricate funding systems that often underpin voluntary sector organisations contracted to deliver government services and the difficulty of establishing the costs as much as the benefits of public programmes (Greenberg and Davis, 2007). The result is that policy makers are perhaps more acutely aware of the gap between aspiration and feasibility than in the past.

- Nevertheless, this largely positive assessment has itself to be tempered by reference to reality. The worlds of policy making and policy evaluation are very different. The adversarial nature of the British political system makes evaluation risky, with ministers aware that the possibility of negative results may give the opposition free ammunition. Political time horizons are short with the next election being defined as long term and Cabinet reshuffles tending to shift priorities. Policy decisions cannot always wait for full evaluation results, so policy is often shaped, or justified, by interim findings. Ministers point to the importance of political mandates and political judgement (Select Committee on Science and Technology, 2006b) and, indeed, the *Modernising government* White Paper (Cabinet Office, 1999) makes clear that evidence is not simply a matter of research and evaluation.

- Not all policies lend themselves to piloting, which is itself costly as well as unpredictable and time consuming. Many policies have multiple objectives, some relating to changes in individual behaviour and others to aggregate effects, and it is difficult to measure all necessary outcomes with equal precision. Increasingly politicians are aware of the need for joined-up governance with common policy goals across different departments but disentangling the contribution of individual policies to outcomes is often as methodologically challenging as it is difficult to secure cross-departmental consensus on policy strategy. This is the reality of policy evaluation in a political context.

- As already noted, the policy-making culture has shifted and it is becoming somewhat easier for politicians to accept negative findings and to learn from them. In practice, evaluation can, for good reasons, provide inconclusive results and, even when outcomes are clear, they rarely point unequivocally in one policy direction. Inconclusive findings sometimes reflect the limited impact of policy; effect sizes – even those lauded from the US – are rarely more than a few percentage points, a salutary reminder of the inconsequential nature of much policy activity (Greenberg and Schroder, 2004; Griggs et al, 2007). Politicians may of course judge that even a small impact is worth having. Sometimes, inconclusive results reflect inadequate sample sizes and poor evaluative design; this clearly emphasises the importance of good evaluation and adequate investment in robust methods, if policy is to depend on its results. The increased emphasis on evaluation has placed increased pressures on evaluators, both within and outside government. In government, this has been reflected in a growth in the number of social science professionals working in government but, even where resources have increased, training has often struggled to keep pace with the demand for ever-more sophisticated evaluation and analysis skills. Similarly, the supply of good evaluators in the wider research and academic community has not kept pace with market demand. The Economic and Social Research Council (ESRC) and others have been active in trying to address this (ESRC, 2006).

• Many of the problems and issues described reflect the inevitable tensions between research and policy. The past 10 years have seen a huge attempt to minimise these tensions through capacity building and development and refinement of state-of-the-art evaluation techniques. The tensions will never completely disappear and no evaluator would ever want to claim that they know everything there is to know about policy evaluation; as with all professions, techniques will continue to evolve. Evaluation findings will only ever be one among many influences on policy decision making. It is easy to point to flaws in the policy–research relationship (and they do exist), but it is certainly true that evaluation now plays a more significant role in the process of policy development and review than ever before.

Further reading

Cabinet Office (2003) *Trying it out: The role of pilots in policy making*, London: Cabinet Office – provides a review and makes recommendations on the use of pilots in government.

Nutley, S.M., Walter, I. and Davies, H.T.O. (2007) *Using evidence: How research can inform public services*, Bristol: The Policy Press – a useful exploration of the ways in which research is used and how it could have a greater impact within and on public services.

PMSU (Prime Minister's Strategy Unit) (2003) *The magenta book: Guidance notes for policy evaluation and analysis*, London: Cabinet Office, PMSU.

Useful websites

The ESRC's National Centre for Research Methods – www.ncrm.ac.uk – provides access to a range of information and resources. Other ESRC-supported sites that are of relevance for this topic are the EPPI-Centre (http://eppi.ioe. ac.uk/cms/) and Evidence Network (www.evidencenetwork.org).

www.policyhub.gov.uk/magenta_book/index.asp – Government Chief Social Researcher's Office – a useful set of guidance including on policy evaluation.

www.gsr.gov.uk – the website of the Government Social Research service contains articles of general interest about the use of evidence in policy and related issues.

TEN

Learning lessons from policy experience

John Hudson

Learning lessons from experience of what works and what does not work is the ninth of the core competencies identified in *Professional policy making for the twenty-first century* (Cabinet Office Strategic Policy Making Team, 1999). It clearly relates strongly to other competencies including 'evaluation' and 'review', so to what extent is it a distinct competency in itself? This chapter:

- examines suggestions that policy makers should learn differntly;
- suggests that the conception of learning advocated in *Professional policy making for the twenty-first century* is overly narrow and instrumental; and
- draws on ideas from complexity theory to point to alternative ways of learning for better policy making.

In the *Modernising government* White Paper, the government argued that policy making could be improved by 'learning from experience ... [by viewing] policy making as a continuous, learning process, not as a series of one–off initiatives' (Cabinet Office, 1999, p 17). To this end, *Modernising government* carried an expectation that learning would be embedded in the policy-making process.

Building on *Modernising government*, the Cabinet Office Strategic Policy Making Team's *Professional policy making for the twenty-first century* identified 'learning lessons' as the final of the nine core competencies at the heart of a professional approach to policy making (1999). However, it advanced a rather vague and muddled view of what 'learning lessons' might entail and, more specifically, how learning lessons might differ in practice from the execution of other core competencies of policy making it identified such as evaluation and review.

Indeed, as noted elsewhere in this book, *Professional policy making for the twenty-first century* did not address the issues of review, evaluation and learning lessons in separate chapters, instead examining them together under the heading of 'learning lessons'. By contrast, each of the six preceding core competencies that it identified were given their own chapters and, consequently, examined at much greater length. This naturally leads to questions about the need for nine separate competencies of professional policy making if evaluation, review and learning lessons are so similar as to make separate consideration of them unnecessary. Could they not be regarded as different aspects of one competency? A cursory reading of *Professional policy making for the twenty-first century* certainly seems to suggest so, not least because, for the most part, its discussion of learning lessons almost exclusively evokes the language of evaluation. Indeed, when describing a learning-based policy process it stated:

> This means that new policies must have evaluation of their effectiveness built into them from the start; established policies must be reviewed regularly to ensure that they are still delivering the desired outcome; and the lessons learned from evaluation must be available and accessible to other policy makers. (Cabinet Office Strategic Policy Making Team, 1999, p 54)

Likewise, it argued that:

> The principal mechanism for learning lessons is through evaluation of new policies and by regular review of existing policies. (p 54)

However, this narrow definition of 'learning lessons' seemingly relegates a supposedly core competency of professional policy making to a mere sub-function of evaluation: 'lessons' are drawn from evaluations of new or existing policies and 'learning' occurs through the dissemination of evaluation study findings. This view is reinforced by the one paragraph in the chapter on learning lessons that does not concern itself with evaluation and review, which begins by noting:

> *Once uncovered*, lessons need to be presented effectively if they are to be absorbed and used. (Cabinet Office Strategic Policy Making Team, 1999, p 59; emphasis added)

While the question of how best to disseminate evaluation findings is undoubtedly an important one – and certainly has some potential to improve policy making – it hardly encapsulates the full extent of the notion of 'learning lessons'. The narrow conception *Professional policy making for the twenty-first century* offers is, perhaps, a consequence of it breaking policy making down into so many core competencies, for much of what might come under this heading – such as learning from abroad or making better use of evidence – had already been covered by the time the final principle of 'learning lessons' was reached. Indeed, while policy analysts in academia have shown an increased interest in 'lesson drawing' in recent years (for example, Rose, 1993, 2005), their discussion has focused almost exclusively on the cross-national transfer of policy ideas (as covered in Chapter Three, this volume).

Yet, as Rose (1993) has argued in his work on cross-national lesson drawing, a wider trawl of the social science literature could draw in new ideas that might help us think through a wider notion of what 'policy learning' might entail. While disciplinary boundaries necessarily constrain us here because some fields are outside of our expertise (there are some potentially very interesting ideas in the mass of material on learning theories to be found in educational studies and the large body of work in social psychology that focuses on how decision makers learn), this chapter aims to challenge the narrow conception of 'learning lessons' found in *Professional policy making for the twenty-first century* and, in so doing, will draw on a somewhat eclectic range of ideas. A major goal of the chapter is therefore to offer some food for thought on the question of *how* policy making might become more of a learning process. As a consequence, the chapter may embrace a slightly more abstract approach than some others in this book, but in part this reflects a relative lack of progress in this area since 1997. As the Centre for Management and Policy Studies (Bullock et al, 2001) found when interviewing senior civil servants about the modernisation of policy making for their *Better policy making* survey, 'A broad range of activities was identified such as: reviewing existing evidence; commissioning new research; piloting initiatives and programmes; evaluating new policies; and inviting experts to advise on specialist areas. Less was mentioned of learning from or disseminating best practice' (p 49).

Learning as feedback: the simple systems approach

As a starting point it is necessary to begin by exploring in more detail the 'narrow view' of policy learning propounded in *Professional policy making for the twenty-first century*. Chapter One of this volume noted that the Blair government's desire to modernise and improve the policy-making process emerges in part from a 'rationalistic view that better policy making can lead to better policies and to better outcomes'. The idea that 'learning lessons' forms the final stage of a recurring 'policy cycle' is at the heart of the so-called 'rational comprehensive model' of the policy process and this perspective itself is very well established within the policy analysis literature (see Parsons, 1995; Hudson and Lowe, 2004; Spicker, 2006). Indeed, the Treasury's *Green Book* (2003) endorses the ROAMEF cycle (Rationale, Objectives, Appraisal, Monitoring, Evaluation and Feedback) in which the feedback of the lessons found in evaluation forms the final stage of policy making (see Figure 10.1).

The suggestion that feedback from evaluation studies provides the main source of policy learning features heavily in many rational comprehensive models of the policy process as a 'policy cycle'. The model echoes classic conceptions of the political system that drew analogies with mechanical systems (such as Easton, 1965), where a central idea was that a feedback loop provides essential information that keeps the system in equilibrium. Talk of feedback and feedback loops features heavily in both the *Modernising government* White Paper and in *Professional policy making for the twenty-first century*, but while the latter concluded that feedback loops were generally weak or absent, it offered few suggestions for repairing broken or blocked loops. Primarily, it focused on the question of how evaluation research

Figure 10.1: HM Treasury *Green Book*: ROAMEF model

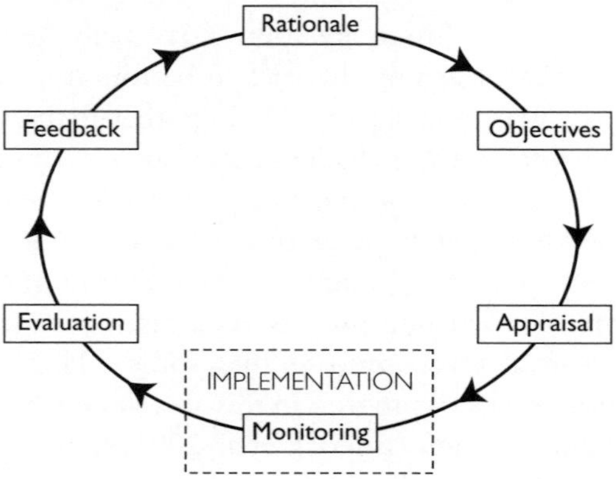

Source: HM Treasury (2003)

might be better disseminated, arguing 'lessons need to be presented effectively if they are to be absorbed and used' (Cabinet Office Strategic Policy Making Team, 1999, p 59).

Presentation does, of course, play an important role in helping research evidence move from between the covers of a report and into political debate. In a review of learning from evaluation studies in the Swiss energy policy sector, Balthasar and Rieder (2000) identified the 'production of a report whose language and scope are appropriate to its intended audience' (p 258), and its presentation in an appropriate forum as one of four key factors positively influencing learning effects. Similarly, in discussing the potential for research to influence policy, Duncan and Harrop (2006) suggested that 'if research is to have an impact with practitioners they need access to particular types of information in ways that fit with how they work … [they] may have little time to read and digest lengthy reports' (p 165). These are certainly themes that *Professional policy making for the twenty-first century* warms to, for it makes the case for a constrained approach to the presentation of lessons on the basis that it will make them easier to absorb:

> Far more useful in many cases will be to focus on a small number of significant and timely lessons for future policy. Completeness can, perversely, become a barrier to learning, both in terms of generating resistance to more critical elements of an evaluation and because of the sheer volume of material involved. With this in mind, a more targeted approach, presenting a few key lessons – both through executive summaries and preferably face to face – to Ministers and top officials is more likely to have an impact. (Cabinet Office Strategic Policy Making Team, 1999, p 59)

It has certainly become fashionable of late to suggest that better decision making may result from the consideration of less rather than more information. Gladwell's (2005) best-selling *Blink* is almost entirely based around the claim that skilled and experienced decision makers are able to act quickly and effectively on the basis of their instincts and a limited amount of information rather than on the basis of a more lengthy consideration of very detailed evidence – a process he dubs 'thin-slicing'. Indeed, Gladwell (2005) claims that 'decisions made very quickly can be every bit as good as decisions made cautiously or deliberately' (p 14) and, moreover, that 'our snap judgements and first impressions can be educated and controlled … [and] just as we can teach ourselves to think logically and deliberately, we can also teach ourselves to make better snap judgements' (pp 15-16). It is a view that may well find some sympathy with Tony Blair; in an interesting exchange during a meeting of the House of Commons Liaison Committee he argued that recourse to detailed research-based evidence was not necessary in many of his most controversial policy decisions and, when pushed on the potential for a more open and evidence-based approach to policy making, suggested that 'my experience of this stuff is that process and debates about process become a substitute often for people making up their minds on the policy' (Liaison Committee, 2004, p 73).

Significantly, academic studies of actual processes of policy learning have often concluded that genuine learning is rare for the simple reason, as Frantz and Sato (2005) put it, that 'policy learning takes time and thought – often more time and thought than policy makers are willing or able to invest' (p 164). Given such a context, it is easy to see why the notion of 'thin-slicing' has had such broad appeal. However, irrespective of the merits of Gladwell's claims that skilled decision makers can and do make good quality decisions largely on the basis of their instincts, there are obvious problems in advocating thin-slicing as an approach to policy making. Chief among these is the worry that decision makers may 'thin-slice' the evidence in a manner that is flawed or skewed towards one particular set of conclusions. For instance, Houghton (1996, 1998a, 1998b) has argued that political leaders use historical analogies in decision making more often than is presumed. Indeed, he suggests that when faced with a high degree of risk or uncertainty, leaders often feel there is a real value in drawing lessons from similar situations faced by their predecessors in the past. However, Houghton suggests that the search for relevant analogous situations is usually somewhat limited in practice, typically involving the examination of just one prominent historical case. While such analogical reasoning can play a key role in promoting a search for lessons – and a reflection on the causes of policy success and failure – it is far from systematic. The danger is that overly simple conclusions can be drawn: every call for action short of war when faced with a military aggressor can be likened to Chamberlain's appeasement of Hitler; every military intervention warned against as a potential Vietnam. The problem in drawing on the past, as Runciman (2006) neatly puts it, is that 'because history does not repeat itself, we need to be careful about what we think it is telling us' (p x). While *Professional policy making for the twenty-first century*'s suggestion that policy lessons be presented in a compact form makes sense on a pragmatic level, there are very real risks that flawed decisions will be made when there is over-reliance on a limited amount of information (see Glees, 2005). At the same time, however, there is no doubting that there are very real limits to the absorptive capacity of the average policy maker, analyst or politician; information does, of course, need to be summarised and we should be wary of simply arguing that more information is always better. Instead, the challenge is to ensure that 'thin-slicing' captures the true richness and complexity of the policy problem that is being examined.

Yet, while government seems more willing to listen to ideas that emerge from evaluations than was often the case in the past (for example, see Chapters Eight and Nine, this volume), there is still some degree of hesitancy on the part of the research community when it comes to the question of how best to ensure the 'key lessons' of evaluation studies might be taken forward. Indeed, Pollitt (2006) has argued that the policy–research nexus remains underdeveloped, not least because academics are often unsure of the role their knowledge ought to play in shaping policy on the ground. Some, such as Duncan and Harrop (2006), have argued strongly that greater emphasis needs to be placed on making policy relevance a central part of any definition of high-quality research in the policy sciences. What this means in practice, they suggest, is that the development of ever-more robust research methodologies needs to be accompanied by a continual dialogue between researchers and policy makers about their respective needs, for good quality policy research should not only be scientifically robust but also have practical value for end users in government. Others raise doubts about such an approach, most notably Pawson (2006), who has argued that 'good quality' research sometimes has little to offer us in terms of concrete policy lessons and that 'poor quality' research can sometimes offer some solid ideas for policy change. The significance of this observation comes in the techniques that might be adopted when synthesising the lessons of a body of evidence; while the standard approach is to summarise the conclusions of the highest 'quality' research – those elements with the most robust methods – Pawson's (2006) view is that the emphasis should be on 'looking for pearls of wisdom rather than acres of orthodoxy' (p 136) because policy relevance and robust methods may not always walk hand-in-hand. In short, even if the view presented in *Professional policy making for the twenty-first century* that 'a more targeted approach, presenting a few key lessons' (p 59) is to be preferred, there remain considerable difficulties in determining which of the many lessons thrown up by evaluation research are 'key'.

In fact, if the yardstick by which quality of evaluation research is to be judged is whether its findings are put into practice, then it may well be that the major issue is not so much what happens in terms of the presentation of findings once the research has been completed but, rather, what happens *before* the research begins. *Professional policy making for the twenty-first century* noted that 'one obstacle [to learning lessons] is defensiveness if lessons are mixed and an evaluator expresses an overall judgement about a specific initiative' (Cabinet Office Strategic Policy

Making Team, 1999, p 59). Certainly this is a view that finds some support in the evaluation literature: van der Meer and Edelenbos (2006) echo this language almost completely when they suggest summative 'evaluation may invoke defensive reactions, which may restrict the learning processes' (p 202). Their view stretches beyond this, for they believe restricted learning arising from defensiveness bedevils the majority of evaluation activities because the emphasis tends to be on accountability and, therefore, clear summative judgements. Indeed, they go so far as to suggest that there may be a fundamental contradiction between the dual goals of evaluation as a tool for accountability and a tool for learning. Likewise, Balthasar and Rieder (2000) have suggested that learning is unlikely to flow from evaluation activities if the affected parties feel they are being subjected to an external process of scrutiny rather than being participants in the process of learning themselves. For both van der Meer and Edelenbos and Balthasar and Rieder, a large part of the solution to this problem is to approach the issue from the bottom up. By involving practitioners in both the design and execution of the evaluation research, the chances of real policy learning taking place will increase for the simple reason that the research itself is more likely to be delivered to a receptive audience. Similar arguments have been made by those who advocate so-called 'appreciative inquiry' (see Coghlan et al, 2003) and 'responsive evaluation' (see Abma, 2004). In short, the key to producing research that speaks the language of decision makers is less likely to be found through questioning the language and format in which the research is presented than in the framing of the actual questions the research explores. Yet, while *Professional policy making for the twenty-first century* points to problems that might arise from defensiveness, it does not embrace the more inclusive approach to evaluation advocated as a solution in much of the literature, a point we will return to later.

While the issues surrounding the presentation of research findings or the framing of research questions certainly provide some challenges for those undertaking evaluation research, there is one more element of *Professional policy making for the twenty-first century*'s strategy for unblocking feedback loops that we have yet to explore and it poses what is probably the biggest headache of all for evaluation research: time. It was noted above that *Professional policy making for the twenty-first century* suggested learning might be aided by focusing on 'a small number of significant and *timely* lessons' (Cabinet Office Strategic Policy Making Team, 1999, p 59; emphasis added). We might reasonably ask what 'timely' means in this context. On the one hand, it might mean earlier presentation of findings. That decision makers and evaluators often work to differing timescales has been well documented in the policy analysis literature. For instance, in his review of the use of pilots in policy making, Jowell (Cabinet Office, 2003) highlighted the tension between policy makers who 'complained that researchers were too seldom willing to recognise how short the optimal time period was in which to roll [new policies] out' and researchers concerned about pressure to work 'to a timetable that was incapable of accurately answering the primary questions being addressed' (p 57). Here, timeliness appears to have two distinct dimensions: speed of delivery and delivery at an opportune moment. While the two may well coincide in practice – research may be commissioned when an issue is politically 'live' and findings needed promptly in order to shape an ongoing debate – this need not be so. Indeed, in the policy analysis literature that concerns itself with the impact of ideas on policy change, a common observation is that new policies often draw on rather old ideas that, for whatever reason, have come into fashion (Hudson and Lowe, 2004). Policy learning is often not so much about the impact of new information as it is about the renewed search for ideas that brings into purview policy proposals that had once been discarded as inappropriate (Hall, 1993; Pemberton, 2004). Moreover, this literature suggests that such a search for ideas is, more often than not, prompted by a crisis in existing policy frameworks that briefly opens up a window for change. Interestingly, in their review of learning from evaluations, Balthasar and Rieder (2000) observed a similar process, noting that the deepest 'learning effects are especially dependent on the occurrence of so-called "windows of opportunity"' (p 258). Yet, as they concluded, the obvious problem evaluators face in aiming to deliver timely findings is that 'these factors are scarcely controllable by evaluators and their commissioners' (p 258).

Learning or lessons?

What the issue of timeliness demonstrates is that the rational comprehensive view of learning in a policy system presented in *Professional policy making for the twenty-first century* has some serious limitations as an analytic device. The policy analysis literature makes it clear that *accidents* of timing often play a hugely important role in triggering policy learning and that, in practice, policy learning and policy change are rather haphazard processes. In short, learning is a far from linear process and a model that sees the policy process as analogous to an autonomous engineered system is unlikely to get us far in terms of promoting a learning approach to policy making.

Yet, that said, the proposals for improving learning that *Professional policy making for the twenty-first century* advances are neither particularly controversial nor especially problematic in themselves: indeed, it seems churlish to argue against the claims that greater consideration of when and how evaluation research is presented can deliver policy gains. The real issue at hand is the question of the *sorts* of gains it might deliver. In seeking to constrain the level of feedback entering the system, encouraging tight timescales for the delivery of lessons and, indeed, by focusing on evaluation research as the main form of learning, legitimate questions can be raised about the depth of learning that is likely to arise.

It is worth noting at this juncture that the academic literature on policy learning has found it necessary to distinguish different *levels* of policy learning and change. (Similar observations are made in the management literature: see Case study 10.1.) The most famous articulation comes from Hall (1993), who points us towards three different levels of policy (or, as he put it, *social*) learning and change:

- *first-order change:* in which policy goals and instruments remain unaffected but the settings of instruments are adjusted;
- *second-order change:* in which policy goals remain unaffected but new policy instruments are introduced in order to achieve these goals;
- *third-order change:* in which the actual policy goals or paradigms are the focus of change.

What is interesting about this articulation of learning and change is that it lays bare the widely varying types of learning that we might expect to find in the political system and, in turn, that we might aim to promote in a professionalised policy-making environment. Political scientists, arguably, have focused most of their attention on deep-level third-order change. It is here that arguments stressing the haphazard and spasmodic opening of 'windows of opportunity' have most currency, because policy paradigms shift on an infrequent basis. By contrast, it is widely accepted that lower orders of change occur on a much more regular basis, not least because they are easier to deliver. The proposals outlined in *Professional policy making for the twenty-first century* seem to be aimed pretty squarely at the more limited learning necessary for first-order change. On the face of it, this seems to be a sensibly pragmatic approach: it makes sense to focus our learning efforts in the places where change can be most readily implemented. Yet, we might well argue that a genuinely learning-based approach to policy making should seek out deeper lessons that not only look to fine-tune the weaknesses to be found in current policy frameworks but also challenge those very frameworks themselves. We have already noted that the policy analysis literature has observed that, in practice, the deepest level of learning and change usually occurs only when existing frameworks are in crisis. It seems perverse, to say the least, that deep-level learning is so often postponed until the last possible moment.

While the distinction between different *levels* of policy learning is useful, we might also draw a distinction between different *types* of policy learning. Johnson (1998) suggests that there are many ways in which evaluation research can be utilised. Three of the most common types of learning that he explores are:

- *instrumental usage:* where results are directly used as the basis for changing policy;
- *conceptual usage:* where evaluation research influences policy makers' thinking about a programme or problem;
- *process usage:* where the act of participating in an evaluation programme alters an actor's understanding of a problem or their behaviour.

Professional policy making for the twenty-first century appears to focus primarily on the instrumental use of evaluation research, proceeding largely on the basis that the key to learning is to disseminate the one or two significant lessons from an evaluation study that need to be acted on. However, conceptual and process uses may be as important – if not more so – in generating real policy learning. When evaluation prompts a conceptual or process-based usage its impacts are harder to measure and difficult to trace; but, by encouraging reflection and a re-evaluation of the decision maker's world view, they put in chain a process of reflexive learning that is qualitatively distinct from the 'absorption' of a 'few key lessons' that *Professional policy making for the twenty-first century* seeks to encourage (cf van der Knaap, 2004, on theory-based evaluation and learning).

Taken together, these differing types and levels of policy learning help shed light on the rather limited view of learning lessons presented in *Professional policy making for the twenty-first century*. Indeed, the functional nature of its approach is further highlighted by the two 'levers for change' it recommends to departments as vehicles for improving learning: developing an evaluation programme that 'corresponds to the priorities set out in PSAs' and ensuring that 'policy makers agree clear, unambiguous statements of desired outcomes at the start of the policy process' (Cabinet Office, 1999, p 76). These levers seem to be more concerned with calling departments to account than encouraging deep reflection and warrant further discussion because they raise significant questions about the real model of learning that underpins *Professional policy making for the twenty-first century*.

For instance, while unambiguous early statements of desired policy outcomes greatly help those evaluators whose job it is to offer a clear, concise and summative judgement of a policy's success or failure in meeting its goals, they often do little to help those policy makers who are trying to find innovative ways of tackling complex, multi-dimensional problems. Indeed, many policy analysts have argued that public policy often engages with 'wicked problems' or 'messes' that defy clear definition, not least because different stakeholders so often carry different but valid interpretations of the problem (Chapman, 2004; Hudson, 2006). What is more, the consensus among those who study 'wicked problems' is that their complex roots require complex solutions that will also defy clear and simple definition; indeed, it is often suggested that the end point of a policy initiative is not when the problem is solved, but when resources allocated to it have run out. Conklin and Weil (1997) are clear in their view that 'a linear approach to solving a wicked problem simply will not work'. Instead, an ongoing, reflexive, adaptive approach is required, in which the definition of the problem and the solution are in a state of flux. In short, continuous learning – not a clear, one-off judgement that offers us some pithy lessons – is required.

Similarly, the recommendation to build evaluation programmes around Public Service Agreements (PSAs) makes it clear that the main focus of learning in *Professional policy making for the twenty-first century* is not learning about policy goals but on how far the settings of existing instruments have moved us towards already agreed policy goals. While it clearly makes sense to measure progress in meeting PSA targets, we might ask whether so doing should be regarded as being one of just two key levers for promoting the learning of lessons. Indeed, the exceedingly narrow focus of so many of the PSA targets is a particular problem in this context. For example, the Department for Education and Skills (DfES) is charged with ensuring that, by 2008, 60% of young people aged 16 achieve the equivalent of five GCSEs at grades A★-C, and the Department for Work and Pensions (DWP) with reducing the average processing time of a Housing Benefit claim to 48 days or less by the end of the same year (HM Treasury, 2004a). While it is *possible* that an evaluation programme based around a consideration of these targets will be built in a manner that allows a broad reflection on the nature of 14-16 schooling or the value of the existing approach to housing support, it seems unlikely. Narrow quantifiable targets too readily lend themselves to a narrow quantitative evaluation.

In short, the suggested 'levers for change' focus very much on producing instrumental lessons that can be used to tweak existing policy instruments. There are some real dangers here, not just in terms of inhibiting a broader approach to learning, but because the kind of feedback it is likely to produce is what some systems theorists call 'positive feedback': information that reinforces, rather than challenges, the status quo (Chapman, 2004). Indeed, Chapman suggests that if evaluations uncover a failure to meet targets without also uncovering the broader failings in a system that have contributed to this failure, then there is a very real risk that the policy response will be more of the same rather than something different altogether. In such circumstances, we enter a vicious circle in which a continued failure to learn leads to the continued reinforcement of a failing policy system.

Case study 10.1: Health inequalities in Australia: using triple loop learning in a policy context

Argyris and Schön (1978) pioneered the idea of 'double loop learning' after frequently observing the inability of senior management in organisations to pick up on major failures that were well known to more junior employees. The problem, they argued, came from poor organisational learning strategies designed to evaluate progress in working towards already agreed goals. Consequently, it was often possible for feedback to directors to indicate that manufacture of a new product was proceeding as planned, while major concerns on the ground about the viability of the product itself remained unreported. 'Double loop learning' addresses these weaknesses by questioning the validity of the frameworks themselves: it asks not only 'are we doing things right?' but also 'are we doing the right things?'. Flood and Romm (1996) advanced the idea of 'triple loop learning', which asserts that power imbalances can act as a barrier to learning. What 'triple loop learning' means in practice is that processes of learning must be able to sweep in a wide range of issues from multiple perspectives, including those that challenge existing frameworks and sources of authority.

McIntyre (2003) observes that despite ranking third in the United Nations' global Human Development Index (UNDP, 2006), Australia has some of the most shocking health inequalities anywhere in the world. At the start of the 21st century, the average life expectancy for the non-indigenous population was 82 for women and 76.6 for men; for the Aboriginal and Torres Strait Islanders population it was 64.8 for women and 59.4 for men (Aboriginal and Torres Strait Islander Social Justice Commissioner, 2005). The causes of these health inequalities are undoubtedly complex and the relationship between inputs and outcomes is often unpredictable. McIntyre (2003) notes that in Alice Springs, which has a substantial indigenous population, the level of human services is almost twice the national average, but the city has significantly below average outcomes in health, education and employment. Single loop learning is ineffective in this context: doing more of the same does not appear to be the answer. McIntyre suggests that double loop learning is also insufficient, for power imbalances have impeded the development of new policy agendas. Drawing on action research in Alice Springs, she argues that the solution lies in the implementation of a programme of deliberative democracy that redresses some of these power imbalances by providing a safe and reflexive environment in which the knowledge of the indigenous population can be brought to the fore. Central to McIntyre's approach is not just devolution of power but the use of a systems thinking methodology designed to capture a holistic view of the policy environment. In particular, she suggests that tools need to be employed for structuring the conversation in a manner that prompts the 'sweeping in' of new ideas and the 'unfolding' of meanings while being 'mindful of values' and ensuring design options are not 'cut off'.

Learning in a complex adaptive system

Many of those who point to the difficulty of dealing with 'wicked' problems often suggest there are inherent flaws in a world view that equates policy making with operating a piece of machinery. Indeed, while *Professional policy making for the twenty-first century* offers us 35 'levers for change to policy making' in order to make its nine core competencies of modern policy making 'stick', Chapman (2004) worries about the 'mechanistic and reductionist thinking' (p 10) that such language betrays. Indeed, he feels that such thinking forms the dominant conceptualisation of policy making, observing that:

> A conversation with a civil servant, politician or senior public sector manager will yield a large number of phrases based upon the notion that government and organisations are machine-like: 'stepping up a gear', 'changing direction', 'driving through change', 'the machinery of government' and 'policy levers' are common examples. (p 10)

For Chapman (2004) – and for others who approach the analysis of policy from a perspective informed by complexity theory (for example, Medd, 2001; Blackman,

2006; Hudson, 2006) – the problem comes not so much from viewing policy as a system, but in the simplistic, reductionist conceptions of a system that are often found in documents like *Professional policy making for the twenty-first century*. Space does not allow for a lengthy review of complexity theory's potential applications to policy analysis in this chapter (see Byrne, 1998, 2001). However, Medd (2001, following Cilliers, 1998) suggests the following themes are central to such an analysis of the (social) policy process rooted in complexity science:

- many (potentially) simple elements make up the whole policy system. While these elements *may* lend themselves to simple analysis, the complex dynamic interactions between these elements do not;
- there are multiple direct and indirect feedback loops that influence the behaviour of the many elements in the system in unpredictable, non-linear ways;
- 'emergent properties' are the focus of analysis: it is not the individual components of the system that we need to understand but the nature of interactions between these components;
- the system is open – it interacts with its environment and adapts on the basis of feedback. It regularly operates far from equilibrium because of environmental changes but can cope with this through learning;
- the system has a memory – a history – that plays a role in coordinating behaviour. However, this memory is distributed throughout the system;
- the system is adaptive – it is self-organising and can adjust without the intervention of an external third party.

These are not simple ideas, but some of their implications can be illustrated fairly simply. To begin with, as Hudson (2006) notes, 'complexity theory consistently emphasises the limitations on our ability to predict, plan and control the behaviour of social systems' (p 14). The unpredictable interactions of the different elements that constitute a system make it difficult to confidently predict the outcomes of action – a change in one part of the system may have an unintended impact on another part that in turn impacts on another and so on. From this perspective, attempts to proceed on a command-and-control basis are often doomed to failure because policy makers neither command nor control the whole of the system. Worse still, attempts to impose command-and-control can end up destroying the system's ability to adapt – or, in other words, restrict its ability to learn and adapt in the face of a changing environment. Plsek (2001) (cited in Chapman, 2004) offers us an excellent metaphor that sums up this predicament neatly:

> ... [compare] throwing a stone with throwing a live bird. The trajectory of a stone can be calculated quite precisely using the laws of mechanics, and it is possible to ensure that the stone reaches a specified destination. However, it is not possible to predict the outcome of throwing the live bird in the same way, even though the same laws of physics ultimately govern the bird's motion through the air. ... [O]ne approach is to tie

the bird's wings, weight it with a rock and then throw it. This will make its trajectory (nearly) as predictable as that of the stone, but in the process the capability of the bird is completely destroyed. (p 18)

Rather than advocating strong central control of the system, those who view policy as a *complex adaptive system* tend to suggest that government ought to foster the dynamic process of learning the system needs in order to adapt. Yet, the strategies that have been promoted to boost 'learning' on the basis of evaluating the evidence of 'what works' make little sense from this perspective (see Chapman, 2004): if systems interact with their environment in unpredictable ways then we can never be sure that what works in one place will work in another; if nested feedback loops result in unpredictable, non-linear behaviour then policy outcomes will be the result of the actions of the *system itself* rather than the external interventions, so attempts to isolate and evaluate the impact of those external interventions will tell us very little; and quantitative measurement of progress in achieving predetermined targets and goals will always mask as much us it reveals, because in measuring only intended actions it cannot tell us anything about important unintended consequences.

Added to this, complexity theory-based perspectives suggest that another major weakness of reductionist approaches comes in the way they break down complex systems into separate components for the purpose of analysis. One of the major insights that complexity theory has provided is that an understanding of change requires us to undertake a whole-systems analysis because it is the interactions between components – rather than the individual components themselves – that are key. By analysing components in isolation from the rest of the system the danger is that we will miss what really matters because 'the very act of simplifying by sub-division loses the interconnections and therefore cannot tackle this aspect of complexity' (Chapman, 2004, p 35). This is a key issue with regard to the summarising – or 'thin-slicing' – of information available to policy makers: in the process of extracting 'a few key lessons' the temptation to focus on one small part of the system, rather than the whole system, should be avoided.

Blackman's (2006) discussion of the causes of smoking offers us a useful example of complexity-rooted analysis in practice that can illustrate some of these points well. Smoking cessation has been one of the key concerns of public health policy in recent years and has also been a prime candidate for evidence-based policy making: indeed, the National Institute for Health and Clinical Excellence (NICE) have supported the prescription of nicotine replacement therapy and bupropion on the basis of a systematic review of their clinical effectiveness (NICE, 2002a, 2002b). However, as Blackman (2006) notes, the increased availability of these treatments has made relatively little progress in reducing smoking rates in deprived communities: a clear demonstration of the non-linear impacts of policy in practice and the importance of neighbourhood effects in shaping policy outcomes. While some have suggested that this is simply because low income itself is one of the main determinants of smoking, through an analysis of detailed survey data of the residents of Middlesbrough, Blackman demonstrates that such a perspective is also overly simplistic for low income and low smoking rates often coincide. What matters more is the *interaction* of low income with a number of other factors and Blackman (2006) finds that: 'Overall, the higher smoking rates appear to start with unhelpful neighbours, rise further with combinations of low liveability and no further education, and then reach their highest level among the workless configurations' (p 45). By adopting a more holistic perspective of the causes of smoking that appreciates the complex interactions between multiple factors, Blackman draws a conclusion that differs radically from NICE's narrower evaluation of medical technologies: 'improving incomes and job opportunities among disadvantaged communities may have a much greater impact than smoking cessation services' (p 45).

Interestingly, whole-systems working has begun to gain some intellectual currency in policy circles, particularly in health and social care, where interorganisational partnerships have acted as a catalyst for thinking about how the different elements of policy delivery networks might work together more effectively (Hudson, 2006). One of the main suggestions that has been made in such contexts is that 'it is necessary ... to accept that completely different evaluations of social systems, their purposes and performance will inevitably exist' and so 'the only way we can get near to a view of the whole system is to look at it from as many perspectives as possible – subjectivity needs to be embraced rather than ignored by the systems approach' (Hudson, 2006, p 15). Rather than using hard systems methodologies that seek to quantitatively measure activity, it is argued that Soft Systems Methodologies (SSM; see Case study 10.2) that try to draw out people's different understandings and encourage an iterative process of reflection and learning are to be preferred (see Checkland and Scholes, 1990; Chapman, 2004; Hudson, 2006). In other words, it is only through seeking to understand and reflect on the multiple connections – the emergent properties – which come together to create the system that true learning can occur. Indeed, we might argue that, in essence, all learning aims to tap into the 'memory' of the system. When the policy process is viewed as a complex adaptive system, however, it becomes clear that the memory does not reside in one place and certainly not in the centre of government alone. Consequently, it is impossible to draw on the system's memory-using techniques that fail to account for the multiple valid perspectives that reside within it.

Case study 10.2: A review of personal taxation: Soft Systems Methodology as a learning tool

In 2003, the Inland Revenue conducted a review of the personal taxation system (Brown et al, 2006). The study combined data mining with the use of Soft Systems Methodology (SSM). SSM was used to guide consultations with key stakeholders to develop an understanding of how they regarded the

---

personal tax system in the UK. Perspectives included external customers such as employees, tax credit recipients, pensioners, employers and accountants; internal stakeholders such as operational staff, information technology (IT) experts and tax policy experts; and civil servants.

The focus was on drawing comparisons between views of the current tax system and the perceived ideal. The methodology encourages divergence and over 90 ideas for both improving the current system and proposing fundamental change to the personal taxation system were generated.

A convergent phase of analysis brought the ideas together and rationalised them through clustering, categorising according to feasibility, and exclusion where the impact was expected to be minor. Four idealised systems were eventually identified. All of the systems were evaluated against: impact on customers; support for the Inland Revenue's current role; ideal features as described by stakeholders; robustness and adaptability to change; and implementation and operational implications. Brown et al (2006) contend that the use of SSM helped in creating shared perceptions about how the Inland Revenue would need to respond in implementing ideas for improvement. This offers hope for the dynamic learning capability so often missing in the evidence-based policy methodologies centred on positivist discovery and discussed by Parsons (2002).

The collaborative methodology used in the Inland Revenue exercise comes closer to achieving learning capability than simply arriving at a solution. In the words of Schön (1983, p 42), 'There is a high, hard ground where practitioners can make effective use of research-based theory and technique, and there is a swampy lowland where situations are confusing "messes" incapable of technical solution. The difficulty is that the problems of the high ground, however great their technical interest, are often relatively unimportant to clients or to the large society, while in the swamp are the problems of greatest human concern'.

The key, Parsons (2002) identifies, is not in government trying to decide what works. Instead, he suggests that 'government has to learn to let go and learn how to learn' (p 52).

In short, viewing the policy process as a complex adaptive system rather than as a machine that can be controlled gives us a radically different world view that problematises much of the approach to learning offered in *Professional policy making for the twenty-first century*. And, because it is a seemingly radical perspective, the prescriptions that might flow from it can seem radical and daunting too. Yet, they need not be. It is to this issue that we now turn.

Towards open systems?

Systems thinking does not offer magic solutions for policy makers because one of its core messages is that systems cannot be easily controlled. Indeed, systems thinking cannot offer substantive prescriptions without contradicting itself, because while it can generate new ideas and approaches:

> ... it is critical to the overall enterprise that they emerge from a learning process in which as many stakeholders, end-users and delivery agents are involved as possible. It is only by integrating their different perspectives and values into the learning process that the resulting actions will deal effectively with inherent complexity, including multiplicity of views and aspirations. (Chapman, 2004, p 89)

In terms of process, however, it can take us forward in a number of areas. First and foremost, it suggests there is a need for the centre to avoid the temptation to adopt a command–and–control approach. For Chapman (2004), greater learning can only arise if greater experimentation is allowed. He argues that while the centre ought to establish boundaries and the general direction of change it requires, more freedom in the use of resources and greater discretion in how goals may be achieved is needed at the local level. It is through experimentation, diversity and reflection, rather than through target setting and measures, he suggests, that learning can be best fostered in complex adaptive systems. One idea that has become increasingly important in New Labour's health and education policies – earned autonomy – gains Chapman's support on the basis that it recognises some of the deficiencies of the target-based culture and because it allows for learning-by-doing to occur organically at the local level.

Obviously such an approach brings risks for policy makers, not least because abandoning central 'control' over policy detail in favour of local experimentation might be seen as a recipe for chaos. However, systems thinking stresses the prominence of disorder and chaos in complex adaptive systems and, because of this, urges responses that acknowledge that order cannot be imposed on the system; instead, it 'provides some ways of understanding disorder and apparent irrationality' (Hudson, 2006, p 4). This, in turn, means that it 'is more about *problem coping* than *problem solving*' (Hudson, 2006, p 21, emphasis in original). This is unlikely to be the sort of advice that those ministers keen to demonstrate strong problem-solving skills will want to hear, but genuine learning must surely involve acknowledging there are limits to what can be achieved. Moreover, if we are keen to encourage a process of learning then this means that we have to be supportive of well-intentioned policy efforts that fail to generate the hoped-for outcomes. In fact, more than this, it must mean allowing both success *and* failure to occur, because *both* are crucial in terms of our learning. Yet, as Chapman (2004) observes, the blame culture in Whitehall makes it difficult for real experimentation to take place. As he puts it: 'while failure is unacceptable, learning is not possible – with the paradoxical result that failures will continue' (p 71).

Relinquishing central control can also seem risky because it appears to involve giving up control over the detail of policy implemented on the ground to other organisations. Yet, systems thinking would suggest this feeling of control is often an illusion and the expansive policy analysis literature examining implementation 'failures' would seem to support this (Hudson and Lowe, 2004). Indeed, the policy analysis literature has, for quite some time, suggested that policy is made and delivered by complex interorganisational networks that, like – or, even, *as* – complex adaptive systems, are self-organising and autonomous entities (Marsh and Rhodes, 1992; Kickert et al, 1997; Marsh and Smith, 2000). The consensus in this literature is that policy makers need to acknowledge these networks, learn about them and work with(in) them. Van der Meer and Edelenbos (2006) apply this same thinking directly to the learning that might flow from policy evaluations, noting that because 'different actors, with different, but related, interests, perspectives, norms and values interact to produce the phenomena we study ... increasing connections between [multiple] evaluation activities is essential if evaluation is to contribute to accountability, learning and co-operation in complex multi-actor policy networks' (p 216). However, networks are not only important in so far as they need to be understood if we are to learn about policy, they can also be a source of learning themselves. Benz and Fürst (2002) have even suggested that it is within policy networks that much of the policy learning we observe takes place – although they are keen to stress that learning is far from automatic and that, consequently, 'networks are no panacea for learning' (p 23). Interestingly, when exploring the role of networks in producing the different levels of policy learning identified by Hall (1993; see above), Pemberton (2004) noted (in the context of British economic policy) that the deeper the level of change, the wider the number of organisations and actors that were drawn into the policy network and the broader the pool of ideas entering the feedback loop.

In a set of reflections on power, penned after he left his role as Director of Policy at 10 Downing Street, Geoff Mulgan (2005b) made two observations that are directly relevant to the discussion in hand. Firstly, he emphasised that governments must draw on independent knowledge, arguing that 'knowledge resides in universities, in international organisations like the OECD or EU, and in government itself. ... [The Blair] Government's greatest successes have generally been in areas in which the knowledge base is strongest and where independent validators of knowledge ... are most powerful'. Here, he points to the decision to make the Bank of England independent – a decision that involved passing management of policy detail to the policy network as systems thinking might advocate – as a key success. Secondly, he concluded that 'dynamic governments remain porous', arguing that:

> ... one of the optical illusions of government is that those inside it think of themselves as the drivers of change. Energetic leaders do

cajole, prod and persuade. Yet most far-reaching ideas and changes come from outside, from social movements and movements of ideas. Governments are more often vehicles than initiators.... This is why it is so important for governments to remain porous – open to the views and ideas of business and NGOs [non-governmental organisations], public servants and the public – and why it is sometimes necessary for even the most powerful politicians to take time out to listen and learn. For the same reasons, the smarter governments around the world realise that they need to build innovation into their everyday working: through experimental zones and pilots, competitive funds and rewards for promising new ideas. And new ideas need time to evolve – preferably away from the spotlight. (Mulgan, 2005b)

Mulgan's ideas here chime precisely with those found in systems thinking. That this is so is not surprising, for he has written in the past (Mulgan, 2001) about the potential for systems thinking to improve policy making and delivery and his earlier work (for example, Mulgan, 1997) was influenced by complexity theory. However, what is surprising is that these ideas had so little impact on the notion of learning outlined in *Professional policy making for the twenty-first century* despite Mulgan's role at the centre of government at the time of its publication. Indeed, Mulgan (2001) himself noted that 'systems thinking – especially in its broader meaning – remains largely foreign to the everyday practice of government', and that 'governments tend to be happier with simple causal relationships, relationships between inputs and outputs, rather than with interdependent phenomena' (p 23).

Part of the reason it has had such a limited impact – as Mulgan (2001) notes – is that 'in the real world of policy making and implementation at current levels of knowledge, systems thinking is usually more useful as a heuristic tool, something more than a metaphor but less than a useable model' (p 28). Certainly it is true that more needs to be done in terms of working through how systems thinking might be utilised by policy makers and how a networked perspective on learning can be facilitated. However, government itself has a key role to play in driving up the supply of such skills by increasing its demand for them. By encouraging greater diversity, innovation and experimentation in policy at the local level, the knowledge base will naturally expand, not just in terms of substantive knowledge about particular policy fields but also in terms of knowledge about how systems can be understood. But government also needs to be more open in order to deliver real learning. This means not only drawing in knowledge from outside, but helping that knowledge to develop by allowing greater access to important information. Chapman (2004) and Mulgan (2005b) both suggest that secrecy has been one of the greatest barriers to learning in the UK government and, in turn, that this secrecy is fuelled by a culture of accountability as apportioning blame and highlighting failure that pervades both our political system and the media.

Faced with complex problems in engineering, computing science has demonstrated that two quite different ways forward (co)exist. One has been to concentrate large amounts of resources in very large organisations that work at length and in secret on a new product until it is ready for launch. The other is to harness the power of the network by making raw program code available for inspection to all from the outset and asking those who can see errors or room for improvement to make or suggest changes (see also Chapter Six, this volume, on inclusive policy making). While the latter approach – known as open source working – may seem like a fantasy, it has already proved adept in creating products that rival those made by the powerful multi-national corporations that dominate information technology (IT): while most home computers use the commercially developed Microsoft Windows® operating system, the open source developed LINUX powers around a quarter of business servers; similarly, while Microsoft's Internet Explorer is the dominant web browser – with around 80% of the market – the recently launched open source-developed Firefox browser commanded around 15% of the market by the end of 2006. Mulgan has recently written about open source methods (Mulgan and Steinberg, 2005), and it has been noted that there is potential for open source-inspired methods to be used in the policy process. Intriguingly, David Cameron has tried to open up the Conservative Party's ongoing policy commissions by allowing members of the public to contribute to debates on individual websites set up for each commission, although it should be noted that few people have taken up the invitation to comment to date. Likewise, as Secretary of State for the Environment, David Miliband has tried to use collaborative web-based tools ('wikis') in the production of an environmental contract, although again with limited success. It has also been reported that the CIA (Central Intelligence Agency) has created a collaborative web-based intelligence tool that allows its agents – and those working for its allies – to create and amend data about a whole range of individuals, organisations and events of relevance to its operations (*Sydney Morning Herald*, 2006).

Conclusions

While, ultimately, as Tony Blair notes, policy is about people making their minds up about which course of action needs to be pursued, he is wrong to suggest that the process by which that decision is arrived at is a substitute for decision making. Indeed, if anything, process is the key phrase for it describes the form that learning must take: a continual learning process rather than the periodic input of lessons. It should also be a more open process than is commonly the case, embrace multiple perspectives and multiple stakeholders, encourage experimentation and be tolerant of failures or dead ends. It is a process with no clear end and is as much about exploration and problem coping as it is about problem solving. Above all else, it must involve relinquishing some control and embracing a broader, more network-based approach. This is, of course, easier said than done. It involves much uncertainty for policy makers, asking them to move out of the comfort zone provided by their current way of thinking, engage with alien perspectives that might run counter to their own world view and allow the agenda for discussion to be (at least partially) set by others. Yet, this is exactly the kind of situation we would expect a good student, keen to learn, to find themselves in. If we really want to encourage a learning-based approach to policy making, should it be any different for policy makers? Overall, this chapter has argued that:

- *Professional policy making for the twenty-first century* advanced a narrow conception of learning that relegated it to a sub-function of evaluation activities.
- Learning can be improved if information is provided in a useable and timely fashion; however, we need to be wary of simplifying complex issues too far and issues of timing are often difficult to control.
- The literature offers useful distinctions between different levels and types of learning; in practice, the focus tends to be on first-order instrumental uses, but deeper and more reflexive learning is possible.
- We should be wary of treating learning as the input of hard 'lessons': learning is better viewed as a process. Gathering evidence is not always the same as learning.
- Understanding the complex interactions between different parts of a policy system is often key in promoting greater learning.
- The use of SSM and whole-systems thinking might help to promote deeper levels of learning.

Further reading

Blackman, T. (2006) *Placing health: Neighbourhood renewal, health improvement and complexity*, Bristol: The Policy Press – this book uses complexity theory to analyse the links between neighbourhood renewal strategies and health improvement in England. In so doing, it demonstrates both the practical applications of complexity theory and the value it can add to our understanding of policy problems.

Brown, J., Cooper, C. and Pidd, M. (2006) 'A taxing problem: the complementary use of hard and soft OR in the public sector', *European Journal of Operational Research*, vol 172, no 2, pp 666-79 – this article is based around a case study of the use of SSM in the Inland Revenue and offers some useful insights into its potential applications – and limits.

Chapman, J. (2004) *System failure: Why governments must learn to think differently*, London: Demos – Chapman's pamphlet – written for the think-tank Demos – is probably the most complete attempt to think through the implications of complexity theory for policy analysis and essential reading for those wanting to gain a fuller understanding of the ideas outlined in this chapter.

Hudson, B. (2006) *Whole systems working: A guide and discussion paper*, London: Integrated Care Network/DH – this short discussion paper provides an accessible guide to whole-systems working, drawing on ideas found in complexity theory but remaining practical in its outlook. A good starting point for those new to complexity theory.

Mulgan, G. (2001) 'Systems thinking and the practice of government', *Systemist*, vol 23, special edition, pp 23-9 – drawing on his unique position as someone who has been both a scholar in the field of complexity thinking and a central player in policy delivery in Downing Street, Mulgan's reflections on the potential – and the limits – of systems thinking are illuminating.

Useful websites

www.policyhub.gov.uk/better_policy_making/learns_lessons.asp – the 'Learns lessons' section of the Policy Hub website provides links to a range of useful government documents, although the nature of the links it carries perhaps underlines the limited definition of 'learning' noted throughout this chapter.

www.demos.co.uk/publications/systemfailure2 – this site carries free access to the full text of Jake Chapman's 'System failure' (see 'Further reading') and links to broader information about his work with the think-tank Demos.

www.whb.co.uk/socialissues/indexvol1two.htm – this special issue of the online journal *Social Issues* carries a series of articles about complexity and social policy.

ELEVEN

Conclusions

Hugh Bochel and Sue Duncan

... there is nothing a government hates more than to be well-informed; for it makes the process of arriving at decisions much more complicated and difficult. (Keynes, quoted in Skidelsky, 1992, p 630)

The discussions throughout this book serve to highlight the key debates over the 'modernisation' of policy making, particularly under New Labour since 1997. While it is clear that changes associated with 'modernisation' have received considerable impetus since 1997, it is also apparent that in many of the key areas there have been developments going back several decades. Such attention to policy making is not unique to the UK, and there are reflections of such an approach in many other states. However, what has perhaps been most new has been the generally consistent drive across government to reform policy making.

The nine elements of policy making, set out in *Professional policy making for the twenty-first century* (Cabinet Office Strategic Policy Making Team, 1999), are not a blueprint for action. Neither, as is clear from the discussions in this book, are the different elements mutually exclusive (for example, issues around 'evidence-based' policy also emerge in relation to virtually all of the key characteristics, with questions over what is considered good evidence, the quality of evidence and the uses to which it is put, or indeed not put). Rather, they are best seen as a set of overlapping and, in many cases, interdependent principles. As the chapters in this book make clear, there are also significant variations in the extent to which the nine competencies have been more fully articulated in subsequent government documentation and guidance. For example, there is a significant literature associated with the 'joined-up' and 'evidence-based' competencies, while others, such as 'learning lessons' and 'innovative, flexible and creative', are less well explained. There are a number of possible reasons for this. It may be that the principles are based on a flawed model of policy making; this would be unsurprising, as despite many attempts the development of a workable model of the policy process has proved somewhat elusive (see, for example, Parsons, 1995; Sabatier, 2006), defying a description that illuminates rather than confuses.

Alternatively, the state of development of the different elements may simply reflect the degree to which those elements were already embedded in existing practice, or the availability of appropriate tools and methods. This is certainly true of 'learning lessons' (Chapter Ten), where it is clear that the more sophisticated tools available are not a routine part of the policy maker's toolkit, and 'forward looking' (Chapter Two), where appropriate techniques are still under development. But even in the case of elements that have, to a greater or lesser extent, a long history, such as 'evidence-based' (Chapter Five) or 'inclusive' (Chapter Six) policy making, there remain problems in operationalising what are still seemingly elusive concepts. This is not an argument for abandoning the ideas underpinning *Professional policy making for the twenty-first century*, but there is certainly a case for further reflection, including on what is meant by each of these terms, how they are appropriately put into practice in a range of often very different contexts, and how the political context in which policy decisions are made influences what happens on the ground. While official guidance may in some cases be unclear and imprecise, equally some of the academic literature criticises performance in modern policy making without fully acknowledging the complexity of the political world in which it operates. The advantage of bringing together academics and civil servants is that we have been able to move closer to integrating the two perspectives. Academic theory has been measured against reality and, conversely, civil servants have been able to view their world through the eyes of an outsider. However, even this process has not always been easy.

Given that they have been a major plank of the policy-making process for nearly a decade, it is perhaps surprising that there has been little recent attention given, either in civil service or academic literature, to refining the nine elements of policy making. Despite a number of flaws *Professional policy making for the twenty-first century* does represent a valuable attempt to systematically analyse some of the key ingredients of the policy process. This current analysis of 'modern' policy making found the model useful in analysing progress and issues, both in terms of the individual competencies and the overall approach; although it identified a range of weaknesses and areas that would benefit from further development, the document and its model provided a sound basis for reviewing the state of the art of policy making. Although not without problems, in both definition and implementation, the nine principles do represent a bold attempt to take forward thinking and to guide practice in policy making across government, and probably deserve further attention. The current emphasis on Professional Skills for Government, which aims, among other things, to clearly position policy making as a professional activity, has not led to a re-evaluation or further development of the nine principles. Indeed current thinking at the individual level setting out core competencies for the senior civil service draws little on the nine competencies; under the Professional Skills for Government banner, a new leadership model is set out; the core skills are people management, financial management, programme and project management, analysis and use of evidence, strategic thinking and communications and marketing (http.psg.civilservice.gov.uk).

While there is some acknowledgement of the nine principles, the broad thrust of Professional Skills for Government involves analysing the core skills of the senior civil service in a very different way, and it is not easy to see how this relates to 'professional policy making'. Of course, not all senior civil servants are engaged in the business of making policy – delivery and corporate functions like human resources (HR) and finance are also important – but at a time when there is an emphasis on developing specialist competency frameworks, it is surprising that *Professional policy making for the twenty-first century* has not been revisited and some of the ideas more clearly incorporated into Professional Skills for Government.

At the organisational level, the most obvious current drivers of civil service reform are the Capability Reviews, which aim to assess how well equipped departments are to meet delivery challenges and provide targeted support to make necessary improvements. The standard model of Capability encompasses three elements – leadership, strategy and delivery – and 10 sub-categories 'designed to focus on the most crucial areas of capability'. A number of these, for example, 'base choices on evidence', 'focus on outcomes', 'plan, resource and prioritise', 'develop clear roles, responsibilities and business model(s)', draw on some of the features identified in 'modern policy making' (www.civilservice.gov.uk/reform/capability_reviews/tools/model.asp).

Again, the Reviews reflect the fact that the activities of departments involve much more than making policy, but it would be reassuring to be clear that the thinking that went into *Professional policy making for the twenty-first century* had contributed to the further development of the modernisation project, and indeed that lessons had been learnt. As a number of the chapters here make clear, progress has certainly been made in embedding and developing some of the elements and, in some cases, new structures have been set up, with, for instance, 'joining up' providing many examples of new ways of working. Yet, taken together, the Capability Reviews, Professional Skills for Government and *Professional policy making for the twenty-first century* seem to leave considerable scope for further coherent and collective action on the ideas that they themselves seek to promote.

The growing awareness of the complexity of contemporary society, and of the structures of governance, as reflected, for example, in the concept of multi-level governance, also have implications for many of the ideas from *Professional policy making for the twenty-first century*, and it remains unclear to what extent these have been embraced, or even accepted, across the different tiers of government in the contemporary UK. While sharing many (although by no means all) of the policy imperatives of Whitehall, the devolved administrations and local government also have their own take on approaches to policy making, as is apparent, for example, in some of the discussions in Chapters Six and Seven (this volume). Many of the drivers of a new approach to policy making have also impinged on local as well as central government. The introduction of Best Value and of a system of performance management, reflecting many of the elements seen in central government, are a clear attempt to carry through some of the central government reforms to the local level. Similarly, notions of citizen empowerment, articulated in the local government White Paper, *Strong and prosperous communities* (Department of Communities and Local Government, 2006), together with organisational change such as the strengthening of Government Offices and the establishment of the Neighbourhood Renewal Unit and the wider emphasis on communities as the focus for policy, are all part of the same theme. There is much discussion throughout this book on how 'real' some of these innovations are in terms of their impact on the ground and, in truth, the balance of power between central and local government is perhaps inevitably a theme that has threaded through analyses of the policy process for many decades.

So, has policy making changed? At present, for a wide variety of reasons, the degree to which the nine principles are embedded in practice is variable. However, the real value of *Professional policy making for the twenty-first century* and the nine competencies has perhaps been in documenting a general direction of travel rather than in setting out new directions. It has also arguably set down some markers against which change can be measured.

There are, however, some more fundamental questions. One of these is 'does the modern approach to policy making lead to better policy?'. Although, at the most superficial level, the nine principles are hard to argue against, falling into the category of common sense, there is little clear evidence that policy is objectively better as a result. This of course begs the question of 'better for whom?'. It is almost certainly true that it is clearer what policies are trying to achieve and whether they are successful, but, at least within central government, this is probably as much a consequence of the Public Service Agreement (PSA) process as of modern policy making. It is also the case that efforts at 'joining up' on various dimensions have resulted in better coordinated policy. Similarly, progress is being made in use of evaluation and other evidence; although the concept 'evidence-based policy making' is still awkward to operate in practice, it *is* firmly embedded in the civil service culture. There are some signs that the 'forward-looking' competency is also starting to become more embedded in some parts of government, although, for a variety of reasons, this is patchy, and the same is arguably true for policy making that is 'outward looking' and 'learns lessons'. As Chapter Eight (this volume) makes clear, there has certainly been a great deal of 'review' of policy in recent years, but there is little clarity over what this should or does entail. Similarly, all tiers of government appear to have taken up 'inclusive' approaches with some enthusiasm, but it is not yet clear whether inclusive approaches have made any significant impact on policy making or outcomes. And, in some respects, the hardest of all to assess is whether policy making is more 'innovative, flexible and creative', in part because to achieve it would be likely to require and reflect the acceptance of the other elements. While it does appear that *Professional policy making for the twenty-first century* has had an impact, we are clearly still some way from being able to assess the extent to which policy making is 'better'.

Another fundamental question, which is reflected in the discussions in a number of the chapters, is the differing pressures that seeking to produce long-term, evidence-based policies may bring, compared with those faced by policy makers who need to respond rapidly to what may be short-term problems, or even to demands for quick responses to long-term problems.

Inevitably, any attempt to rationalise the process of policy making and identify good practice has to take account of the context in which these activities are set. Politics, rightly, muddies the waters, as politicians seek to assert their responsibilities as our elected representatives. In doing this, they take account of a range of influences, including political ideology and, specifically, manifesto commitments, and the need to be responsive to public opinion and the electorate more widely. Party politics and the ballot box are an ever-present influence and mean that, however good any blueprint for effective policy making might be, it will need to be sufficiently flexible to adapt in response to the immediate political situation. This is not an argument against developing good practice models for policy making, but simply a reflection of the real world, where policy makers need to anticipate and respond to the needs of those who ultimately make decisions. This will sometimes mean adapting an ideal-typical model to fit particular circumstances.

There is therefore perhaps an inevitable tension between some of the goals and approaches set out in *Professional policy making for the twenty-first century* in the real world inhabited by politicians and other policy makers, but in any attempts to produce a rationalistic approach of policy making it is important to be aware of the pressures that arise from it. Ultimately policy making is political, and the view expressed by the Secretary of State for Trade and Industry, Alistair Darling, to the House of Commons Select Committee on Science and Technology remains powerful:

> You want to take into account all the available evidence; but, at the end of the day, a Minister's job, Parliament's job is to reach a judgement as to whether or not a particular policy ought to be pursued.... I strongly defend my right, as the Secretary of State, a Member of an elected Government, to form a judgement as to what I think is the right thing to do, and the Commons and Lords will decide. (Select Committee on Science and Technology, 2006b, p 71)

Bibliography

'T Hart, P. and Wille, A. (2006) 'Ministers and Top Officials in the Dutch Core executive, living together, growing apart?', *Public Administration*, vol 84, no 1, pp 121–46

Abma, T (2004) 'Responsive Evaluation: The Meaning and Special Contribution to Public Administration', *Public Administration*, vol 82, no 4, pp 993–1012.

Aboriginal and Torres Strait Islander Social Justice Commissioner (2005) *Social Justice Report 2005* (http://www.hreoc.gov.au/social_justice/sjreport05/index.html).

Appleby, J. and Coote, A. (2002) *Five Year Health Check: A Review of Health Policy, 1997-2002*, London: King's Fund.

Argyriades, D. (2006) 'The Rise, Fall, and Rebirth of Comparative Administration: The Rediscovery of Culture', *Public Administration Review*, vol 66, no 2, pp 281–4.

Argyris, C., and Schön, D. (1978) *Organizational learning: A theory of action perspective*, Reading, MA: Addison Wesley.

Arnstein, S.R. (1969) 'A Ladder of Citizen Participation', *Journal of the American Institute of Planners*, vol 35, no 4, pp 216–24.

Ashworth, K., Cebulla, A., Davis, A. Greenberg, D. and Walker, R. (2005) 'When Welfare-To-Work Programs Work Well: Explaining why Riverside and Portland shine so brightly', *Industrial and Labor Relations Review*, vol 59, no 1, pp 34–49.

Ashworth, K., Cebulla, A., Greenberg, D., and Walker, R. (2004) 'Meta-evaluation: Discovering what works best in welfare provision', *Evaluation*, vol 10, no 2, pp 193–216.

Audit Scotland (2006) *Community planning: an initial review*, Edinburgh: Audit Scotland.

Australian Public Service Commission (2004) *Connecting Government: Whole of Government Responses to Australia's Priority Challenges*, Canberra: Commonwealth of Australia.

Bache, I. and Flinders, M. (2004) 'Multi-level Governance and the Study of the British State', *Public Policy and Administration*, vol 19, no 1, pp 31–51.

Bagley. C., Ackerley, C. and Rattray, R. (2004) 'Social exclusion, Sure Start and organizational social capital: evaluating inter-disciplinary multi-agency working in an education and health work programme', *Journal of Education and Policy*, vol 19, no 5, pp 595–607.

Balthasar, A. and Rieder, S. (2000) 'Learning from Evaluations: Effects of the Evaluation of the Swiss Energy 2000 Programme', *Evaluation*, vol 6, no 3, pp 245–260.

Barker, A. with Byrne, I., and Anjuli, V. (1999) *Ruling by Task Force*, London: Politico's in association with Democratic Audit.

Barker, K. (2006) *Barker Review of Land Use Planning*, London: HM Treasury.

Barnett, N. (2003) 'Local Government, New Labour and 'Active Welfare': A Case of 'Self Responsibilisation'?', *Public Policy and Administration*, vol 18, no 3, pp 25-38.

Beard, R. (1999) *National Literacy Strategy: review of research and other related evidence*, London: DfEE.

Beard, R. (2000) 'Research and the National Literacy Strategy', *Oxford Review of Education*, vol 26, nos 3-4, pp 421-36.

Becker, S. and Bryman, A. (2004) (eds), *Understanding Research for Social Policy and Practice*, Bristol: The Policy Press.

Bee, A. (2007) *An Examination of the Ethical and Legal Issues of 'Piloting' in its Widest Sense in DWP*, London: Social Security Advisory Committee.

Bennett, C.J. (1997) 'Understanding Ripple Effects: The Cross-national Adoption of Policy Instruments for Bureaucratic Accountability', *Governance*, vol 10, no 3, pp 213-33

Benz, A. and Fürst, D. (2002) 'Policy Learning in Regional Networks', *European Urban and Regional Studies*, vol 9, no 1, pp 21-35.

Berthoud, R. (1984) *The Reform of Supplementary Benefit*, London: PSI.

Birch, D. and Powell, R. (2004) *Meeting the challenges of Pigot: Pre-trial cross-examination under s.28 of the Youth Justice and Criminal Evidence Act 1999*, London: Home Office.

Blackman, T. (2006) *Placing health: Neighbourhood renewal, health improvement and complexity*. Bristol: The Policy Press.

Blair, T. (1998) 'Europe's left-of-centre parties have discovered the "Third Way"', *Independent*, 7 April, cited in A. Coote, J. Allen, and D. Woodhead (2004) *Finding out what works: Understanding complex, community-based initiatives*, London: Kings Fund.

Blunkett, D. (2003) *Active Citizens, Strong Communities: Progressing Civic Renewal*, London: Home Office.

Blustein J. (2005) 'Toward a more public discussion of the ethics of federal social program discussion', *Journal of Policy Analysis and Management*, vol 24, no 4, pp 824-46.

Boaz, A. and Pawson, R. (2005) 'The perilous road from evidence to policy: five journeys compared', *Journal of Social Policy*, vol 24, no 2, pp 175-94.

Bochel, C. (2006) 'New Labour, Participation and the Policy Process', *Public Policy and Administration*, vol 21, no 4, pp 10-22.

Bochel, C. and Bochel, H. (2004) *The UK Social Policy Process*, Basingstoke: Palgrave Macmillan.

Bogdanor, V. (2005) *Joined-up Government*, Oxford: Oxford University Press.

Borins, S. (2001) *The Challenge of Innovating in Government*, Arlington, VA: PriceWaterhouseCoopers Endowment for the Business of Government.

Borins, S. (2002) 'New Public Management, North American Style', in K. McLaughlin, S.P. Osborne and E. Ferlie (eds), *New Public Management: Current Trends and Future Prospects*, London: Routledge.

Bottomley, D. and Walker, R. (1996) *Experimental Methods for Policy Evaluation*, Loughborough: CRSP Working Paper 276S.

Bovaird, T. (2003) 'E-government and E-governance: Organisational Implications, Options and Dilemmas', *Public Policy and Administration*, vol 18, no 2, pp 37-56.

Bovaird, T. and Löffler, E. (2003) 'The Changing Context of Public Policy', in T. Bovaird and E. Löffler (eds), *Public Management and Governance*, London: Routledge.

Brewer, M., Clark, T. and Myck, M. (2001) *Credit Where It's Due? An Assessment of the New Tax Credits* Commentary 86, London: Institute for Fiscal Studies.

Brown, B. and Liddle, J. (2005) 'Service Domains – the New Communities: A Case Study of Peterlee Sure Start, UK', *Local Government Studies*, vol 31, no 4, pp 449-73.

Brown J., Cooper, C. and Pidd, M. (2006) 'A taxing problem: the complementary use of hard and soft OR in the public sector', *European Journal of Operational Research*, vol 172, no 2, pp 666-79.

Bullock, H., Mountford, J. and Stanley, R. (2001) *Better Policy Making*, London: Centre for Management and Policy Studies.

Bulmer, M. (1978) *Social Policy Research*, London: Macmillan.

Bulmer, S. and Padgett, S. A. (2005) 'Policy Transfer in the European Union: an Institutionalist Perspective', *British Journal of Political Science*, vol 35, no 1, pp 103-26.

Butler, E., Deaton, S., Hodgkinson, J., Holmes, E. and Marshall, S. (2005) *Quick but not dirty, Rapid Evidence Assessments as a decision support tool in social policy*, London: Government Social Research Unit (www/gsr.gov.uk/downloads/gsrnews/quickdirty.pdf).

Byrne, D. (1998) *Complexity Theory and the Social Sciences: An Introduction*, London: Routledge.

Byrne, D. (2001) 'Complexity Science and Transformations in Social Policy', *Social Issues*, vol 1, no 2 (www.whb.co.uk/socialissues/db.htm).

Cabinet Office (1994) *The civil service: Continuity and change*, London: The Stationery Office.

Cabinet Office (1996) *government.direct*, London: The Stationery Office.

Cabinet Office (1999) *Modernising Government*, London: The Stationery Office.

Cabinet Office (2000) *Be the Change: Peer Review Report of the Cabinet Office Role in Modernising Government*, London: Cabinet Office.

Cabinet Office (2002a) *Viewfinder: A Policy Maker's Guide to Public Involvement*, London: Cabinet Office.

Cabinet Office (2002b) *Involving the Front Line in Policy Making*, London: Cabinet Office (www.policyhub.gov.uk/docs/front_line-staff2.pdf).

Cabinet Office (2003) *Trying It Out: The Role of Pilots in Policy Making*, London: Cabinet Office.

Cabinet Office (2007) *Building on Progress: Public Services*, London: Cabinet Office.

Cabinet Office Strategic Policy Making Team (1999) *Professional Policy Making for the Twenty First Century*, London: Cabinet Office.

Cambridge Policy Consultants, SOLAR at the University of the West of England and Arwel Jones Associates (2006) *Action Research Report 2: Cluster Groups, part of the interim evaluation of the Welsh Assembly Government Communities First Programme*, Cardiff: Welsh Assembly Government.

Campbell, D.T. (1969) 'Reforms as experiments', *American Psychologist*, vol 24, no 4, pp 409–29.

Campbell, H. (2002) 'Evidence-based policy: The continuing search for effective policy processes', *Planning Theory and Practice*, vol 3, no 1, pp 89–90.

Capability Reviews Team (2006a) *Capability Reviews: The Findings of the First Four Reviews*, London: Cabinet Office.

Capability Reviews Team (2006b) *Capability Reviews: Tranche 2: Common Themes and Summaries*, London: Cabinet Office.

Capability Reviews Team (2006c) *Capability Review of the Department for Work and Pensions*, London: Cabinet Office.

Capability Reviews Team (2006c) *Capability Review of the Department for Education and Skills*, London: Cabinet Office.

Capability Reviews Team (2006e) *Capability Review of the Home Office*, London: Cabinet Office.

Capability Reviews Team (2006f) *Capability Review of the Department for Communities and Local Government*, London: Cabinet Office.

Carr, F. and Massey, A. (2006) *Public Policy and the New European Agendas*, Cheltenham: Edward Elgar.

Carroll, P. and Steane, P. (2002) 'Australia, the New Public Management and the New Millenium', in K. McLaughlin, S.P. Osborne and E. Ferlie (eds), *New Public Management: Current Trends and Future Prospects*, London: Routledge.

Casey, B and Gold, M (2005) 'Peer review of labour market programmes in the European Union: what can countries really learn from one another?' *Journal of European Public Policy*, vol 12, no 1, pp 23–43.

Castle, B. (1980) *The Castle Diaries 1974-76*, London: Weidenfeld and Nicolson.

Cebulla, A. (2005) 'The road to Britain's "New Deal"' in A. Cebulla, K. Ashworth, D. Greenberg and R. Walker (eds) *Welfare-to-Work: New Labour and the US Experience*, Aldershot: Ashgate.

Cebulla, A., Ashworth, K., Greenberg, D. and Walker, R. (eds) (2005) *Welfare-to-Work: New Labour and the US Experience*, Aldershot: Ashgate.

Central Advisory Council for Education (1967) *Children and their Primary Schools*, London: HMSO.

Central Policy Review Staff (1975) *A Joint Framework for Social Policies*, London: HMSO.

Challis, L., Fuller, S., Henwood, M., Klein, R., Plowden, W., Webb, A., Whittingham, P. and Wistow, G. (1988) *Joint Approaches to Social Policy: Rationality and Practice*, Cambridge: Cambridge University Press.

Chalmers, D. and Lodge, M. (20023) 'The Open Method of Co-ordination and the European Welfare State', *CARR Discussion Paper Series* Centre for Analysis of Risk and Regulation, LSE DP11, London: London School of Economics.

Chancellor of the Duchy of Lancaster (1993) *Realising Our Potential*, London: HMSO.

Chapman, J. (2004) *System Failure: Why Governments Must Learn to Think Differently*, London: Demos (www.demos.co.uk/publications/systemfailure2).

Checkland, P. (1981) *Systems Thinking, Systems Practice*, Chichester: Wiley.

Checkland, P. and Scholes, J. (1990) *Soft Systems Methodology in Action*, Chichester: Wiley.

Chief Information Officer (2005) *Transformational Government: Enabled by Technology*, London: The Stationery Office.

Chilvers, M. and Weatherburn, D (2004) 'The New South Wales "Compstat" Process: Its Impact on Crime', *Australian and New Zealand Journal of Criminology*, vol 37, no 1, pp 22-48.

Cilliers, P. (1998) *Complexity and postmodernism: understanding complex systems*, London: Routledge.

Civil Service Management Board (2005) *Professional Skills for Government: Progress report from The Civil Service Management Board* (http://psg.civilservice.gov.uk/uploaded_files/6/Progress%20report.pdf).

Clarence, E. (2002) 'Technocracy Reinvented: The New Evidence Based Policy Movement', in *Public Policy and Administration*, Special Issue, Evidence Based Policy, vol 17, no 3, Autumn 2002, pp 1-11.

Clarke, J. (2004) *Changing Welfare, Changing States*, London: Sage.

Clarke, J., Gewirtz, S., Hughes, G. and Humphrey, J. (2002) 'Guarding the Public Interest?', in J. Clarke, S. Gewirtz and E. McLaughlin (eds), *New Managerialism, New Welfare?*, London: Sage.

Coghlan, A., Preskill, H. and Tzavaras Catsambas, T. (2003) 'An Overview of Appreciative Inquiry in Evaluation', *New Directions For Evaluation*, no 100, Winter 2003, pp 5-22.

Cohen, N. (2004) *Pretty Straight Guys*, London: Faber and Faber.

Commission of the European Communities (2001) *European Governance: A White Paper*, Brussels: Commission of the European Communities.

Commission on Social Justice (1994) *Social Justice: Strategy for National Renewal* (Borrie Report), London: Vintage/ IPPR.

Conklin, J. and Weil, W. (1998) *Wicked Problems: Naming the Pain in Organisations* (www.3m.com/meetingnetwork/readingroom/gdss_wicked.html).

Cope, N. (2004) 'Intelligence Led Policing or Policing Led Intelligence?', *British Journal of Criminology*, vol 44, no 2, pp 188-203.

Coxall, B. (2001) *Pressure Groups in British Politics*, Harlow: Pearson.

Croft, S. and Beresford, P. (1992) 'The Politics of Participation', *Critical Social Policy*, no 35, pp 20-44.

Davies, P. (1999) 'What is evidence based education?' *British Journal of Educational Studies*, vol 47, no 2, pp 108-121.

Davies, H.T.O. and Nutley, S. (2002) 'Evidence based policy and practice: moving from rhetoric to reality', Research Unit for Research Utilisation, University of St. Andrews, Discussion Paper 2.

Davies, H.T.O., Nutley, S.M. and Smith, P. (2000a) 'Introducing evidence-based policy and practice in public services' in H.T.O. Davies, S.M. Nutley and P.C. Smith (eds) *What works? Evidence-based policy and practice in public services*, Bristol: The Policy Press.

Davies, H.T.O., Nutley, S. and Smith, P.C. (eds) (2000b) *What Works? Evidence-Based Policy and Practice in Public Services*, Bristol: The Policy Press.

Davies, H.T.O., Nutley, S.M. and Smith, P. C. (1999) 'Editorial: What works? The role of evidence in public sector policy and practice', *Public Money and Management*, vol 19, no 1, pp 3-5.

Davies, P. (2004a) 'Is evidence-based government possible?', Jerry Lee Lecture 2004, 4th Annual Campbell Collaboration Colloquium, Washington DC.

Davies, P. (2004b) 'Policy Evaluation in the United Kingdom', Paper presented at the KDI International Policy Evaluation Forum, Seoul, Korea, 19-21 May.

Davies, P. (2004c) *Rapid Evidence Assessments: A tool for policy making*, London: Government Chief Social Researcher's Office (www.gsr.gov.uk/newresearch/archive/rae.asp).

De Bruijn, J.A. and ten Heuvelhof, E.F. (1997) 'Instruments for Network Management', in W.J.M. Kickert, E-H, Klijn and J.F.M. Koppenjan (eds), *Managing Complex Networks: Strategies for the Public Sector*, London: Sage.

Deakin, N. and Parry, R. (2000) *The Treasury and Social Policy: The Contest for Control of Welfare Strategy*, London: Macmillan.

Defra (Department of the Environment, Food and Rural Affairs) (2006) *Our Approach to Evidence and Innovation*, London: Defra.

Defra (2007) *Looking Back at Looking Forwards: Next Steps for Horizon Scanning and Futures*, London: Department for Environment, Food and Rural Affairs.

Defra (undated) 'Evidence-based policy making' (www.defra.gov.uk/science/how/evidence.htm).

Department for Work and Pensions (2006) *A fresh start: Child support redesign – the Government's response to Sir David Henshaw*, London: The Stationery Office.

Department of Communities and Local Government (2006) *Strong and Prosperous Communities – The Local Government White Paper*, London: The Stationery Office.

Department of Health (1989) *Working for Patients*, London: HMSO.

Department of Health and Social Security (1985) *Reform of Social Security: Programme for Change*, London: HMSO.

Department of Health (2002) *The NHS Plan – A Progress Report: The NHS Modernisation Board's Annual Report 2000-2001*, London: Department of Health.

Department of the Environment, Transport and the Regions (1998a) *Modern Local Government: In Touch with the People*, London: The Stationery Office.

Department of the Environment, Transport and the Regions (1998b) *Modernising Local Government: Local Democracy and Community Leadership*, London: The Stationery Office.

DiMaggio, P. and Powell, W. (1983) 'The Iron Cage Revisited: Institutional Isomorphism and Collective Rationality in Organizational Fields', *American Sociological Review*, vol 48, no 2, pp 147-60.

Disability Rights Commission (2006) *Policy Development*, Central Government Guidance Bulletin, October 2006, London: Disability Rights Commission.

Dixon, D. and Maher, L. (2005) 'Lessons for Australia from the "New York miracle"', *Criminal Justice*, vol 5, no 2, pp 115-43.

Dolowitz, D. (1998) *Learning from America: Policy Transfer and the Development of the British Workfare System*, Brighton: Sussex Academic Press

Dolowitz, D. P. and Marsh, D. (1996) 'Who Learns What from Whom: a Review of the Policy Transfer Literature', *Political Studies*, vol 44, no 2, pp 343-57.

Donahue, J. D. (2005) 'Dynamics of Diffusion: Conceptions of American Federalism and Public Sector Innovation' (www.innovations.harvard.edu/showdoc.html?id=6771).

Dorey, P. (2005) *Policy Making in Britain*, London: Sage.

Dror, Y. (1964) 'Muddling Through – Science or Inertia?', *Public Administration Review*, vol. 24, no. 3, pp. 153-7.

DTI (Department for Trade and Industry) (2003) *Competing in the global economy: The innovation challenge*, DTI Innovation Report, London: DTI.

Duncan, S. (2005) 'Towards evidence inspired policy', *Social Sciences*, no 61, pp 10-11.

Duncan, S. and Harrop, A. (2006) 'A User Perspective on Research Quality', *International Journal of Social Research Methodology*, vol 9, no 2, pp 159-74.

Easton, D. (1965) *A Systems Analysis of Political Life*, New York: J. Wiley and Sons.

Education and Skills Committee (2005) *Teaching children to read*, London: The Stationery Office.

Efficiency Unit (1988) *Improving management in government: The next steps*, London: HMSO.

EMCDDA (2001) 'Drug Coordination Arrangements in the EU Member States', Lisbon: European Monitoring Centre for Drugs and Drug Addiction (www.emcdda.europa.eu/).

ESRC (July 2006) *Annual Report and Accounts 2005-2006*, London: The Stationery Office.

Etzioni, A. (1967) 'Mixed Scanning: A "Third" Approach to Decision Making', *Public Administration Review*, vol 27, no 5, pp 385-92.

Evans, M. (ed) (2004) *Policy Transfer in Global Perspective*, Aldershot: Ashgate.

Fabian Society Commission on Taxation and Citizenship (2004) *Paying for Progress: A New Politics of Tax for Public Spending*, London: Fabian Society.

Federal Register (1991) 'The Federal policy for the protection of human subjects', Tuesday, 18 June, vol 56, no 117, pp 28002-32.

Flinders, M. (2002) 'Governance in Whitehall', *Public Administration*, vol 80, no 1, pp 51-75.

Flood, R. L. and Romm, N.R.A. (1996) *Diversity Management: Triple Loop Learning*, Chichester: Wiley.

Ford, J. and England, J. (2000) *Data and literature on mortgage interest*, London: Social Research Branch, Department of Social Security.

Frantz, J. and Sato, H. (2005) 'The Fertile Soil for Policy Learning', *Policy Sciences*, vol 38, nos 2-3, pp 159-76.

Freud, D. (2007) *Reducing dependency, increasing opportunity: options for the future of welfare to work*, Leeds: Corporate Document Services.

Friend, J.K., Power, J.M. and Yewlett, C.J.L. (1974) *Public Planning: the Inter-corporate Dimension*, London: Tavistock.

Fulton Committee (1968) *Report of the Committee the Civil Service 1966-68, vol 1*, London: HMSO.

Gains, F. (2003) 'Surveying the Landscape of Modernisation: Executive Agencies Under New Labour', *Public Policy and Administration*, vol 18, no 2, pp 4-20.

Game, C. (2002) 'Britain's "5 Percen" Local Government Revolution: the Faltering Impact of New Labour's Modernization Agenda', *International Review of Administrative Sciences*, vol 68, no 3, pp 405-17.

Gavigan, J. P. and Scapolo, F. (1999) 'A comparison of national foresight exercises', *Foresight*, vol 1, no 6, pp 495-517.

Gibson, C. and Duncan, G. (2002) 'Lessons learned: The advantages of mixed methods in program evaluation', Paper presented at the American Association of Policy Analysis and Management, Annual Conference, Dallas, 8th November

Giddens, A. (1998) *The Third Way: The Renewal of Social Democracy*, Oxford: Polity Press.

Giles, C. and Timmins, N. (2007) 'Brown's bequest: a mighty Treasury contemplates the waning of its power', *Financial Times*, 22 March.

Gladwell, M. (2005) *Blink: The Power of Thinking without Thinking*, London: Penguin.

Glees, A. (2005) 'Evidence-Based Policy or Policy-Based Evidence? Hutton and the Government's Use of Secret Intelligence', *Parliamentary Affairs*, vol 58, no 1, pp 138-155.

Glendinning, C., Powell, M. and Rummery, K. (eds) (2002) *Partnerships, New Labour and the governance of welfare*, Bristol: The Policy Press.

Gould, P. (1998) *The Unfinished Revolution*, London: Little, Brown and Company.

Government Social Research Unit (2005) *GSR Professional Guidance: Ethical Assurance for Social Research in Government*, Cabinet Office/GSRU report (www.gsr.gov.uk/downloads/professional_guidance/ethical_guidance.pdf).

Grant, W. (2000) *Pressure Groups and British Politics*, Basingstoke: Macmillan.

Gray, A. and Jenkins, W. (2002) 'Government and Administration: Reasserting Public Services and their Consumers', *Parliamentary Affairs*, vol 55, no 2, pp 235-53.

Greater London Assembly (2005) *Our London. Our Future. Planning for London's Growth II*, London: Greater London Assembly.

Greenberg, D. and Davis, A. (2007) *The NDDP Cost Benefit Analysis (CBA)*, London: Department for Work and Pensions.

Greenberg, D and Schroder, M. (2004) *Digest of Social Experiments*, Washington DC: Urban Institute Press.

Griggs, J., Noble, M., McLennan, D., Walker, R. and Whitworth, A. (2007) *Working with People and Places: A review of the evaluative evidence*, York: Joseph Rowntree Foundation..

Guest, M. (2003) *The Nature of Community Involvement*, Birmingham, BANF.

Hall, N., Hoggart, L., Marsh, A., Phillips, J., Ray, K. and Vegeris, S. (2005) *The Employment Retention and Advancement scheme: Report on the implementation of ERA during the first months. Summary and conclusions*, London: Policy Studies Institute.

Hall, P. (1993) 'Policy Paradigms, Social Learning, and the State: the Case of Economic Policy Making in Britain', *Comparative Politics*, vol 25, no 3, pp 275-96.

Harrison, S. (1998) 'The politics of evidence-based medicine in the United Kingdom' *Policy & Politics*, vol 26, no 1, pp 15-31.

Harrison, M. (2006) 'E&IS Moving Forward Workshop' (www.defra.gov.uk/science/how/documents/EIS14JuneWorkshopPresentation1.pdf.)

Hart, C. (1998) *Doing a Literature Review*, London: Sage.

Hasluck, C. (2000) *The New Deal for Lone Parents: A review of the evaluation evidence*, Employment Service Report ESR51, Sheffield: Employment Service.

Hasluck, C. and Green, A. (2007) *What Works For Whom: A review of evidence and meta-analysis for the Department for Work and Pensions*, Research Report 407 London: Department for Work and Pensions.

Health Committee (2007) *Work of the Committee 2005-06*, London: The Stationery Office.

Healy, A. (2002) 'Commentary: Evidence-based policy – the latest form of inertia and control?', *Planning Theory and Practice*, vol 3, no 1, pp 97-8.

Heclo, H. (1974) *Modern Social Politics in Britain and Sweden: From Relief to Income Maintenance*, New Haven, CT: Yale University Press.

Held, D. (2003) 'From Executive to Cosmopolitan Multilateralism' in D. Held and M. Koenig-Archibugi (eds) *Taming Globalization*, Cambridge: Polity Press.

Henley Centre (2001) *Understanding Best Practice in Strategic Futures Work: A report for the Performance and Innovation Unit*, London: Henley Centre.

Henshaw, D. (2006) *Recovering Child Support: Routes to Responsibility*, London: The Stationery Office.

Heywood Committee (1965) *Report of the Committee on Social Studies*, London: HMSO.

HM Treasury (1988) *Policy Evaluation: A guide for Managers*, London: HMSO.

HM Treasury (1997) *Appraisal and Evaluation in Central Government, 'The Green Book'*, London: HM Treasury.

HM Treasury (1998) *Public Services for the future; modernising, reform, accountability – Comprehensive Spending Review; Public Service Agreement 1999-2002* (www.hm-treasury.gov.uk/pub/html/psa/csrpsa.pdf).

HM Treasury (2000) *Spending Review 2000; Service Delivery Agreements 2001-2004: A guide* (www.hm-treasury.gov.uk/SI2000/sda/index.html).

HM Treasury (2003) *The Green Book: Appraisal and Evaluation in Central Government*, London: The Stationery Office.

HM Treasury (2004a) *Public Service Agreements 2005-9*, London: HM Treasury.

HM Treasury (2004b) *Risk Management Assessment Framework: A tool for Departments*, London: HM Treasury.

HM Treasury (2004c) *The Orange Book: Management of risk - principles and concepts*, London: HM Treasury

HM Treasury (2005) *Managing risks to the public: Appraisal guidance*, London: HM Treasury.

HM Treasury (2006) *Opportunities and Challenges for the UK: Analysis for the 2007 Comprehensive Spending Review*, London: HM Treasury.

HM Treasury (2007) *Economic and Fiscal Strategy Report*, London, HM Treasury.

HM Treasury and Cabinet Office (2004) *Devolved Decision Making: delivering better public services: refining targets and performance management* (www.hm-treasury.gov.uk/media/9B9/20/devolving_decision1_409.pdf).

Hogwood, B. (2000) 'The consideration of social experiments in the UK: Policy, Political, Ethical and Other Concerns', Paper to ESRC Conference on Social Experiments, 9-10 November.

Hogwood, B.W. and Gunn, L.A. (1984) *Policy Analysis for the Real World*, Oxford: Oxford University Press.

Home Office (1998) *Speaking up for Justice*, London: Home Office.

Home Office (2004a) *Firm Foundations: The Government's Framework for Community Capacity Building*, London: Civil Renewal Unit.

Home Office (2004b) *Facilitating community involvement: practical guidance for practitioners and policy makers*, London: Research, Development and Statistics Directorate.

Hood, C. (1991) 'A Public Management for All Seasons', *Public Administration*, vol 69, no 1, pp 3-19.

Hood, C. (2006) *The Politics of Public Sector Bargains: Reward, Competency, Loyalty – and Blame*, Oxford: Oxford University Press.

Hood, C. and Lodge, M. (2006) *The Politics of Public Service Bargains: Reward, competency, loyalty – and blame*, Oxford: Oxford University Press.

Houghton, D. (1996) 'The Role of Analogical Reasoning in Novel Foreign Policy Situations', *British Journal of Political Science*, vol 26, no 4, pp 523-52.

Houghton, D. (1998a) 'Historical Analogies and the Cognitive Dimension of Domestic Policymaking', *Political Psychology*, vol 19, no 2, pp 279-303.

Houghton, D. (1998b) 'Analogical Reasoning and Policymaking: Where and when is it used?', *Policy Sciences*, vol 31, no 3, pp 151-176.

House of Commons Library (undated), Research Paper 02/35, *Select Committees*, London: House of Commons

Huby, M. and Dix, G. (1992) *Evaluating the Social Fund*, Research Report 9, London: Department of Social Security.

Hudson, B. (2006) *Whole Systems Working: A Guide and Discussion Paper*. London: Integrated Care Network/DoH.

Hudson, J. and Lowe, S. (2004) *Understanding the Policy Process: Analysing Welfare Policy and Practice*, Bristol: The Policy Press.

Hughes, O. E. (2003) *Public Management and Administration*, Basingstoke: Palgrave Macmillan.

Humphreys, P. and Padgett, S. (2006) 'Globalization, the European Union, and Domestic Governance in Telecoms and Electricity', *Governance*, vol 19, no 3, pp 383-406.

Ibbs, R. (1988) *Improving Management in Government: The Next Steps: Report to the Prime Minister*, London: HMSO.

IBM (2006) *Global Innovation Outlook 2.0*, New York, NY: International Business Machines Ltd.

Innes, J. (2002) 'Improving policy making with information', *Planning Theory and Practice*, vol 3, no 1, pp 102-4.

IPPPR (Institute for Public Policy Research) (2001) *Building Better Partnerships*, London: IPPR.

Jacoby, W. (2001) *Imitation and Politics: Redesigning Modern Germany*, Ithaca NY: Cornell University Press.

James, O. and Lodge, M. (2001) 'The Limitations of "Policy Transfer" and "Lesson Drawing" for Public Policy Research', *Political Studies Review*, vol 11, no 2, pp 179-93.

Jasanoff, S. (2005) *Designs on Nature: Science and Democracy in Europe and the United States*, Princeton: NJ: Princeton University Press.

Johnson, M. and Griffiths, R. (2001) 'Developing Evidence-Based Clinicians', *International Journal of Nursing Practice*, vol 7, no 2, pp 109-18.

Johnson, R. (1998) 'Toward a Theoretical Model of Evaluation Utilization', *Evaluation and Program Planning*, vol 21, no 1, pp 93-110.

Jones, T. and Newburn, T. (2002) 'Policy convergence and crime control in the USA and the UK: Streams of influence and levels of impact', *Criminal Justice*, vol 2, no 2, pp 173–203.

Jones, T. and Newburn, T. (2007) *Policy Transfer and Criminal Justice*, Maidenhead: Open University Press.

Jordan, A., Wurzel, R. and Zito, A. (eds) (2003) *New Instruments of Environmental Governance*, London: Frank Cass.

Jordan, G (2007) 'Policy Without Learning: Double Devolution and Abuse of the Deliberative Idea', *Public Policy and Administration*, vol 22, no 1, pp 48-73.

Kajermo, K.N., Nordstrom, G., Krusebrant, A. and Björvell, H. (2000) 'Perceptions or Research Utilization: Comparisons Between Health Care Professionals, Nursing Students and a Reference Group of Nurse Clinicians', *Journal of Advanced Nursing*, vol 31, no 1, pp 99-109.

Karagiannaki, W. (2007) 'Exploring the effects of integrated benefits systems and active labour market policies: evidence from JobCentre Plus in the UK', *Journal of Social Policy*, vol 36, no 2, pp 177-95.

Kelemen, R.D. and Sibbitt, E.C. (2004) 'The Globalization of American Law', *International Organization*, vol 58, no 1, pp. 103-36.

Kelly, R. (2006) Speech to the Local Government Association Conference' 5 July.

Kickert, W, Klijn, E. and Koppenjan, J. (1997) *Managing Complex Networks: Strategies for the Public Sector*, London: Sage.

King, D. (2006) *Anticipating Technological Change* (www.foundation.org.uk/events/pdf/20060524_King.pdf).

King, D. and Wickham-Jones, M. (1999) 'From Clinton to Blair: The Democratic (Party) Origins of Welfare to Work', *The Political Quarterly*, vol 70, no 1, pp 62–74.

Kingdon, J. (1984) *Agendas, Alternatives and Public Policies*, New York: HarperCollins.

Klevmarken, N.A. (1997) *Behavioral Modelling in Micro-simulation Models*, Working Paper 31, Uppsala: Department of Economics, Uppsala University.

Koch, P. and Hauknes, J. (2005) *Innovation in the Public Sector*, Oslo: NIFU STEP.

Lasswell, H. (1958) *Who Gets What, When and How*, Cleveland, OH: Meridian Books.

Leicester, G. (1999) 'The seven enemies of evidence-based policy', *Public Money and Management*, vol 19, no 1, pp. 5-7.

Leitch Review (2006) *Prosperity for All in the Global Economy – World Class Skills*, London: The Stationery Office.

Levitt, R. and Solesbury, W. (2005) *Evidence-informed policy: What difference do outsiders in Whitehall make?* Working Paper 23, London: ESRC UK Centre for Evidence Based Policy and Practice

Lewis, J., Mitchell, L., Sanderson, T., O'Connor, W. and Clayden, M. (2000) *Lone parents and personal advisers: roles and relationships. A follow-up study of the New Deal for Lone Parents Phase One prototype*, Research Report No 122, London: Department for Work and Pensions.

Liaison Committee (2004) *Minutes of Evidence*, 3 February, London: House of Commons.

Lindblom, C.E. (1959) 'The Science of "Muddling Through"', *Public Administration Review*, vol 19, no 2, pp 78-88.

Ling, T. (2002) 'Delivering joined-up government in the UK: dimensions, issues and problems', *Public Administration*, vol 80, no 4, pp 615-43.

Lipsey, M.W. and Cordray, D.S. (2000) 'Evaluation Methods for Social Intervention', *Annual Review of Psychology*, vol 51, pp 345–375.

Loumidis, J., Stafford, B., Youngs, R., Green, A., Arthur, S., Legard, R., Lessof, C., Lewis, J., Walker, R., Corden, A., Thornton, P. and Sainsbury, R. (2001) *Evaluation of the New Deal for Disabled People Personal Adviser Pilots*, Research Report 144, London: Department of Social Security.

Loveridge, D. and Street, P. (2003) *Inclusive Foresight*, PREST Discussion paper 03-13. Manchester: PREST, University of Manchester.

Ludlam, S. (2000) 'What's published is what counts', *British Journal of Politics and International Relations*, vol 2, no 2, pp 264-76.

Margetts, H. (2006) 'E-Government in Britain – A Decade On', *Parliamentary Affairs*, vol 59, no 2, pp 250-65.

Marsh, D. and Rhodes, R. (1992) *Policy Networks in British Government*, Oxford: Clarendon Press.

Marsh, D. and Smith, M. (2000) 'Understanding policy networks: towards a Dialectical Approach', *Political Studies*, vol 48, no 1, pp 4-21.

Massey, A. (2005) 'Multilevel Governance: Administering Global Governance in a Differentiated Political Context', in G. F. Moleketti (ed), *The World We Could Win: Administering Global Governance,* Amsterdam: IOS Press.

Massey, A. and Pyper, R. (2005) *Public Management and Modernization in Britain*, Basingstoke: Palgrave Macmillan.

Mayer, K. and Lassnigg, L. (2006) 'Lernprozesse in der Politik am Beispiel der Etablierung des Fachhochschulsektors in Österreich', Institut für Höhere Studien, März, Wien Reihe Soziologie.

McIntyre, J (2003) 'Participatory Democracy: Drawing on C. West Churchman's Thinking When Making Public Policy', *Systems Research and Behavioural Science*, vol 20, no 6, pp 489-498.

Medd, W. (2001) 'Making (Dis)Connections: Complexity and the Policy Process?', *Social Issues*, vol 1, no 2 (www.whb.co.uk/socialissues/wm.htm).

Middleton, S., Perren, K., Maguire, S., Rennison J., Battistin, E., Emmerson, C. and Fitzsimons, E. (2005) *Evaluation of Education Maintenance Allowance Pilots: Young People Aged 16 to 19 Years. Final Report of the Quantitative Evaluation*, Nottingham: Department for Education and Skills.

Miliband, R. (2006) 'Speech to the Future Services Network's Three Sectors Summit', 22 June 2006.

Moore, M.H. (1995) *Creating Public Value: Strategic Management in Government*, Cambridge, MA: Harvard University Press.

Morris, A. (2005) 'Evidence Initiatives: Aspects of Recent Experience in England', *Evidence & Policy*, vol 1, no 2, pp 257-67.

Morris, S., Greenberg, D., Riccio, J., Mittra, B., Green, H., Lissenburgh, S. and Blundell, R. (2004) *Designing a Demonstration Project. An Employment retention and advancement demonstration for Great Britain*, London: Government Chief Social Researcher's Office, Cabinet Office.

Moss, P. (2004), 'Sure Start', *Journal of Education Policy*, vol 19, no 5, pp 631-4.

Mossberger, K. (2000) *The Politics of Ideas and the Spread of Enterprise Zones*, Washington DC: Georgetown University Press.

Mulgan, G. (1997) *Connexity: How to Live in a Connected World*, London: Chatto and Windus.

Mulgan, G. (2001) 'Systems Thinking and the Practice of Government', *Systemist*, vol 23, Special Edition, November, pp 23-29.

Mulgan, G. (2005a) 'Government, knowledge and the business of policy making: the potential and limits of evidence-based policy', *Evidence and Policy*, vol 1, no 2, pp 215-26.

Mulgan, G. (2005b) 'Lessons of Power', *Prospect*, Issue 110, May (www.prospect-magazine.co.uk/article_details.php?id=6888).

Mulgan, G. (2005c) *Joined-up government: Past, present and future*, London: The Young Foundation (online at www.youngfoundation.org.uk/node/223).

Mulgan G. and Albury, D. (2003) *Innovation in the Public Sector*, London, Prime Minister's Strategy Unit (ver 1.9, October 2003).

Mulgan, G. and Lee, A. (2001) *Better Policy Delivery and Design: A Discussion Paper*, London: Cabinet Office Performance and Innovation Unit.

Mulgan, G. and Steinberg, T. (2005) *Wide Open: Open Source Methods and their Future Potential*, London: Demos.

Nakano, K. (2004) 'Cross-National Transfer of Policy Ideas: Agencification in Britain and Japan', *Governance*, vol 17, no 2, pp 169-88.

National Audit Office (2001a) *Modern Policy-Making: Ensuring Policies Deliver Value for Money*, London: The Stationery Office.

National Audit Office (2001b) *Measuring the Performance of Government Departments*, London: The Stationery Office.

National Audit Office (2001c) *Joining up to Improve Public Services*, London: The Stationery Office.

National Audit Office (2002) *Better Public Services through e-government*, London: The Stationery Office.

National Audit Office (2004) *Evaluation of Regulatory Impact Assessments Compendium Report 2003-04*, London, National Audit Office.

National Audit Office (2005) *Joint Targets*, London: The Stationery Office.

National Audit Office (2006a) *Delivering Efficiently – Strengthening the Links in Public Service Delivery Chains*, London: The Stationery Office.

National Audit Office (2006b) *Achieving Innovation in Central Government Organisations*, London: The Stationery Office.

National Audit Office (2006c) *Child Support Agency – Implementation of the Child Support Reforms*, London: The Stationery Office.

National Evaluation of Sure Start (NESS) (2000), *Getting Sure Start Started*, London: Institute for the Study of Children, Families and Social Issues.

Newman, J. (2001) *Modernising Governance: New Labour, Policy and Society*, London: Sage.

Newman, J., Barnes, M., Sullivan, H. and Knops, A. (2004) 'Public Participation and Collaborative Governance', *Journal of Social Policy*, vol 33, no 2, pp 203-23.

NHS Institute for Innovation and Improvement (2006) *Blue Book*, London NHS Institute.

NICE (National Institute for Health and Clinical Excellence) (2002a) *Guidance on the Use of Nicotine Replacement Therapy (NRT) and Bupropion for Smoking Cessation: Technology Appraisal Guidance No 39*, London: NICE.

NICE (2002b) *A Rapid and Systematic Review of the Clinical and Cost Effectiveness of Bupropion SR and Nicotine Replacement Therapy (NRT) for Smoking Cessation*, London: NICE.

Northern Ireland Review of Public Administration (2006) *Better Government for Northern Ireland: Final Decisions of the Review of Public Administration*, Belfast: Review of Public Administration of Northern Ireland.

Nutley, S. (2003) 'Bridging the policy/research divide: Reflections and lessons from the UK', Keynote paper presented at 'Facing the Future: Engaging stakeholders and citizens in developing public policy', National Institute of Governance Conference, Canberra, Australia, 23-24 April.

Nutley, S. and Webb, J. (2000) 'Evidence and the Policy Process' in H.T.O. Davies, S.M. Nutley and P.C. Smith (eds) *What works? Evidence-based policy and practice in public services*, Bristol: The Policy Press.

Nutley, S.M., Walter, I and Davies, H.T.O (2007) *Using evidence: How research can inform public services* Bristol: The Policy Press.

O'Toole, B. (2006) *The Ideal of Public Service: Reflections on the higher civil service in Britain*, London: Routledge.

OECD (2004a) *Public Sector Modernisation: Modernising Public Employment, Policy Brief*, Paris: OECD.

OECD (2004b) *Public Sector Modernisation: Changing Organisational Structures, Policy Brief*, Paris: OECD.

OECD (2005a) *Public Sector Modernisation: Open Government, Policy Brief*, Paris: OECD.

OECD (2005b) *Public Sector Modernisation: Modernising Accountability and Control, Policy Brief*, Paris: OECD.

Office for Science and Innovation (undated) *Strategic futures planning – a toolkit*. Available at http://www.foresight.gov.uk/HORIZON_SCANNING_ CENTRE/Toolkit/Toolkit.html (accessed 21 November 2006).

Orr, L. (1998) *Social Experiments Evaluating Public Programs with Experimental Methods: Evaluating Public Programs with Experimental Methods*, New York: Sage.

Page, E., Wolman, H. and Connelly, D. (2005) 'Policy study visits: Policy learning in Practice', Paper presented at the American Political Science Association Annual Meeting, Washington DC, August.

Palumbo, D. (ed) (1987) *The Politics of Program Evaluation*, Newbury Park, CA: Sage.

Parker, R. (2007) 'Networked governance or just networks? Local governance of the knowledge economy in Limerick (Ireland) and Karlskrona (Sweden)', *Political Studies*, vol 55, no 1, pp 113-32.

Parker, S. and Gallagher, N. (eds) (2007) *The Collaborative State: How working together can transform public services*, London: Demos.

Parry, J. and Scully, E. (2003) 'Health Impact Assessment and the consideration of Health Inequalities', *Journal of Public Health and Medicine*, vol 25, no 3, pp 243-245.

Parry, R. (2005) 'The Civil Service Response to Modernisation in the Devolved Administrations', *Financial Accountability and Management*, vol 21, no 1, pp 57-74.

Parsons, W. (1995) *Public Policy: An Introduction to the Theory and Practice of Policy Analysis*, London: Edward Elgar.

Parsons, W. (2002) 'From Muddling Through to Muddling Up – Evidence Based Policy Making and the Modernisation of British Government', *Public Policy and Administration*, vol 17, no 3, pp 43-60.

Parsons, W. (2003) 'Modernizing policy-making for the twenty-first century: the professional model,' in T. Butcher and A. Massey (eds), *Modernizing Civil Services*, Cheltenham: Edward Elgar.

Parsons, W. (2004) 'Not Just Steering but Weaving: Relevant Knowledge and the Craft of Building Policy Capacity and Coherence', *Australian Journal of Public Administration*, vol 63, no 1, pp 43-57.

Patton, M. (2002) *Qualitative Research and Evaluation Methods*, Thousand Oaks: CA: Sage Publications.

Pawson, R. (2006) 'Digging for Nuggets: How "Bad" Research Can Yield "Good" Evidence', *International Journal of Social Research Methodology*, vol 9, no 2, pp 127-42.

Pawson, R. and Tilley, N. (1997) *Realistic Evaluation*, London: Sage.

Paxman, J. (2003) *The Political Animal*, Harmondsworth: Penguin.

Pearce, N. and Dixon, N. (2005) 'New model welfare', *Prospect*, 19 April.

Pemberton, H. (2004) *Policy Learning and British Governance in the 1960s*, London: Palgrave.

Pensions Commission (2004) *Pensions: Challenges and Choices. The First Report of the Pensions Commission*, London: The Stationery Office.

Pensions Commission (2006) *Implementing an Integrated Package of Pension Reforms*, London: Pensions Commission.

Percy-Smith, J., Burden, T., Darlow, A., Dowson, L., Hawtin, M. and Ladi, S. (2001) *Promoting change through research: The impact of research in local government*, York: Joseph Rowntree Foundation.

Performance and Innovation Unit (1999) *The Future and How to Think About It*, London: Performance and Innovation Unit.

Performance and Innovation Unit (2000a) *Adding It Up*, Performance and Innovation Unit, London.

Performance and Innovation Unit (2000b) *Wiring It Up*, Performance and Innovation Unit, London.

Performance and Innovation Unit (2000c) *Reaching Out: The Role of Central Government at Regional and Local Level*, London: The Stationery Office.

Performance and Innovation Unit (2000d) *Adoption: Issues for Consultation*, London: Performance and Innovation Unit

Performance and Innovation Unit (2000e) *Recovering the Proceeds of Crime*, London: Performance and Innovation Unit

Phillips, Lord (2000) *The BSE Inquiry*, London: The Stationery Office.

Pigot, T. (1989) *Report of the Advisory Group on Video Evidence*, London: Home Office.

Plsek, P. (2001) 'Why won't the NHS do as it's told', Plenary address, NHS Confederation Conference, 6 July.

Plowden Report (1967) *Children and their Primary Schools*, London: HMSO.

PMSU (Primr Minister's Strategy Unit) (2003) *The Magenta Book: Guidance Notes for Policy Evaluation and Analysis*, London: Cabinet Office, Prime Minister's Strategy Unit, Government Chief Social Researcher's Office (www.policyhub. gov.uk/magenta_book/index.asp).

Pollitt, C. (1996) 'Justification by works or by faith: Evaluating the new public management', *Evaluation*, vol 1, no 2, pp 133-54.

Pollitt, C. (2003) 'Joined-up Government: A Survey', *Political Studies Review*, vol 1, no 1, pp 34-49.

Pollitt, C. (2006) 'Academic Advice to Practitioners – What is its Nature, Place and Value Within Academia?', *Public Money and Management*, vol 26, no 4, pp 257-64.

Pollitt, C. and Bouckaert, G. (2004) *Public Management Reform. A Comparative Analysis*, Oxford: Oxford University Press.

Pollitt, C., Girre, X., Lonsdale, J, Mul, R., Summa, H. and Waerness, M. (1999) *Performance or Compliance? Performance Audit and Public Management in Five Countries*, Oxford: Oxford University Press.

Powell, M. (ed) (1999) *New Labour, New Welfare State? The 'Third Way' in British Social Policy*, Bristol: The Policy Press.

Powell, M. (ed) (2002) *Evaluating New Labour's Welfare Reforms*, Bristol: The Policy Press.

Pratt, J. (2004) *The 'Accreditation' Model: Policy Transfer in Higher Education in Austria and Britain*, Oxford: Symposium Books.

PREST (2006) *Evaluation of the United Kingdom Foresight Programme: Final Report*, Manchester: PREST, University of Manchester.

Prime Minister's Strategy Unit (2002a) *Health Strategy Review. Analytical Report*, London: Prime Minister's Strategy Unit.

Prime Minister's Strategy Unit (2002b) *Risk – improving government's capacity to handle risk and uncertainty*, London: Prime Minister's Strategy Unit.

Prime Minister's Strategy Unit (2004) *Strategy Survival Guide*, Prime Minister's Strategy Unit, London.

Prime Minister's Strategy Unit (2006) *The UK Government's Approach to Public Service Reform*, London: Cabinet Office.

Public Administration Committee (2005) *Government by Inquiry*, London: The Stationery Office.

Public Administration Committee (2006) 'Evidence heard in Public Questions 358-405', Minutes of Evidence, Governing the Future (www.publications. parliament.uk/pa/cm200506/cmselect/cmpubadm/c756-iv/c75602.htm).

Public Administration Committee (2007) *Governing the Future*, London: The Stationery Office.

Public Service Committee (1998) *Public Service – Report*, London: House of Lords.

Putnam, R. (2000) *Bowling Alone. The Collapse and Revival of American Community*, New York: Simon and Schuster.

Rawnsley, A. (2001) *Servants of the People*, Harmondsworth: Penguin.

Redfern, S. and Christian, S. (2003) 'Achieving Change in Health Care Practice', *Journal of Evaluation in Clinical Practice*, vol 9, no 2, pp 225-38.

Rennison, J., Maguire, S., Middleton, S. and Ashworth, A. (2005) *Young People Not in Education, Employment or Training: Evidence from the Education Maintenance Allowance Pilots Database*, London: Department for Education and Skills.

Rhodes, R.A.W. (1997) *Understanding Governance: Policy Networks, Governance, Reflexivity and Accountability*, Buckingham: Open University Press.

Rhodes, R.A.W., Carmichael, P., McMillan, J. and Massey, A. (2003) *Decentralizing the Civil Service: from Unitary State to Differentiated Polity in the United Kingdom*, Milton Keynes: Open University.

Ritchie, J. and Lewis, J. (2003) *Qualitative Research Practice: A guide for social science students and researchers*, London: Sage.

Ritchie, J. and Matthews, A. (1982) *Take-up of Rent Allowances: An In Depth Study*, London: Social and Community Planning Research.

Ritchie, J. and Matthews, A. (1985) 'Problem definition: Attitudes to benefits', in R. Walker (ed) *Applied Qualitative Research*, Aldershot: Gower.

Rose, J. (2006) *Independent review of the teaching of early reading* (Final Report) London Department for Education and Skills (www.standards.dfes.gov.uk/phonics/earlyreading/).

Rose, R. (1993) *Lesson Drawing in Public Policy: A Guide to Learning Across Time and Space*, Chatham NJ: Chatham House.

Rose, R. (2001) 'Ten Steps in Learning Lessons from Abroad', London: Future Governance Paper No 1 (www.hull.ac.uk/futgov/Papers/PubPapers/RRPaper1.pdf).

Rose, R. (2005) *Learning from Comparative Public Policy. A Practical Guide* London, Routledge.

Rothschild Report (1971) *The Organisation and Management of Government Research and Development*, London: HMSO.

Rouse, J. and Smith, G. (2002) 'Evaluating New Labour's Accountability Reforms', in Powell, M. (ed), *Evaluating New Labour's Welfare Reforms*, Bristol: The Policy Press.

Royal Commission on Long-Term Care (1999) *With Respect to Old Age: Long-term Care – Rights and Responsibilities* (The Sutherland Report), London: The Stationery Office.

Royal Commission on the National Health Service (1979) *Report*, London: HMSO.

Royal Society (2002) *Foot and Mouth Disease 2001: Lessons To Be Learned Inquiry*, London: Royal Society.

Runciman, D. (2006) *The Politics of Good Intentions: History, Fear and Hypocrisy in the New World Order*, Woodstock: Princeton University Press.

Sabatier, P. (ed) (2006) *Theories of the Policy Process: 2*, Boulder: Co; Westview Press.

Sackett, D.L., Rosenberg, W.M.C., Gray, J.A.M., Haynes, R.B., Richardson, W.S. (1996) 'Evidence based medicine: what it is and what it isn't', *British Medical Journal*, vol. 312, pp 71-2.

Sainsbury, R. (2004) 'Policy ignoring research: the case of housing benefit appeals and a new deal', in S. Becker and A. Bryman (eds) *Understanding Research for Policy and Practice*, Bristol: The Policy Press.

Sampson, A. (2005) *Who Runs this Place?*, London: John Murray.

Sanderson, I. (2000) 'Evaluation, policy learning and evidence-based policy making', *Public Administration*, vol 80, no 1, pp 1-22.

Sanderson, I. (2002) 'Making sense of "what works": evidence based policy making as instrumental rationality', *Public Policy and Administration*, vol 17, no 3, pp 61-75.

Sanderson, I. (2003) 'Is it "what works" that matters? Evaluation and evidence-based policy-making', *Research Papers in Education*, vol 18, no 4, pp 331–45.

Schön, D (1983) *The Reflective Practitioner*, New York, NY: Basic Books.

Schultz, W (2006) 'The cultural contradictions of managing change: using horizon scanning in an evidence-based policy context', Oxford: Infinite Futures.

Schwartz, P. (1996) *The Art of the Long View: Planning for the Future in an Uncertain World*, New York: Bantam Doubleday Dell.

Science and Technology Committee (2006a) *Scientific advice, risk and evidence based policy making*, London: The Stationery Office.

Science and Technology Committee (2006b) *Scientific Advice, Risk and Evidence Based Policy Making, Seventh Report of Session 2005-6, Volume II Oral and Written Evidence HC900-11*, London: The Stationery Office.

Scott, A. (2003) 'A Review of the Links Between Research and Policy', Lewes: The Knowledge Bridge.

Scottish Executive Central Research Unit (2000) *Assessment of Innovative Approaches to Testing Community Opinion*, Edinburgh: Scottish Executive.

Secretary of State for Work and Pensions (2006) *A Fresh Start: Child Support Redesign – the Government's Response to Sir David Henshaw*, London: The Stationery Office.

Shaxson, L. (2005) 'Is Your Evidence Robust Enough? Questions for Policy Makers and Practitioners', *Evidence & Policy*, vol 1, no 2, pp 101-11.

Simon, H. (1945 and 1957) *Administrative Behaviour*, New York: Free Press.

Simon, H. (1960) *The New Science of Management Decision*, Englewood Cliffs, NJ: Prentice Hall.

Skidelsky, R. (1992) *John Maynard Keynes: A biography. Volume 2: The economist as saviour 1920-1937*, London: Macmillan.

Slaughter, R. (2002) 'From forecasting and scenarios to social construction: changing methodological paradigms in futures studies', *Foresight*, vol 4, no 3, pp 26-31.

Smith, A.F.M. (1996) 'Mad cows and ecstasy: Chance and choice in an evidence-based society', *Journal of the Royal Statistical Society, Series A*, vol 159, no 3, pp 367-83.

Smith, T.A. (1979) *The Politics of the Corporate Economy*, London: Martin Robertson.

Social Exclusion Unit (2000) *National Strategy for Neighbourhood Renewal: a framework for consultation*, London: Cabinet Office.

Social Exclusion Unit/CMPS (2002) *The Social Exclusion Unit's Policy Action Team Approach to Policy Development: The Views of Participants*, London: Social Exclusion Unit/CMPS.

Social Security Committee (1999) *The 1999 Child Support White Paper*, London: House of Commons.

Solesbury, W. (2001) 'Evidence based policy: Whence it came and where it's going', London: ESRC UK Centre for Evidence Based Policy and Practice.

Spencer, L., Ritchie J., Lewis, J. and Dillon, L. (2003) 'Quality in qualitative evaluation: A framework for assessing research evidence', London: National Centre for Social Research.

Spicker, P. (2006) *Policy Analysis for Practice: Applying Social Policy*. Bristol: The Policy Press.

Stafford, B., Greenberg D. and Davis, A. (2002) *A Literature Review of the Use of Random Assignment Methodology in Evaluations of US Social Policy Programmes*, In-house report 94, London: Department for Work and Pensions,

Stern, N. (2007) *The Economics of Climate Change: The Stern Review*, Cambridge, Cambridge University Press.

Stewart, J. (1996) 'A dogma of our times – the separation of policymaking and implementation', *Public Money and Management*, July–September, pp 33-40.

Stewart, J. (2004) *Taking Stock. Scottish Social Welfare after Devolution*, Bristol: The Policy Press.

Stratford, N., Farrell, C., Natarajan, L. and Lewis, J. (2005) *Taking part in a randomised control trial: A participant's eye-view of the Job Retention and Rehabilitation Pilot* Research Report 273, London: Department for Work and Pensions, .

Strickland, P. (1998) 'Working Families Tax Credit and Family Credit', London: House of Commons Library Research Paper, 98/46.

Stuart, M. (1998) *Douglas Hurd: The Public Servant – An Authorised Biography*, Edinburgh: Mainstream.

Sulitzeanu-Kenan, R. (2006) 'If they get it right: an experimental test of the effects of the appointment and reports of UK Public Inquiries', *Public Administration*, vol 84, no 3, pp 623-53.

Sutton, P. K. (2006) *Modernizing the State: Public Sector Reform in the Commonwealth Caribbean*, Kingston, Jamaica: Ian Randle

Sydney Morning Herald (2006) 'Intellipedia is a Wikipedia for spooks', Tech Section, 1 November (www.smh.com.au/news/web/wikipedia-for-spooks/2 006/11/01/1162339891881.html).

Taylor, D. (2005) 'Governing through evidence: participation and power in policy evaluation', *Journal of Social Policy*, vol 34, no 4, pp 601-18.

Thatcher, M. (1993) *Thatcher: The Downing Street Years*, London: HarperCollins.

Thompson, G., Frances, J., Levacic, R. and Mitchell, J. (eds) (1991) *Markets, Hierarchies and Networks: The co-ordination of social life*, London: Sage.

Thornton, P. and Corden, A. (2002) *Evaluating the Impact of Access to Work: A Case Study Approach*, WAE138, Sheffield: Department for Work and Pensions.

Timmins, N. (2001) *The Five Giants*, London: HarperCollins

Toynbee, P. and Walker, D. (2005) *Better or Worse? Has Labour Delivered?* Harmondsworth: Penguin.

Treasury and Civil Service Committee (1986) *Civil Servants and Ministers: Duties and Responsibilities*, London: House of Commons.

UNDP (2006) *Beyond Scarcity: Human Development Report 2006*, UNDP: New York.

Van den Bulck, J. (2004) 'The relationship between television fiction and fear of crime: An empirical comparison of three causal explanations', *European Journal of Communication*, vol 19, no 2, pp 239-248.

Van der Knaap, P. (2004) 'Theory-based Evaluation and Learning: Possibilities and Challenges', *Evaluation,* vol 10, no 1, pp 16-34.

Van der Meer, F. and Edelenbos, J. (2006) 'Evaluation in Multi-Actor Policy Processes: Accountability, Learning and Co-operation', *Evaluation*, vol 12, no 2, pp 201-18.

Varney, D. (2006), *Service Transformation: A better service for citizens and businesses, a better deal for the taxpayer*, London: HM Treasury.

Walker, R. (2000) 'Welfare policy: tendering for evidence', in H. Davies, S. Nutley and P. Smith (eds) *Evidence and Public Policy*, Bristol: The Policy Press.

Walker, R. (2000b) 'Learning if Policy Will Work', *Policy Studies*, vol 21, no 4, pp 313-45.

Walker, R. (2001) 'Great Expectations: Can social science evaluate New Labour's Policies?', *Evaluation*, vol 7, no 3, pp 305-30.

Walker, R. (2004) 'Evaluation: Evidence for Public Policy', in *Evaluating Policies for Local Economic and Employment Development*, Paris: OECD.

Walker, R. and Wiseman, M. (1997) 'The Possibility of a British Earned Income Tax Credit', *Fiscal Studies*, vol 18, no 4, pp 401-25.

Walker, R and Wiseman, M (2001) *Britain's New Deal and the Next Round of U.S. Welfare Reform*, Institute for Research on Poverty Discussion Paper no 1223-01, US, IRP.

Walker, R. and Wiseman, M. (2006) 'Managing evaluations', in I. Shaw, J. Greene and M. Mark (eds) *Handbook of Policy Evaluation*, London: Sage.

Walker, R., Hoggart, L., Hamilton, G. with Blank, S. (2006) *Making random assignment happen: Evidence from the UK Employment Retention and Advancement (ERA) demonstration*, Research Report No 330, London: Department for Work and Pensions.

Wallace, A., Croucher, K., Bevan, M., Jackson, K., O'Malley, L. and Quligars, D. (2006) 'Evidence for policy making: some reflections on the application of systematic reviews to housing research', *Housing Studies*, vol 21, no 2, pp 297-314.

Wallace, A., Croucher, K., Quilgars, D. and Baldwin, S. (2004) 'Meeting the challenge: developing systematic reviewing in social policy', *Policy and Politics*, vol 32, no 4, pp 455-70.

Walter, I., Nutley, S. and Davies, H. (2005) 'What Works to Promote Evidence-Based Practice? A Cross-Sector Review', *Evidence and Policy*, vol 1, no 3, pp 335-63.

Wanless Report (2003) *Securing Good Health for the Whole Population: Population Health Trends*, London: HM Treasury.

Wanless, D. (2002) *Securing our Future Health: Taking a Long-term View. Final Report*, London: The Stationery Office.

Wanless, D. (2006) *Securing Good care for Older People*, London: King's Fund.

Warren, D. (2000) *A Chronology of State Medicine, Public Health, Welfare and Related Services in Britain 1066–1999*, London: Faculty of Public Health Medicine of the Royal Colleges of Physicians.

Weiss, C.H. (1979) 'The many meanings of research utilization', *Public Administration Review*, vol 39, no 5, pp 426-31.

Welsh Assembly Government (2004) *Making the Connections: Delivering Better Services for Wales*, Cardiff: Welsh Assembly Government.

Welsh Assembly Government (2005) *Delivering the Connections: From Vision to Action*, Cardiff: Welsh Assembly Government.

Welsh Assembly Government (2006a) *Making the Connections: Building Better Customer Service – Core Principles for Public Services*, Cardiff: Welsh Assembly Government.

Welsh Assembly Government (2006b) *Beyond Boundaries: Citizen-centred Local Services for Wales*, Cardiff: Welsh Assembly Government.

Westney, E. (1987) *Innovation and Imitation: The Transfer of Western Organizational Patterns to Meji Japan*, Cambridge, MA: Harvard University Press.

Weyland, K. (2005) 'The Diffusion of Innovations: How Cognitive Heuristics Shaped. Bolivian Pension Reform', *Comparative Politics*, vol 38, no 1, pp 21–42.

Weyland, K. (ed) (2004) *Learning from Foreign Models in Latin American Policy Reform* Washington DC: Woodrow Wilson Center Press.

Wilson, J. Q. and Kelling, G. L. (1982) 'Broken Windows', *Atlantic Monthly*, vol 249, no 3, pp 29-38.

Wolman, H. and Page, E. (2000) *Learning from the Experience of Others: Policy transfer among local regeneration partnerships*, York: Joseph Rowntree Foundation.

Wolman, H. and Page, E.C. (2002) 'Policy diffusion among local governments: An information-theory approach', *Governance*, vol 15, no 4, pp 477-501.

Women and Equality Unit (2002) *Gender Impact Assessment*, London: Women and Equality Unit/Department of Trade and Industry.

Work and Pensions Committee (2005) *The Performance of the Child Support Agency*, London: House of Commons.

Wurzel, R.K.W. (2002) *Environmental Policy-Making in Britain, Germany and the European Union: The Europeanisation of Air and Water Pollution Control*, Manchester: Manchester University Press.

Wyatt, A. (2002) 'Evidence based policy making: the view from a centre', *Public Policy and Administration*, vol 17, no 3, pp 12-28.

Yanow D. (1999) *Conducting Interpretive Policy Analysis*, Qualitative Research Methods Series, 47, Thousand Oaks, CA: Sage.

Young, K., Ashby, D., Boaz, A. and Grayson, L. (2002) 'Social Science and the Evidence-Based Policy Movement', *Social Policy and Society*, vol 1, no 3, pp 215-24.

Index